The Métis of Senegal

The Métis of Senegal

URBAN LIFE AND
POLITICS IN FRENCH
WEST AFRICA

———✦✦✦———

Hilary Jones

INDIANA UNIVERSITY PRESS

Bloomington and Indianapolis

This book is a publication of

Indiana University Press
601 North Morton Street
Bloomington, Indiana 47404-3797 USA

iupress.indiana.edu

Telephone orders　800-842-6796
Fax orders　812-855-7931

Manufactured in the
United States of America

Library of Congress Cataloging-in-
Publication Data

Jones, Hilary, [date]
The métis of Senegal : urban life and politics in French West Africa / Hilary Jones.
pages cm.
Includes bibliographical references and
index.
ISBN 978-0-253-00673-8 (cloth : alkaline
paper)
ISBN 978-0-253-00674-5 (pb : alkaline
paper)
ISBN 978-0-253-00705-6 (eb)
1. Racially mixed people—Senegal—
Saint-Louis—Social conditions—19th
century. 2. Sociology, Urban—Senegal—
Saint-Louis. 3. Assimilation (Sociol-
ogy)—Senegal—Saint-Louis. 4. Elite
(Social sciences)—Senegal—Saint-Louis.
5. Metropolitan government—Senegal—
Saint-Louis—History—19th century. 6.
Political leadership—Senegal—Saint-
Louis—History—19th century. 7. Saint-
Louis (Senegal)—Social conditions—
19th century.8. Saint-Louis (Senegal)
—Politics and government—19th century.
9. France—Colonies—Africa—Adminis-
tration. I. Title.

DT549.9.S24 J66　　　2013
307.760966301　　　2012025896

1 2 3 4 5　18 17 16 15 14 13

For Janet, Virgil, and Alyson,
and in memory of
Estelle Bailey Webster.

CONTENTS

ACKNOWLEDGMENTS

This study would not have been possible without the generosity of many people and agencies. My initial research for this project came about with the assistance of a Social Science Research Council International Pre-Dissertation Award. A Fulbright-Hays fellowship allowed me to carry out field research in Senegal and France. The Dubois-Rodney-Mandela post-doctoral fellowship from the Center of Afro-American Studies at the University of Michigan afforded me the space for me to begin to conceptualize the book. A Graduate Research Board summer award from the University of Maryland facilitated research in the Library of Congress and financial support from Macalester College permitted me to conduct additional research at the Spiritains archives in France. I am grateful for the support of people at these institutions as well as the intellectual communities that shaped my thinking and encouraged the development of this study. I owe a debt to the Africana Studies program and the History Department at the University of Notre Dame as well as colleagues at Macalester College and the University of Maryland, College Park.

I benefited enormously from Senegalese *teranaga* or hospitality. Many people welcomed me, responded enthusiastically to my project, and patiently helped me to navigate unfamiliar terrain. The staff of the National Archives, especially directors Saliou Mbaye and Boubacar Ndiaye as well as Mamadou Ndiaye, assisted me by asking the right questions of the archival collections and affording me access to key documents. At University Cheikh Anta Diop, historians Penda Mbow, Ibrahima Thioub, and Boubacar Barry provided valuable guidance. I also benefited from conversations with Charles Becker, Fatou Sow, Pathe Diagne, Fadel Dia, and Souylemane Bachir Diagne. I am indebted to Wilma Randle, Marie Florence Diokh,

Ibrahima Thiaw, and Marieme Diawarra for their friendship. The staff of the West African Research Center in Dakar provided important logistical support. My first lessons in Wolof language and culture came as a student at the Baobab Center in Dakar. I am grateful to the administrative staff and instructors who provided me with a firm foundation to build upon.

In Saint Louis, I aimed to get a sense of life in the town during its heyday by talking with long term residents and seeking out little known sources. I am grateful for the assistance of former director of CRNS, Abdoul Haidir Aïdara, Anne and Youssef Coulibaly, faculty at University Gaston Berger, as well as Monseigneur Pierre Sagna and the staff of the Catholic diocese of Saint Louis. Many *doomu Ndar* (sons and daughters of Saint Louis) were instrumental in my thinking, including Rabi Wane, Aminata Dia, Paul Ouattara, Moustapha Crespin and family, Marie Madeline Diallo, Aicha Fall, Madeline Thiouth, and Ibrahima Diallo. I am especially grateful to Louis Camara for sharing his connection to the historic city and assisting me with identifying and interviewing key subjects. Other informants, mentioned by name in the bibliography, offered me a window into métis society and valuable insight into their family histories. Several individuals passed away during the course of completing this work. I am grateful to Almamy Mathieu Fall, André Guillabert, Georgette Bonet, Alfred d'Erneville, and Sarita Henry for their insights.

This book also draws on archival sources from France. The staff of the Archives Nationales d'Outre-Mer in Aix-en-Provence, the Bibliothèque Nationale in Paris, the Spiritains Archive, the Gironde Departmental Archives, the Bordeaux municipal archives, and the Bordeaux Chamber of Commerce assisted in my research. I am also grateful to Yves Pehaut and Roger Pasquier for alerting me to key resources in France.

A number of people read all or part of this manuscript at various stages. Their critiques and comments proved invaluable. My thanks to David Robinson, Darlene Clark Hine, Leslie Moch, Martin Klein, and Ray Silverman as well as Heran Sereke-Brhan, Cheikh Babou, Ghislaine Lydon, Kalala Ngalamulume, Emily Osborn, Rachel Jean-Baptiste, Lorelle Semley, Wendy-Wilson Fall, and Fiona McLaughlin. Mamadou Diouf, Elsa Barkley Brown, Madeline Zilfi, Ira Berlin, and Valerie Orlando read the work at critical points and offered invaluable suggestions. The two anonymous reviews of the book helped enormously in shaping the final product, as did the patient and diligent work of Dee Mortensen, the editor at Indiana University Press, who shepherded this work to completion. Two copyeditors, Catherine Siskos and Elaine Durham Otto, polished the final product. Don Pirius of dpmaps. com made the maps for this book. The images have been reprinted with generous permission from Georges Crespin, Christian Valantin, and the Senegal National Archives. A. Dolidon transcribed recorded interviews. Ultimately all of the words and ideas put forth here are my own as are any mistakes, omissions, or oversights.

My family and friends have been a great source of support and encouragement. Alyson and Janet Jones have seen this work through from its very beginning. Words cannot express the depth of my gratitude. I must thank my network of friends and family in Detroit, East Lansing, Ann Arbor, Philadelphia, and Washington, D.C., who listened to me, commiserated with me, and inspired me.

Finally, this study would never have been conceived without Carolyn Jones's insistence that I study francophone Africa as a student at Cass Technical High School, and had it not been for the guidance of teachers at Spelman College, especially Margery Ganz and Michael Gomez. Estelle Bailey Webster planted the seed with her love of African history and culture, before I was old enough to remember. This work is dedicated to her.

The Métis of Senegal

Introduction

In 1960, when Senegal achieved independence from France, several descendants of mixed-race families who traced their roots to Saint Louis, the colonial capital, assumed prominent roles in the new nation. The first president, Léopold Sédar Senghor, appointed members of these families to ambassadorships in Paris, London, and the Vatican. Some served as the first generation of lawyers, magistrates, journalists, and educators. André Guillabert became minister of foreign affairs and ambassador to France. Prosper Dodds became the first Senegalese bishop to preside over the Catholic diocese of Senegal and Gambia. Others served among the country's first high-ranking military officers. Still others held elected office in the cities, towns, and the National Assembly. Although some left Senegal for France, others remained to play important roles in the new country.[1]

For those familiar with Senegal's modern political history, the role of the *métis* in the postcolonial nation comes as no surprise. Indeed, the political history of Senegal's nineteenth-century colonial towns is a history of the métis. Descendants of African women called *signares* and European merchants or soldiers who resided in the fortified coastal depots, the métis formed a self-conscious group in mid-eighteenth-century Senegal. Saint Louis, an island port located where the Senegal River meets the Atlantic, became the nexus of métis society, although the métis also trace their origins to Gorée Island on the Cap Vert Peninsula off the coast of Dakar. Shaped by the expansion of French colonial rule, they became the first mayors, city councilors, newspapermen, and local advisors to the colonial administration in the nineteenth century.

An inward-looking group, the métis spoke French, attended Catholic schools, and adopted the dress, tastes, and habits of the French bourgeoisie.

At the same time, they spoke Wolof, maintained a network of kin and clients in the interior, understood the customs of the towns, and had an intimate familiarity with the region's politics. In the early nineteenth century, métis men dominated the export trade in gum arabic from the Senegal River valley. By 1850, they had suffered financial setbacks because of the collapse of the price of gum for guinées (a blue trade cloth) in the river trade centers. The abolition of slavery in the towns, increasing competition by Muslim Saint Louis traders for control over the middleman niche of the colonial economy, and the introduction of peanut culture by Bordeaux merchants seeking to exploit cash crop production in the interior caused an economic crisis for the métis elite. As the primary French-educated population, they took advantage of the Third French Republic's expansion of electoral institutions. In the late nineteenth century, the métis elite turned to urban politics to reassert their influence in colonial affairs. Between 1880 and 1920, they transformed the local assemblies into an arena of negotiation and contestation with colonial authorities. In the process, they articulated a vision of modern Senegal that differed from that espoused by metropolitan capitalists and the colonial administration.

The role of the métis population in Senegalese history raises intriguing questions about the nature of French colonialism, the formation of new urban societies on West Africa's Atlantic coast, and the meaning of racial identity in Senegal. Who are the métis? What kind of society did they build in the nineteenth century, and how did they interpret colonial rule? As a group long affiliated with French culture and politics, the métis are often seen as synonymous with the colonial regime. In 1960, observers considered them culturally the same as the French. One writer went so far as to suggest that the métis so strongly identified with the French that their attitudes toward Africans reflected the same chauvinism and paternalism of French shopkeepers, professionals, and civil servants in the country.[2] Senegalese writers also grappled with the problem of métis identity. Published in 1957, Abdoulaye Sadji's novel Nini: Mulâtresse du Sénégal tells the ill-fated love story of a métis woman during the colonial period who is rejected in marriage by a European and who also rejects an African suitor. The novel suggests that the métis suffered from an internal conflict of not belonging fully to either one of these societies, thus inhibiting their survival.[3] The idea of métissage (interracial mixing sexually and socially) provoked class resentments and racial anxieties in both Senegalese and European societies of the twentieth century. In Senegal's colonial towns, racial tensions tended to escalate during political campaigns.

The image of the métis of Senegal is thus indicative of the two hundred years of French colonial rule that produced thorny contradictions, paradoxes, and tensions. Their history is not unlike that of similar groups who were caught between the worlds of the colonizer and the colonized. The métis of Senegal faced a similar "predicament of marginality" as free people of color faced in Brazil, New Orleans, Martinique, or Réunion.[4] Although universal ideals of enlightenment guided France's encounter with Africa, the métis also experienced exclusion from the French nation. Colonial empires of the era used rigid categories for race, class, ethnicity, and nationality to impose colonial control, and yet as one informant reminded me, being "Creole" in Senegal is not the same as being Creole in the West Indies.[5]

This book reexamines Senegal's modern political history through the lens of the métis population. It examines how and why a distinct métis identity emerged in Senegal's colonial towns from their origins in the late eighteenth century to the consolidation of colonial rule in Senegal by World War I. In 1920, French authorities succeeded in closing Senegal's venerable republican assembly, the General Council, and replacing it with a hybrid institution called the Colonial Council. This political shift coincided with the end of métis dominance in urban politics. The examination of métis society and identity sheds light on urban life in nineteenth-century West Africa and allows for a reconsideration of politics in Senegal's colonial capital from the perspective of Muslim traders, African women, black Catholics, slave women, their masters, African clergy, and French women of religious orders rather than the governors and merchants who are commonly seen as the nexus of colonial power. Examining the métis' role in Senegal's urban community reveals the class tensions, anxieties, contradictions, and power struggles that constituted urban life in the colonial towns from the nineteenth to early twentieth century.

Urban Life, Politics, and French Colonialism

The Métis of Senegal brings together separate strands in the historiography of nineteenth-century Senegal to understand the transformations that occurred in society and identity in a West African port during the nineteenth century. This research examines the intersection of scholarship on the encounter between Africa and Europe in the age of the Atlantic slave trade, the role of Saint Louis in Senegal's economic history during the era of "legitimate trade," and the evolution of democratic politics in Senegal's colonial towns (also known as the Four Communes). The history of Africans and European relations in the coastal locations of precolonial Senegambia is well documented.[6] European travelers offered vivid descriptions of signares, their customs, and their material wealth. Signare, a title given to African women of property and social standing along the Senegambian coast, symbolizes the history of cooperation and interaction between African women and European men in the era of mercantile trade. The subject of European travelers' accounts, historical novels, and films, these women have fascinated historians concerned with the politics of interracial sexuality in contact zones, the role of African women entrepreneurs, and their position as the primary slaveholders in these communities. In the eighteenth century, European visitors wrote of their fascination and attraction to signares, but their accounts rendered African women as the anonymous objects of male desire. Signares and the societies they formed appear as a backdrop to the grand narratives of European exploration of Africa, geopolitics, and imperialist expansion.

In the late eighteenth and early nineteenth centuries, Senegal's coastal communities became thriving, cosmopolitan ports that attracted people from a variety of national, ethnic, linguistic, and religious backgrounds. Historian Ira Berlin's term *Atlantic Creole* captures the meeting of Africans, Europeans, and Americans along the Atlantic littoral, who "by experience or choice as well as by birth" became part of a new culture.[7] Africans and Europeans in Saint Louis and Gorée exhibited the linguistic dexterity, knowledge of Atlantic commerce, and the political acumen that came from the interactions of peoples in these locales and their responses to the political changes affecting the Atlantic world. While there is great fascination with Atlantic ports as sites of African urbanism, cosmopolitanism also operated in Africa's interior. Marrying and producing children across ethnic, religious, and cultural lines constituted what anthropologist Jean Loup Amselle refers to as the "originary logic," of African societies. Strategic marriages between ruling families of Walo on the south bank of the Senegal and Trarza in today's Mauritania, for example, produced "mixed" identities.

European men who arrived in Senegal fought in the Indian wars of North America. They lost fortunes in the wake of the revolutions in France and Haiti and sought adventure abroad during the Napoleonic Wars. In

1807, Bruno Devès left Bordeaux for North America when his family faced bankruptcy, passing through Philadelphia en route to Senegal.[8] Atlantic developments had a profound effect on Africans of the towns, but inhabitants of these locations also turned their attention to Africa's interior. Saint Louis residents' knowledge of Islam, the trade of the southwest Sahara and the Senegal River valley, and the politics of the Wolof kingdoms of the mainland placed them in key positions to mediate between African merchants and European sea captains. In Senegal's coastal towns, Atlantic Creole identity looked to the Atlantic, but had firm roots in the particular social, cultural, and political environment of the African mainland.

While several works address the heyday of métis activity, few consider transformations in their society and identity after 1850. The golden age of métis prosperity occurred during the transition from the slave trade to legitimate trade.[9] Gum harvested from acacia trees along the Senegal River became the most valuable commodity exported from the region to Europe in the late eighteenth century. Saint Louis served as the primary location of French warehouses for imports of *guinées* and gum acquired in the *escales* (the river trade depots) that were controlled by the Trarza Moors on the north bank of the Senegal. Métis trade houses became the primary intermediaries between French merchants and Trarza caravan leaders and emirs who exchanged gum for guinées during the trade season on the lower and middle Senegal. Economic histories of nineteenth-century Senegal concentrate on the relationship between metropolitan capital firms and the Saint Louis trade houses in the long-term structural shifts that paved the way for conquest and resulted in the subjugation of African rulers and middleman traders in the colonial economy.[10]

In 1850, Senegal's middleman traders faced an economic crisis that led to the imposition of peanut culture by Bordeaux merchant firms and financial losses for the slaveholding elite of the towns. Historians of Senegal's middleman traders considered this moment as the nadir of the Saint Louis elite.[11] Recent research demonstrates that while métis gum traders lost ground during the crisis, Muslim traders seized upon changes in the colonial economy to emerge as the dominant middleman traders in the peanut basin after 1850.[12] Gaps remain, however, in our understanding of the ways in which Senegal's métis commercial houses, the best capitalized during the gum trade era, responded to the economic crisis facing town residents. Considering how métis traders continued to operate in commerce by mobilizing their kin and client networks and moving their operations to the frontiers of French expansion suggests that métis traders were more resilient than previously assumed. They used their knowledge of the country to act as agents for French firms and took advantage of the ambiguity of French antislavery laws to recruit labor for commercial activities and household production. Examining their strategies in the second half of the nineteenth century indicates that the economic crisis did not result in the complete financial ruin and collapse of the métis.

As the descendants of European men and African women, Senegal's métis population also sat at the intersection between French colonial expansion and African rulers and clerics who resisted French encroachment of their sovereign territories. In the mid- and late nineteenth century, the Senegal colony changed from a remote commercial outpost to a place where France launched wars for territorial conquest. Saint Louis served not only as the capital of French military forces and the colonial bureaucracy but also as the place where the French envisioned their civilizing mission would spread. The métis occupied key positions in the bureaucracy and military and as representatives of French merchant firms, but they focused their attention on achieving positions of power in the electoral institutions. In this capacity, they acted as a check on abuses of power and, at times, as a thorn in the side of colonial authorities.

Colonialism is an act of conquest or domination by one state over another forged through violence. In Africa, the colonial state was primarily concerned with enforcing its authority and achieving its imperialist aims.[13] While some research depicts the colonial state as all-powerful, other studies have drawn attention to its weakness and permeability. In Kenya, for example, the British were constrained by a lack of financial resources and the difficulty of managing the interests of various groups within the colony while upholding their ideological position of being neutral, benevolent arbiters of state power.[14] Colonialism in West Africa evolved as a process of negotiation between foreign rulers and strategic cooperation with Africans who employed strategies to accommodate one another and respond to the situation as it unfolded on the ground.[15] In Senegal, colonial rule operated through networks of accommodation between French authorities in Saint Louis and clerics, rulers, traders, and urban elites in the country.

The traditional notion of colonial power views it as the work of men operating in a masculine environment of governors and commandants, interpreters and traders, priests and pastors, kings and clerics.[16] And yet colonialism worked its way into the intimate spaces of home, courtyard, kitchen, and bedroom occupied predominately by women. Senegal's nineteenth-century colonial towns emerged as locations where women played determinant roles in creating new Afro-European households while also defining urban society. French authorities viewed women as the key to reproducing colonial society and achieving the cultural aims of colonial rule. In official records, signares and their métis daughters are mentioned as the subjects of conversion and models of republican ideals of womanhood in the colony. In separating the public and private spheres, depictions in the administrative record render women invisible in the formation of an urban political class in the colony. Examining the intersections of race, class, and gender in Senegal's colonial capital shows the complex and subtle ways in which colonial power operated as well as the gendered strategies that urban communities adopted in response to the expansion of French rule.[17]

Histories of French imperialism have dwelled on the economic, nationalist, political, or military questions while African studies tend to underestimate the cultural and ideological aspects of colonial rule.[18] Both fields neglect the role of urban communities in shaping colonial practices and influencing how colonialism played out in African societies. Understanding urban elites through the prism of collaboration and resistance is too simplistic. Christian missionary schools, European commercial firms, and the colonial bureaucracy served as avenues of socioeconomic mobility for urban Africans in the colonial era. In the British West African colonies, individuals rose to positions of prominence in the Protestant missions or as members of the limited representative institutions called legislative councils. Christian marriage advanced one's socioeconomic standing.[19] In Senegal, African and Muslim residents of the colonial towns argued for legal recognition as French citizens and participated in the republican political institutions. Articulating their status as citizens of France entitled to the same rights and responsibilities as metropolitan Frenchmen gave town residents far more extensive privileges within the colonial system. While *originaires* (African residents of the Four Communes) fought for recognition as citizens, the métis used their cultural and biological ties with France to insert themselves into the decision-making apparatus of the colonial administration.[20]

Because electoral politics in Senegal evolved from structures of colonial rule, the history of democratic institutions in the country is tied to the emergence of modern nationalism. In 1914, Blaise Diagne won election to the Chamber of Deputies in the National Assembly in Paris. According to the nationalist narrative, this moment marked the beginning of Senegalese national consciousness. Supported by the mobilization of a politicized African youth in the urban community, Diagne's victory stands out as the defining event because of the urban community's use of electoral politics for anticolonial resistance. Diagne not only broke the métis monopoly over the democratic institutions but also succeeded in passing legislation that confirmed the legal status of African and Muslim town residents as French citizens.[21]

While the first wave of Africanist scholarship on politics in the colony confirmed the integrity of newly formed nations, the literature neglected to show how politics actually operated in the colony.[22] Métis men appear in the history of urban politics in colonial Senegal as predecessors to the rise of authentic nationalist leaders such as Blaise Diagne, Galandou Diouf, and Lamine Gueye. Viewing urban politics in racialized terms relegates métis contributions to nationalist prehistory. In addition, this approach reinforces the administrative structures of the colonial regime that walled off European citizens in the colonial towns from the rural masses governed by the arbitrary practices of the colonial regime in the rural "customary sphere." The colonial administration sought to exclude the majority of African people from civil society by restricting them to the rural protectorate governed by administrative decree, not republican law.[23] While this provided a convenient framework for colonial authorities, it could not account for the ways in which urban communities crossed this divide and used electoral institutions to interact with rural elites and shape the outcomes of events in the interior.

From the perspective of the town residents, the consolidation of French rule involved a struggle between the urban elite and French officials for influence over Africans in the interior. Between 1880 and 1920, the métis relied on a complex web of social, economic, and political ties in their interactions with Africans in the towns and frontier regions of the colony. They used their ability to gain exclusive access to democratic institutions to strengthen their authority with African rulers, traders, and families in the countryside. The métis also capitalized on their familiarity with French culture, knowledge of French law, and ties to Bordeaux merchants, French lawmakers, and colonial officials to shape the outcome of colonial policies. By conforming to the cultural expectations of the French bourgeoisie, métis women bolstered the symbolic capital of their families and carved out their niche in public debate as the voice of morality in urban politics.

Métis Identity under French Rule

Who are the métis of Senegal exactly? Defining them is difficult. People of mixed-racial ancestry do not fit neatly into specific categories of analysis. They were not all subjects of colonial rule or rulers of empires. They were not all rich, but neither were they poor. Physically some could be described as black, while others appeared white. Far from a monolithic group, some métis adhered closely to colonial doctrine, while others broke from the administration and metropolitan merchants. In the literature, they are referred to alternatively as EurAfrican, Afro-European, Creole, or mulatto. The term *Creole* signifies cultural mixing that emphasizes place of birth. In French, Creole describes Europeans born in the colonies. From the stand-point of nineteenth-century ideas of race, the term *mulatto* became the catch-all phrase for the offspring of people of different racial types.[24] *Mulatto,* derived from the Spanish word for mule, carried with it a notion of degeneracy and biological inferiority. The Wolof term for mulatto, *militaar,* consequently become a part of Wolof spoken in Saint Louis. I use the French term *métis* because it is free of the negative, outdated connotations associated with the word *mulâtre.*

The problem of métis identity also raises thorny questions about racial classification in colonial Senegal. The métis of Senegal's coastal towns all carried the last names of their European fathers. Most were the children of African women who came to Saint Louis or Gorée from Wolof, Soninke, Peul, Serer, or Lebu extraction. The fathers of these children included not only French but also British, Irish, Alsatian, Portuguese, and American. Official records, moreover, never used the terms *mulâtre* or *métis,* but usually employed *français* or *indigène* (native) to distinguish between European and African inhabitants of the colonial towns. As a result, the métis easily became conflated with metropolitan French men and women. The slippery nature of classification also meant that people of mixed race could move easily between racial categories. Alfred Gasconi served as Senegal's representative in Paris from 1879 to 1889. In the 1960s, residents of Gorée identified Gasconi as a metropolitan Frenchman even though he was born in Saint Louis, the son of a naval captain from Marseille.[25] Historians speculate that his mother was Signare Elisa Fleuriau. Adding to the confusion, other métis relocated to regions of Senegal's interior, adopted Islam, married, and integrated with Africans in the countryside, leaving little trace of their métis identity.

These questions of definition and identification reveal the contradictions and paradoxes of modern thinking about race. Racial ideology, as current research shows, is a social construction rather than a biological fact.[26] Ideas about race and color emerge in a particular context and are given meaning by specific social, political, and economic circumstances. The notion of race, as historian Barbara Fields points out, is a historical product. Racial identity changes over time. Postcolonial and colonial studies research shows that sexuality across the color line and the mixed race populations that issued from these unions served as critical sites for the emergence of new identities. And yet historians are only beginning to take seriously the meaning of mixed race identity in Africa under colonial rule.[27] Examining the origins of Senegal's métis population shows how this group emerged as symbols of French cultural hegemony while embodying the potential for disruption and subversion of the racial order during the consolidation of French rule. The contingent and often contested ways in which Europeans and Africans in the colony were linked to one another through kin ties complicated colonial policy that sought to create neat divisions between African and European, colonizer and colonized.

In the nineteenth century, the universal ideas and expectations associated with the ideology of assimilation made the attainment of equal status with metropolitan French an option for people of mixed race. In the twentieth century, as Owen White demonstrates, métissage provoked anxieties in French West Africa.[28] Racial thinking became part of the logic of colonial control as officials sought to erect fixed, immutable boundaries separating Europeans from Africans. In French West Africa, European men did not recognize the paternity of their children by African women.[29] Colonial ethnographers argued that the métis suffered alienation from both African and European societies, threatening the stability of the colonial system. The most effective solution to interracial mixing in the colony, in their view, involved removing métis children from colonial society by either confining them to orphanages under the care of the state or removing them from Africa with the goal of integrating them into metropolitan society. In the 1950s, an association called the EurAfricans published a newspaper in French West Africa protesting the denial of French citizenship to métis individuals in the colonies who lacked paternal recognition.[30] The dilemma for this population differed from that of the métis of the nineteenth-century Atlantic towns who had already established their paternity by virtue of carrying the surnames of their European fathers.

I have chosen to use *métis* as a term of identification and analysis. The métis of nineteenth-century Senegal developed a distinct group identity based on their ability to trace their descent to a signare and a European merchant or official who lived in the coastal towns of Saint Louis and Gorée in the eighteenth or early nineteenth centuries. The métis of Senegal developed a common sense of affiliation based on endogamy, identification with the Catholic Church, and conformity to the expectations of the French bourgeoisie. In the nineteenth century, inhabitants of Senegal's towns identified one another by occupation, surname, or household affiliation. Today natives of Saint Louis use the euphemism *doomu Ndar* (children of Saint Louis) to evoke pride in belonging to what Abdoul Hadir Aidra refers to as the "symbiotic culture" of a town that reconciled the "positive values of the Judeo-Christian West and the richness of Islam." Occasionally referred to as *enfants du pays* (children of the soil), the métis of Senegal occupied both worlds, a product of the African and European encounter unique to Senegal's coastal towns.[31]

Civil Society and Symbolic Capital in Saint Louis

The concept of civil society has recently generated a great deal of attention in debates on state-society relations and the meaning of democracy in Africa, Latin America, and Eastern Europe.[32] Although the intellectual discourse about civil society developed in response to the rise of nation-states in Western Europe, scholars of politics and the postcolonial state in Africa use the idea of civil society to explain how non-state actors put pressure on the state to respond to the interests of particular groups. Islamic orders in present-day Senegal, for example, play a stabilizing role in Senegal's current political system.[33] This work considers the historical roots of these practices. Questions such as how and why interest groups emerged in Senegal's colonial towns and to what degree they succeeded in asserting their interests at the highest level of authority deserve further attention.

What happens when we apply the concept of civil society to the study of urban politics in colonial Senegal? Examining this problem from the perspective of a French-educated, republican-minded group reveals the complex patterns of negotiation and contestation between colonial officials and members of the urban community that shaped the process of colonial conquest and the consolidation of French rule. The métis, along with Muslim traders and members of the Catholic and Protestant clergy, emerged as interest groups in the Saint Louis community who used their access to the administration to articulate their concerns and demand action from French officials. The métis dominated electoral politics in the late nineteenth century and considered the local assemblies as their arena. Métis responses to colonial rule through these institutions illustrate the struggle for power between the urban community and the administration that defined the era of conquest and consolidation of French power. Métis activities in the local assemblies, moreover, shed light on the process of establishing colonial hegemony by limiting the power of democratic institutions and suppressing the mobilization of civil society in the colony.[34]

I define civil society as institutions that have some autonomy from the state and thus act as a mediating force between the populace and the government. Institutions of civil society appeared in relation to a state authority that was represented by the colonial administration in Senegal, on the one hand, and the Third Republic, on the other. Late nineteenth-century Senegal presents a unique case for the operation of civil society because the electoral institutions afforded commune residents a political voice beyond the administrative apparatus of colonial rule, which employed authoritarian practices and used violent reprisal to enforce its control. Métis politicians, who knew French law, used their position in these institutions to take conflicts with colonial officials directly to Paris lawmakers for resolution. Métis women relied on their reputation as the moral voice of the community to organize in civil society. In forming an active and engaged citizenry, métis leaders helped shape the political culture of Senegal's colonial towns and began the process of articulating a vision for modern Senegalese politics that differed from that imagined by the colonial state.

In his analysis of political society in Brazil, Alfred Stepan calls electoral politics the "arena of political contestation."[35] For commune residents, that arena involved political institutions that could be distinguished from the administration. The organizations of civil society, in this view, consist of the political arena of electoral politics and the social arena of family, associations, social movements, and forms of public communication. For the métis, the social dimension of civil society was represented through family alliances, membership in the Catholic Church or Masonic lodges, schools, and the short-lived independent press. In the late nineteenth century, the inhabitants of the colonial capital understood their position as republican citizens despite the ambiguities that their citizenship presented for metropolitan society and the colonial state. In the twentieth century, colonial authorities sought to deal with the problem of an empowered citizenry in the colony by restricting the power of democratic institutions to interfere in colonial affairs.

Pierre Bourdieu's sociological theories provide a useful framework for understanding how social behavior and cultural orientation function in response to new situations. Bourdieu uses *habitus* instead of culture to explain how socialization, tradition, and an individual's earliest experiences provide mechanisms for responding to change.[36] Métis men and women constantly reinforced their connection to the metropole by sending their children to France for secondary education and by maintaining residences and business partnerships in Bordeaux or Marseille. At the same time, they used their fluency in Wolof and their familiarity with Muslim practices to forge alliances with influential African residents in the cities and Muslim clerics and African rulers in the interior. Schools, civic associations, and the Church provided the structures that nurtured common group identification despite individual differences. The métis capitalized on their dual identity to solidify their elite status and seek advantages from metropolitan capitalists, colonial officials, African trade partners, rulers, and employees. Doing so mitigated their survival but also created class and race tensions.

Bourdieu's concept of symbolic capital clarifies the close relationship between the public and private spheres in nineteenth-century Saint Louis.[37] A successful marriage alliance in kin-based societies, according to Bourdieu, depends upon the material and symbolic or cultural capital that each party possesses. Marriage for the métis served as a strategy for accumulating wealth and power. The ability to mobilize and effectively use these resources to negotiate the most advantageous union for the family bolstered the credibility of all individuals in their public activities. For métis families, the honor and prestige of the household influenced their ability to mobilize all of the people associated with it. A household's reputation served as an avenue for producing and expanding symbolic capital, which in turn generated greater economic resources and bolstered the family's credibility with important segments of the population during elections. An understanding of how these various forms of capital could be used as resources to gain access to power in the political arena shows the complexity of social life in Senegal's colonial capital and its implications for obtaining and maintaining power.

Sources and Methodology

The history of the métis in nineteenth-century Senegal is one of families. Individuals within the urban community knew one another by family name and reputation. For the métis, tracing one's ancestry to an eighteenth-century signare and a European soldier or merchant conferred respectability and acceptance within the upper echelons of the group. The proper family connections ensured one's social standing within the community and even determined the ability of male leaders to assert power. Like other groups, the interrelated nature of these families commonly produced rivalries and competition in both the political and private realms.

In order to explore these dynamics, I have organized this study using family histories. Sketching the family profiles of leading individuals shows the interrelated nature of this community and also highlights the strategies that the métis developed through family alliances to build and maintain their position as power brokers in the changing environment of colonial expansion. While a small population of these families' descendants exists today, they cannot produce firsthand accounts of the late nineteenth century, and only a few can remember the community in the 1920s. I conducted interviews with ten descendants of métis and originaires of Saint Louis and Gorée, who provided key details of their family lineages and associations.

These interviews and the informal conversations I had with other individuals alerted me to the important role that African women who founded these Afro-European lineages played, even though they are often forgotten by history and rendered anonymous in depictions of urban life.[38] While informants' reminiscences cannot fully capture the period studied, these conversations made me aware of the importance of family collections. Hidden histories contained in photo albums, letters, and journals often kept in tin trunks constitute key archives of the urban experience. For the métis in Senegal, unpublished genealogies serve as a means of recording and remembering the African branches of European families from this era. Increasingly, descendants of Senegal's métis families are making these materials available through new technologies in a way that guarantees the survival of their family names even as elder members pass on.[39]

After 1900, the decline of Saint Louis resulted in the migration of Saint Louis residents to the ports of Senegal's peanut basin (Dakar and Rufisque), Paris, and other key locations of the French Empire. The recent reemergence of Saint Louis as a historically and culturally important location has generated new interest by all "children of Ndar" in recovering documents contained in private family collections.

This study recasts Senegal's modern political history by examining the impact of social organization and cultural practices on urban politics. I focus on the strategies that métis men and women employed to respond to the changes brought about by the colonial regime and to secure their position as citizens of the republic. Examining the intricacies of marriage alliances and educational paths to uncover the network of social relationships that influenced the political process illustrates the tight relationship between the public and private worlds of the urban community. Official reports for Saint Louis are extensive. French soldiers and companies kept records about their interests in trade and the administration of the fort that date to the early eighteenth century. The private writings and papers of members of the colonial judiciary, explorers, geographers, and clergy provide the perspective of European visitors or representatives of European institutions. Governor Louis Faidherbe, the architect of colonial rule in Senegal, wrote extensively about the country, as did the governors and governors general who were responsible for consolidating French rule and establishing the administration of French West Africa between 1890 and 1920. These accounts, however, contain inherent biases that are grounded in notions of African inferiority shaped by the dominant discourse on the slave trade and France's unique civilizing mission. Eighteenth-century observers borrowed race and class terminology from plantation societies of the French Caribbean and applied it to social formations in Senegal's Atlantic towns. Even nineteenth-century accounts by Senegal's indigenous clergy and métis writers reflect common assumptions about the necessity of modernizing and westernizing Africa according to European enlightenment ideas.

To move beyond the limitations of foreign accounts and the official record, I placed particular emphasis on private archival sources. In addition to collecting official reports of the republican institutions and their activities in trade centers and administrative depots of the protectorate, I consulted the records of the Catholic Church in Saint Louis for correspondence between the clergy and the administration, parish registries of marriages and births, and school enrollments. I collected information from the official newspaper published by the administration called the *Moniteur du Sénégal et Dépendances,* but also sought out extant copies of the independent press that appeared in Saint Louis in the 1880s and again in the 1890s.[40]

I examined published accounts of the proceedings of annual meetings of Senegal's General Council and studied the correspondence between the Masonic Lodge in Saint Louis and the Grand Orient in Paris during the secular debates of the 1870s and 1880s. Research in the archives of the Spiritains in Paris as well as in the Gironde departmental archives (Bordeaux) and the Bordeaux Chamber of Commerce yielded valuable information about the lives of métis students and the financial dealings of metropolitain merchants. Civil registries of marriages and births, notarized documents of property transactions, and official reports about slavery, forced labor, and education in the colony provided valuable information about the social networks that bound urban residents together as well as controversies that involved the métis elite. The private papers of the Devès family, a little-explored collection in the Senegal archives, offered new insights into their role and their responses to conflicts with the administration. These documents clarify the interconnected nature of French power with the métis in the early period of formal colonial control.

This study focuses on the town of Saint Louis, located where the Senegal River empties into the Atlantic Ocean. The river travels from its origins in the highlands of present-day eastern Guinea, meets tributaries at the Faléme, and continues westward, forming what colonial observers described as a natural boundary between "black Africa" and the Arab-Berber populations of the southwestern edge of the Sahara Desert. In the nineteenth century, Saint Louis served as Senegal's colonial capital and the most important French port. Métis families considered Saint Louis the nexus of their social, cultural, and political life. Even as they established ties with other mixed-race groups along the coast from Gorée to Banjul, métis families sent their children to school in Saint Louis. They supported the Church in the capital and returned there to participate in politics. Interrelated by blood and marriage, the métis of Saint Louis shared a common history with métis families of Gorée. In the 1860s, Dakar and Rufisque gained importance as modern ports strategically located to take advantage of the boom in cash crops from Senegal's peanut basin. The four colonial towns (Saint Louis, Gorée, Dakar, and Rufisque) constituted the administrative distinct known as the Four Communes. As

Dakar and Rufisque gained importance, Saint Louis's declined. By World War I, métis families and Saint Louis traders relocated to Dakar and Rufisque, as well as secondary towns like Kaolack and Louga, which replaced the escales along the Senegal River. The interests of residents came to dominate the local assemblies.

Histories of urban politics concentrate on the Four Communes. Saint Louis, Gorée, Rufisque, and Dakar held the same legal status as communes in metropolitan France. Political scientists have considered this administrative structure as evidence of the bifurcation, and thus weakness, of the colonial state.[41] Approaching the history of Senegal's colonial towns through the lens of this arbitrary administrative designation reinforces the separation of town and country created by colonial administrators. It also obscures the particular characteristics of each place and the pattern of interaction that existed between commune residents and the inhabitants of the interior.[42] Focusing on Saint Louis allows for a reexamination of the history of Senegal's colonial towns not as European enclaves distinct from the countryside but as places uniquely shaped by their relationship to neighboring territories of the interior.

Chapter 1 traces the roots of métis identity and society by paying attention to the role of women in the formation of Afro-European households and the cultural environment that emerged in Saint Louis from the period of mercantile company rule to the first period of British occupation in 1758. I consider the effects of the French Revolution, the Atlantic slave trade, the Napoleonic Wars, and British occupation on the development of the Saint Louis community.

Chapter 2 examines the economic foundations of métis society during its golden age. This chapter focuses on the transition from the slave trade to legitimate trade in gum beginning in the late eighteenth century. I consider the reoccupation of Senegal by France after the Napoleonic Wars and the impact of the gum trade on *habitant* prosperity to analyze the rise of métis traders as middlemen and their fall as a result of the crisis in the exchange rate of gum for textiles called guinées. I reevaluate assumptions about the collapse of the métis in commerce in the wake of the gum crisis, the end of slavery, and competition from Saint Louis's Muslim traders. This chapter shows the strategies that métis merchants used to recover from the economic crisis and maintain their position as power brokers as French commercial interests moved from the Senegal River valley to the peanut basin.

Chapters 3 and 4 explore the social and cultural environments that shaped métis identity in the nineteenth century. I examine the visible markers that métis families adopted to bolster their affiliation with the property-owning classes of metropolitan France and the implications these choices had for reordering colonial society. Both chapters investigate the gendered way that French rule operated through education and religion as well as the gendered responses of the métis through marriage, domestic consumption, education, professionalization, and their associations. Chapter 4 considers the emergence of an independent press that provided a new voice for opposition in the urban community.

Chapter 5 illustrates the paradox between republican citizenship and colonial rule that existed in Senegal as formal colonial rule unfolded. This chapter focuses on the uneasy tension between colonial conquest and administrative systems that subjugated the vast populations of people in the interior to the arbitrary laws of the protectorate while French laws and republican institutions were reestablished and expanded for inhabitants of the colonial towns. Chapters 6 and 7 address the rise of métis leadership in urban politics and the ways in which it constituted an active and engaged citizenry between 1870 and 1914. I consider the emergence of the Devès and Descemet groups in electoral politics and their impact on affairs of the interior. Chapter 7 looks at the struggle between métis assemblymen and those of the first arrondissement (Saint Louis) who created problems for French officials in their desire to enforce colonial control and consolidate French rule in the region. The work concludes by considering the implications of the closing of Senegal's General Council, a venerable republican institution. In 1920, France announced the closing of the assembly and the establishment of a less powerful institution called the Colonial Council, thereby entering a new phase of development in its West African empire.

Senegal is one of the few regions of West Africa to have been shaped by centuries of direct contact with the Islamic world via trans-Saharan trade networks and the Atlantic world through transatlantic commerce. This book explores the emergence and development of nineteenth-century urban life in Senegal's colonial capital by paying particular attention to the role that people of mixed race played. Forming a group identity and using their position as intermediaries to assert power, the métis influenced French rule during Senegal's transition from remote commercial outpost to the center of French colonial rule in West Africa.

1

Signares, Habitants, and Grumets in the Making of Saint Louis

Signare Cathy Miller rose to prominence as a woman of wealth and high social standing in the town of Saint Louis. She was born in 1760 to Jean Miller, a trader who arrived in Senegal during the British occupation (1758–1783), and an unknown African woman. She married Charles Jean-Baptiste d'Erneville, the son of a Norman naval captain who participated in wars of conquest along the Mississippi.[1] Born in New Orleans, d'Erneville left Louisiana to join his father in France and train as an artillery captain. He served two years in debtors' prison before rejoining the military. In February 1780, at the age of twenty-seven, he arrived in Senegal with a regiment organized to reestablish French control of Saint Louis after Britain lost the territory during the American Revolution. D'Erneville advanced quickly by leading successful military expeditions to upper Senegal. His country-style marriage to Cathy Miller produced four children who achieved notable status as property owners and Senegal River traders. Nicholas (1786–1866) founded a trade house and became the mayor of Saint Louis in 1851. He married Adelaide Crespin, the daughter of Signare Kati Wilcok and Benjamin Crespin, a merchant from Nantes. His brothers, Jean-Baptiste Crespin (1781–1838) and Pierre Crespin (1783–1848) married two daughters of the mayor of Saint Louis, Charles Thevenot.

In 1789, d'Erneville left Saint Louis to assume responsibility for the administration of Gorée, where he established a household with Helene Pateloux. He died there on 2 March 1792. *Mariage à la mode du pays,* the name given for these unions with African women, typically ended upon the death or permanent departure of the husband from Senegal, thereby allowing a signare the freedom to remarry. Following d'Erneville's departure,

Cathy Miller wed Jean-Baptiste Dubrux, an employee of the mercantile company. Their union produced one son, named after his father. On 28 September 1825, he married Desirée Alain, the daughter of Signare Marie Paul Bénis and notable habitant Jean-Jacques Alain, called L'Antillais after his birthplace in Martinique.[2] Signare Cathy Miller witnessed the golden age of métis society in Saint Louis. She lived to see the expansion of new lineages and the growth of a self-conscious métis population during the height of the gum trade. On 10 September 1834, she died in Saint Louis in her seventy-fourth year.

Signares and their métis children gave rise to the development of Creole society in Saint Louis. Signares gave birth to an intermediary class who had the cultural dexterity to move between British, French, or African authorities. Habitants and grumets who developed close ties to European powers used their knowledge of European and African languages, their skill in navigating the Senegal River, and their ability to negotiate with people in the upriver trade depots to play a part in the flow of capital to Europe, Africa, and the Americas. Africans and Europeans participated in the major political events that shaped Western Europe and their colonies in the Americas. French and British soldiers and merchants experienced the Indian wars in North America and geopolitical conflict in Europe as well as the American Revolution, the French Revolution, and a slave revolt in Haiti that transformed colonial society in the French Caribbean. Inhabitants of Saint Louis, like others who lived and worked in port towns across the Atlantic world, absorbed information and developed their responses to the realities they confronted accordingly.

Although Saint Louis emerged as a vibrant port during the transatlantic slave trade and shared commonalities with ports in the Atlantic world, Creole societies did not all operate in the same way. Urban life in Saint Louis developed in relation to the presence of Islam in the Senegal River valley and the migration and settlement of slaves and freepersons from the interior. In addition, the development of Saint Louis as a mercantile port depended on the role that free propertied women played in establishing household life. Signares, their daughters, and the slave women who lived in their households not only provided for the domestic needs of European men but also established the systems needed to organize and facilitate commerce. As the "country wives" of European soldiers and traders, signares produced a group of men and women familiar with the region's social and cultural environment who remained loyal to British and French authorities. The métis, in particular, had the advantage of blood ties to European men that could be evoked in order to claim political power. Colonial ideologies of race, class, and gender afforded métis men the ability to assume positions of leadership within the Saint Louis community.

European travelers who visited the region viewed signares as exotic, seductive beauties. Novelists and filmmakers have perpetuated this tradition, and historians have not done much better as they tend to consider these women either successful entrepreneurs who capitalized on their sexuality or conspirators who facilitated and profited from the slave trade that drew European men to Senegal's island towns.[3] While women's history has made great advances, the gendered aspects of imperialism remain underappreciated. Histories of commercial relations between Europe and Africa and the formation of colonial towns are too often told through the lens of male power and privilege.[4] In the late eighteenth-century, imperialism operated as much through the private, intimate spheres of marriage, household, and sexuality as it did through French policies and practices enacted in its overseas possessions. Saint Louis would not have existed as a viable port town if not for the role that African women played in facilitating commerce, providing domestic services for European men, and producing a class of individuals with the cultural dexterity required to serve as intermediaries and cultural brokers.

Eighteenth-century soldiers and traders left little record of the African women who gave birth to the first métis generation. Genealogical records emphasize patrilineal descent, leaving African women anonymous. Women such as Cathy Miller emerge in the historical record as the overseas companions of European men. Notations in the civil registry, church records, court cases, and family genealogies as well as population statistics provide clues about their names, their professions, their spouses, and the métis lineages that emerged from these interactions, yet they also conceal crucial information. Who was Signare Cathy's mother? Could she have been a grumet (black Catholic)? What kind of household did she grow up in? How did women negotiate their interactions with European soldiers and officials who resided in the island town temporarily? What was their relationship to the increasing numbers of free African migrants who settled in the towns and the slaves who were brought involuntarily to the coast to labor in signare and habitant households? The gendered nature of documentation both conceals and reveals the role that women played in the emergence of the urban community.

Saint Louis society developed as a result of European imperialism and Atlantic commerce, but signares, habitants, grumets, free Muslim Africans, and slaves shaped urban life. Despite the absence of strict racial segrega- tion, social and economic mobility depended on one's proximity to Euro- pean authority, and biological kinship to European men conferred access to political power. In this fashion, signares, habitants, and grumets consti- tuted the propertied and privileged class of the late eighteenth century. At the same time, autonomy from metropolitan control facilitated the growth of an independent-minded urban community that looked outward to the Atlantic world while remaining firmly connected to African societies of the Senegal River valley. The people of Saint Louis observed the Wolof tradi- tions of the lower Senegal while adopting an outward-looking approach that embraced participation in Atlantic commerce. An urban Wolof town, Saint Louis neither replicated European society nor directly corresponded to the societies of Senegal's mainland.

European Authority in a West African Town (1758–1809)

Saint Louis was founded in the seventeenth century to secure French trade interests on the Senegal River. Located where the river empties into the Atlantic Ocean, Saint Louis was uniquely situated between a natural har- bor, called the *langue de barbarie* on the Atlantic Ocean, and the *petit bras* or little branch of the Senegal River to the east (map 1). The source of the 1,020-mile-long river is located in the highlands of eastern Guinea, where the river meanders north and west through the grassy plains of the savan- nah and arid expanses of the Sahara's southwestern edge. The river empties at the mouth of the Senegal in the delta region at Saint Louis. The rich floodplains of the river form a natural semiarid boundary known as the *sahel*. Foreigners understood the river as the frontier between pastoral Bidan (white Moors) who claimed Arab-Berber descent and (black) Wolof, Fulbe, and Soninke people of the pastoral and agricultural settlements on the south bank.[5] For the people of the Senegal River valley, trade, intermar- riage, political alliances, and religious affiliation brought Moor, Wolof, Fulbe, and Soninke into regular contact for centuries.

By the mid-sixteenth century, the region of the lower Senegal included three Wolof kingdoms: Walo, Cayor, and Baol.[6] The Denyanke kingdom ruled over the semipastoral Pulaar-speaking population of Fouta Toro in the middle Senegal valley (also known as Toukolor). A multilayered population of Soninke, Mandinka, and Khassonke inhabited the upper Senegal, which was controlled by the Soninke Gajaaga kingdom. Gajaaga's close proximity to the Bambuk gold fields along the Niger River bend as well as all the major trade routes of this region bolstered the kingdom's power as an exporter of slaves, gold, and other commodities.

In 1659, France erected a fort on the island, making Saint Louis the first European fortified trade post on the Senegal. Called Ndar by the Wolof of Walo, Saint Louis offered European ship captains strategic access to human and material commodities controlled by African rulers in the interior. It also offered a suitable climate for European soldiers and the mercantile company employees who were seeking slaves, ivory, gold, and hides.[7] In the seventeenth century, the delta region of the lower Senegal remained sparsely populated. The Wolof kingdoms of Walo and Cayor considered the area a prime location for collecting salt and fishing. The Wolof village of Gandiole, located on the mainland, exercised some autonomy but paid tribute to the Damel of Cayor. Gandiole also supplied salt and provisional goods to foreigners conducting ship-to-shore trade. Inhabitants of Gandiole were probably among the first free African people to establish relations with Europeans and settle in Saint Louis.

One story of the island's origins holds that it was uninhabited before Europeans arrived, except for a few cotton fields that belonged to the Brak of Walo. Other explanations suggest that the territory belonged to Dyambar Diop, the son and successor of the Brak, who ruled over the adjacent island called Sor. A third tale of origin posits that Saint Louis belonged to the head of a semi-independent state attached to Walo that was required to supply soldiers to the king when called upon. One final explanation suggests that the town got its name from a farming village named N'da that once existed as an important market on the salt flats of Leybar before it was displaced by the Saint Louis market.[8] The French named the town after King Louis XIV, but African town residents continued to call it Ndar.

Portuguese navigators located the mouth of the Senegal in 1445. During the sixteenth century, European sailors used this location for an annual ship-to-shore trade. In 1633, when Richelieu decided to embark on a new era of French colonization, he offered a charter to a Norman company. In 1658, the Compagnie du Cap Vert replaced the Normans and received a charter that allowed merchant-investors from Rouen exclusive rights to trade along the Senegal. The company established a base on the nearby island of Bocos, but the settlement suffered from floods that inundated the makeshift fort. In 1659, Dyambar Diop (known to French writers as Jeanne Barre) ceded Ndar to the French. The company built a permanent fort on the island to house employees and supply ships with goods. The French Crown initially administered the settlement through soldiers sent to provide security and oversee the operation. In 1677, Paris granted the Compagnie du Sénégal the exclusive right to export slaves from the Senegal River for sale to plantations in the Caribbean. In exchange, the company agreed to manage the settlement and provide their own security. Appointed by the Crown, the company's director had the authority to negotiate treaties, declare war against European rivals, and administer local justice.

From 1659 to 1758, eight different mercantile companies administered the settlement at Saint Louis. They maintained and staffed the fort, policed the waters, and organized trade.[9] Company policy prohibited cohabitation with African women and did not allow company employees to bring families with them to the colonies. Although not widespread, some company employees looked to African women for domestic needs. In 1716, the Compagnie du Sénégal became part of the operating division of the Compagnie des Indes. The new company opened trade in the region to all French ships that paid a tax. These reforms allowed the company to focus its attention on the river trade rather than the ocean trade. The company's director concentrated on securing and transporting goods from the river posts, called *escales*, to independent shippers on the coast.

Two years earlier, André Brue, the company director, established Fort Saint Joseph at Galam, where the Senegal River meets one of its tributaries, the Falémé.[10] The fort served as a strategic base for French trade with the Soninke of Gajaaga, who held a monopoly on slave trading in the region. After 1850, Gajaaga became an increasingly important source of gum arabic from acacia trees along the Senegal. The French position at Gajaaga became even more valuable when gum overtook the slave trade in the volume of French exports. Establishing a fort at Galam, moreover, allowed the small staff of French soldiers to intercept English caravans headed toward the Gambia River.[11]

Company rule dissolved when Britain's victory in the Seven Years' War ousted France from Senegal. British occupation marked a turning point in the growth and development of the coastal towns.[12] French officials armed the free African residents who lived in close proximity to the fort and who fought to defend the settlement from British attack. In 1758, Britain seized Gorée, and Saint Louis fell shortly thereafter. During the period of British occupation, Saint Louis residents sought protection under British law, perhaps opting for security under European rule rather than recognizing the sovereignty of the Wolof kingdoms over the territory of Ndar. Although European rule remained inherently unstable and unpredictable, residents expressed loyalty to France but considered British officials the new authority of the port town.

Geopolitical conflict spurred by war in Europe that was followed by the American Revolution, the French Revolution, and the Napoleonic Wars, had significant repercussions for the colonies of the *ancien régime*. In Saint Louis, most of the permanent residents were African, England and France depended heavily on them to maintain their holdings and carry out the business of trade on the West African coast. Company rule gave way to the British Crown, which imposed its system of law and governance on the outpost. Britain officially recognized the free status of "negroes and mulattos of both sexes" and the rights of free Africans to hold property and practice their religion.[13] At the same time, London left administration of the territory to military officials without oversight from the metropole. A petition dated 22 August 1775 by the inhabitants of Senegal to London details the abuses committed by Colonel Charles O'Hara, who was appointed to govern the colony. According to the petition, O'Hara attempted to abolish the Catholic Church and prevent Africans from receiving a Catholic burial. He also arbitrarily sold household slaves and free people in the transatlantic trade as a means of judicial punishment. Among the list of grievances, petitioners claimed that O'Hara insulted women, used racial insults against townspeople, and seized the property of free Africans to provide a residence for his "concubine," Coumba Poole.[14] Residents saw these actions as an affront to the normal customs of their society and as a sign of the illegitimacy of British rule.

The American Revolution ended British occupation. France seized control of Saint Louis on 30 January 1779. The 1783 Treaty of Versailles , which officially ended the war in North America, ceded Saint Louis and Gorée to the French. The return of French authority raised new questions about the nature of company rule and the importance of territory in Senegal for the *ancien régime*. Louis XVI had little interest in pursuing imperialism. War in Europe and the seeds of the French Revolution undoubtedly distracted the monarchy from paying attention to colonial interests, let alone the concerns of African residents in remote West African outposts. In the late eighteenth century, gum from the Senegal River valley began to replace slaves as the dominant export. In 1785, Louis XVI granted a new mercantile company exclusive rights to the gum trade along the Senegal River. In addition, he placed a military officer in charge of administering civil, military, and judicial law while carrying out diplomatic relations between France and neighboring African states.

Paris appointed the chevalier Stanislas-Jean de Boufflers, a naval officer and renowned novelist and poet, as governor of Senegal.[15] Boufflers arrived in Saint Louis on 21 January 1786 to assume responsibilities from former governor Louis Legardeur Repintigny, who had been chased out of the country after a fire, supposedly the revenge of Muslim clerics, which destroyed 200 straw dwellings on the island. Boufflers remained in Saint Louis for a few months and then left for Gorée, where he established the new French capital. Silvester Golbéry, chief engineer, arrived on the ship *Rossignol* with Boufflers and Geoffroy de Villeneuve, a sous-lieutenant and second-in-command to Boufflers. Jean Baptiste Leonard Durand served as the chief resident agent of the company. Dominique Harcourt Lamiral, an independent French trader who had worked for the company, resided in Saint Louis from 1786 to 1789.[16] All of these men wrote narratives of their travels in Senegal, their observations of economic and social life in the towns, and their impression of signares and other notable Africans.

Despite the concerns that French observers expressed about the company's control over the trade on the Senegal, which resulted in the end of its monopoly over trade in the escales, Paris paid little attention to Senegal. The French Revolution drew state resources away from trade interests in West Africa. François Blanchot served as governor from 1787 to 1809. In 1801, Blanchot left for France. In October 1802, he returned to serve a second term. In total, Blanchot resided almost twenty years in Senegal, more than any other French official in history. He died in Saint Louis on 12 September 1807. As head administrator for the colony, Blanchot provided continuity throughout the revolutionary era, the First Republic, and Napoleon Bonaparte's rise to power. He expressed grave concern over Saint Louis's rapidly expanding population and the danger of being unable to secure enough provisions to feed town residents, French officials, and employees as well as the growing number of slaves that free residents owned.

The Declaration of the Rights of Man and of the Citizen gave birth to a language of universal rights and freedoms that fundamentally altered the political culture of metropolitan France and had significant implications for the nature and legitimacy of French rule in her overseas territories. The language of inalienable rights, individual liberty, and equality for all raised complicated questions about slavery's legitimacy and the extension of French rights to people of color in the Grandes Colonies of Guyana, Guadeloupe, Martinique, and Réunion. The revolution led by slaves in Saint Domingue forced France to grapple with the contradiction of upholding the idea of universal human rights, while protecting the right of slave owners to their property.[17] In March 1792, the revolutionary assembly granted political rights to all *gens de couleur* (people of color) in the colonies. On 4 February 1794, France abolished slavery in its empire. The constitution of the republic not only made the Grandes Colonies departments of France but also conferred the rights of French citizenship to all adult male inhabitants of France's overseas territories, no matter their social status or racial identity. In doing so, the republic called for a new order in which all people, regardless of race, were entitled to the same rights.

Although the debate over slavery and republican rights had a negligible impact on Saint Louis and Gorée, metropolitan policies that sought to expand the political and legal rights of people of African descent in the French West Indies had unforeseen implications. News of the revolutions in France and the West Indies certainly reached the inhabitants of Senegal's coastal towns. Arriving in Senegal in the late 1780s and 1790s, French soldiers and company employees experienced the upheaval of revolution. Some participated in wars for territory in North America. The Alain family may have been part of an exodus from the French West Indies to other regions of the Francophone Atlantic as a result of the conflict in the Caribbean. In addition, France deported a number of soldiers to Senegal for fighting under Toussaint L'Ouverture, but they were expelled after they threatened Governor Pierre Lassere (1807–1809).[18]

Free and property-owning residents of Saint Louis entered the debate over including colonial subjects in the new nation, where they would have the right to participate equally in the export trade. In 1789, the habitants of Saint Louis sent a letter to the Estates-General outlining their grievances against the mercantile company. They argued that Paris should dissolve the Senegal Company's monopoly over the gum and slave trade in order to allow town residents to compete openly as export middlemen.[19] Paris abolished the monopoly over trade in the escales but did not extend full legal and political rights to the inhabitants. Dominique Lamiral, an independent trader who presented the letter to the legislative assembly in Paris, expressed the paternalistic attitude that defined relations between the West African settlement and the metropole. Lamiral described the people of Saint Louis as brothers of those who live "on the banks of the Seine," yet he viewed political rights as something the inhabitants of Senegal's towns should aspire to in the future.[20] Nevertheless, the revolutionary moment had unforeseen consequences for the Saint Louis elite by providing a basis for asserting their interests and challenging the company's monopoly over trade in the river posts.

In 1802, the First Republic came to an abrupt end when Napoleon Bonaparte gained power. He rescinded the decree abolishing slavery, legalizing the institution in the French Empire. The Napoleonic Wars brought a new era of disruption and insecurity for Saint Louis residents. In 1800, British forces took control of Gorée and imposed a naval blockade that prevented French forces from reaching Saint Louis, effectively cutting off all communication with France and preventing provisions from reaching the town. On 13 July 1809 the British reoccupied Saint Louis. Great Britain held control over the two Senegalese coastal territories until the treaty ending the Napoleonic Wars restored Senegal to France in January 1817.

Urban Life in Saint Louis

Urban society grew substantially between 1758 and 1817. Social stratification deepened, and the institutions and practices that defined the town's culture were solidified. In 1736, 127 Frenchmen, a little more than one hundred free African laborers, and ninety-four slaves owned by the mercantile company lived in and around the fort.[21] By the end of the eighteenth century, the number of permanent residents increased as a result of an influx of free African workers as well as slaves. At a time when European authority vacillated between French and British rule, Africans constituted the majority of permanent residents and provided a stable workforce for the settlement.

Africans from the lower Senegal came to work for the French company, settling just outside the fort. Some served as *maitres des langues* (interpreters) between the French and Africans on the mainland. The company employed

Africans as soldiers, sailors, deckhands, and helmsmen on ships sailing along the coast and as riverboat crew. Africans who adopted Christianity came to be known as *grumets*.[22] The close ties that free African town residents developed with European officials afforded this group the opportunity to enter into contractual arrangements with the company to buy plots of land. Those who lived in close proximity to the fort, called *l'habitation,* came to be known as *habitants.* The ability to build a house close to the fort served as the basis for establishing social hierarchy in the town.

The role of signares expanded as European trade with Senegal increased in the second half of the eighteenth century. Signares organized the domestic lives of company employees and European officials. Their métis offspring served as translators and intermediaries for French and English officials. Métis men entered the local provisional trade in grains from the lower Senegal. They also inherited property from their fathers. They rented their ships, canoes, and slaves to company officials for upriver trade expeditions. The term *habitant* now also referred to the descendants of grumets, maitres des langues, and signares who acquired capital and could enter into business for themselves.[23]

In the 1730s, the company turned to slave labor to replace skilled European workers. Company employees routinely suffered from disease and illness because of the harsh climate they encountered in the interior.[24] These conditions proved especially devastating for the skilled workers who died during the two-week voyage from Saint Louis to Fort Saint Joseph when the trading season began in July. The company lost additional personnel who remained in the river trade depots until October, when the trading season ended. The company decided to replace them with slaves who were trained as carpenters, coopers, gunsmiths, and sail makers. This solved the problem of relying on either an undependable European workforce or on free African labor that could prove difficult to control.

By the 1750s, habitants rather than the mercantile company owned most of the slaves. In 1754, the company gathered population data for the last time before British occupation.[25] Because officials were primarily concerned with counting the "useful" residents (male workers, not women and children), the data does not reflect the population in normal times. Beginning in 1751, the region was struck by a famine that lasted four years. The report shows that while the number of slaves belonging to the company declined, the number owned by habitants increased. The total Saint Louis population reportedly amounted to 2,500 persons, but officials counted only 800 men as "useful." The population of interest to the company included 15 habitant ship captains, 15 first mates (presumably habitant), 36 grumets, 3 chief interpreters, 36 apprentices, and 98 slaves owned by the company who received their food and three francs a month in wages.[26] Habitants owned 550 slaves that the company rented for upriver trade missions. In addition, 100 free people from Walo and Cayor, who officials reported "are attached to us by their cohabitation with women of the island," lived permanently in the town. The remaining residents undoubtedly constituted women and children.

By the time the French returned in the mid-1780s, the permanent population numbered between 5,000 and 6,000.[27] The free population amounted to approximately 2,500, while the rest served as slaves in the households of free town residents. A significant increase in domestic slavery accounted for the growth in the Saint Louis population during this time. Household slaves, according to Golbéry, lived on the master's ground, "intermarrying and serving within the bounds of his domains."[28] Signares, rather than company officials, became the dominant slave owners. Women controlled a retinue of household slaves that could be used for trade on the owner's behalf or to fulfill the domestic needs of European traders and officials who resided temporarily in the country. Marie Gonefall owned 67 slaves, the largest number belonging to any individual in the town in the late eighteenth century.[29]

The social hierarchy that developed in Saint Louis centered on occupation, specifically one's position in the commercial system, but also intersected with French ideas about racial difference borrowed from the wider Atlantic world. Men who became traders constituted the top rank, followed by interpreters. Grumets who served as boat captains made up the next rank, followed by free African riverboat workers, called *laptots*. Artisans, unskilled workers, and slaves occupied the lowest level. Signares and their métis offspring had more access to capital than grumets and also derived their social status from their familial ties to European men. As a result, métis men tended to dominate the middleman trade niche but did not exclusively control it. Grumets gained notable standing because of their positions as captains of sailing vessels. Their identification with Christianity also marked their close association with European merchants and authorities. A grumet named Blondin worked as a boat captain for Signare Coumba Poole and earned enough capital to enter the river trade. Pierre Dubois became the wealthiest grumet in town. Both men achieved notable standing by establishing themselves in trade. Free African workers, originating from the lower or upper Senegal, had greater social standing than household slaves, but unlike the habitants, they could be subjected to arbitrary enslavement and export in the Atlantic trade.[30] Their position as unskilled labor without property set some free Africans and slaves apart from habitants.

The social hierarchy of Saint Louis is evident in the pattern of household building and settlement that developed.[31] Poorly constructed and barely livable, the fort was located in the center (map 2). Company directors began leasing small parcels of land around the fort to habitants and signares, who conveniently built houses where European men either rented accommodations or purchased land for their spouses to build a home. Habitants typically lived in one-story houses described as *maisons en dur,* while African workers lived in straw dwellings with a conical roof. The working-class African and Muslim neighborhood on the north side of the island became known as *lodo* in Wolof, which means "place of people from the countryside." Habitants lived in the neighborhood south of the fort known by Wolof speakers as the *quartier Kretien,* or the Christian neighborhood, where the "*mulâtres, mulâtresses, quarterons*" plus the "*négresses libres*" and their captives lived.[32] Household slaves lived in conical dwellings within their master's courtyard.

A daily market at the center of the island brought people from the Atlantic fishing villages of Guet Ndar and the mainland farming regions of Gandiole and Leybar to the town to sell produce, meat, fish, and salt. Habitant traders specialized in the grain trade. They acquired millet from producers in the lower Senegal for sale to ship captains or for local consumption. Habitants also cultivated garden plots where they reportedly "grew vegetables from Europe."[33] Food supplies remained a constant source of anxiety for Saint Louis residents as blockades prevented French ships from arriving with imported provisions during periods of conflict, such as during the American Revolution and the Napoleonic Wars. The threat of periodic famine and the increase in the domestic slave population raised official concern over the town's ability to provide adequate food. A hospital, church, Christian cemetery, and twenty brick houses existed in the town by the late eighteenth century.

The development of local traditions of democratic politics also defined the urban community during this period. Residents of Saint Louis and

Gorée took up arms to defend the settlement from British attack in an expression of loyalty to the French Crown. Habitants used the practice of writing petitions to express their concerns and complaints to officials in London and Paris. Saint Louis and Gorée residents also chose a notable habitant to serve as mayor, the beginning of a local tradition of democratic institution building. French law did not recognize municipal government for Senegal's towns until the end of the nineteenth century. Like other Atlantic African trade societies, influential families derived power from their success in commerce by establishing strong patron-client networks.[34] An individual's position in commerce, status as a respected property owner, and affiliation with the Church bolstered his standing as a leader in the community.

Habitants thus emerged as spokesmen for the urban community in their dealings with European authorities. The tradition of appointing a notable habitant as mayor developed during the period of company rule. When Britain gained control of Gorée in 1758, Reverend Lindsay noted that an "island gentleman (although a negroe) of good education" presented an address on behalf of the urban community to the Crown. Mayor Charles, Lindsay wrote, "may truly be stil'd their king, priest and lawgiver."[35] Mayors, in the Saint Louis and Gorée tradition, came from a notable habitant family and typically obtained a degree of Western education beyond their peers. In the absence of a permanent priest, the mayor performed mass and other Roman Catholic rites. The mayor also provided security for the local marketplace and administered justice. In the 1790s, the habitants, under the direction of the governor, organized local councils to advise French officials on matters concerning the territories' administration and mobilized conscripted labor for public works.[36] British and French officials depended on the cooperation of town residents to carry out the daily functions of government, which reduced the need for substantial European personnel in their West African settlements.

The *Cahier de doléances,* signed by the habitants of Saint Louis and presented to the Estates-General by Dominique Lamiral, offers rare evidence of habitant responses to the revolutionary era.[37] As France sought to reconcile its claim to universal rights with slaveholding in its plantation colonies, metropolitan debates about slavery's legitimacy and the rights of free people of color in the new republic did not include the implications of these legal and political questions for Senegal's habitant population. French officials considered household slavery in Senegal benign and outside the scope of reforms to the planter system of the West Indies. Habitants, moreover, constituted the slave-owning class of the island towns, and officials in Senegal and Paris had little concern about the implications of antislavery laws for the people of Saint Louis. The debates over universal rights sweeping metropolitan France and her colonies manifested itself in Senegal as a struggle for habitants to compete equally with the mercantile company in the export trade.

Senegal's habitants directed to the revolutionary assembly their complaints about the abusive practices of the mercantile company. In 1786, when France regained control of Saint Louis and Gorée from the British, Louis XVI granted the French company exclusive rights to carry out trade in the escales and to export slaves to supply markets in the West Indies. By 1789, the gum trade with Trarza who controlled the gum trade on the north bank gained in profitability over slave exports. The monopoly denied habitant traders participation in the gum trade by giving the company exclusive access to trade in the escales. Lamiral, an independent trader with his own grievances against the company, delivered a statement to the revolutionary council on behalf of the free property-owning Christian residents of Saint Louis, expressing their abiding loyalty to France while also demanding equal protection and justice under French law like all other subjects of the king. The habitants complained about the abusive practices of the company, which sought to reduce the profits of local middlemen by excluding them from the gum trade. The habitants argued that the middleman trade constituted their only means of subsistence and that the French regime had a duty to protect them from mercantile companies that sought to eliminate them from the export economy.

The opening line of the petition inserted Senegal into the French body politic by stating, "The king assembled you to hear . . . the complaints of his people," for those who live "on the fortunate banks of the Seine, those who made flourish the Atlantic Islands, those who live in the beautiful climate of India as well as those who live on the arid banks of the Niger."[38] The petition demanded that the revolution's universal values of equality and brotherhood as well as the universal laws espoused in the Declaration of the Rights of Man should be extended to the people of the colonies, regardless of race. The habitant petition read, "Negres or Mulâtres, we are all French, because it is French blood which runs through our veins and those of our progeny."

The habitants declared their loyalty to the French nation by claiming that they were entitled to the same rights and protections as French citizens, even if the republic did not recognize them as such.

Paris responded to habitant concerns by abolishing the company's monopoly and by opening trade in the escales to habitant merchants. The habitants also outlined a plan for municipal government and representation in the national assembly. Consistent with colonial ideologies of race and citizenship, the plan for municipal government outlined in the petition limited voting rights to French, métis, and "assimilated Africans." The language of the plan reflected French thinking about the political and legal rights of people of color in which political rights corresponded to specific cultural markers of Frenchness. In Lamiral's view, mulâtres were people "born under a different sky," who had the education and morals necessary to enjoy such "social liberties" but could not be citizens of the nation. Their children, he argued, could aspire to the same legal status as metropolitan French. "Blacks," Lamiral maintained, were not "civilized enough" to participate in political life.[39]

The habitants' demand did not expand their political rights and institutions, but it did formalize democratic traditions already established in the towns. Nevertheless, the republic did not grant Saint Louis or Gorée municipal status or the right to elect a legislative representative. In Senegal, French officials recognized the habitant practice of selecting a mayor and provided a salary for the position. In the 1790s, Governor Blanchot organized local advisory councils consisting of notable habitants to advise him on local matters. While colonial policy did not formally recognize the legal or political rights of habitants, town residents wrote letters and petitions to articulate their interests with authorities in Paris and to assert their claim to leadership positions within the urban community.

Signares and the Formation of the Urban Community

By the late eighteenth century, most European men who lived in Senegal as soldiers or company employees entered into temporary unions with African women. Signares played key roles in shaping the social and cultural environment of the towns and in establishing the systems that facilitated trade between European merchants and kin-based societies of Senegal's interior. Signares embraced the new cultural influences coming from the Atlantic world but also upheld continuity with the social and cultural values of Senegal's mainland. Derived from the Portuguese word *senhora,* the title of signare signified a woman of high social standing who owned property and maintained a proper, respectable household.[40] The title applied equally to African women and women of mixed racial ancestry who entered unions, called mariage à la mode du pays, with European men. Marriage to a high-ranking military officer or merchant, rather than to a company employee, further expanded a signare's opportunity for social prominence and wealth (fig. 1).

Signares exercised authority over the household, yet their activities had effects beyond the woman's sphere of home and private life. The household served as the central location to exchange ideas and circulate capital between visiting foreigners and African townspeople. Establishing households for European men also enhanced their companions' survival in the unfamiliar, harsh environment of the sahel.[41] Giving birth to sons, moreover, produced a network of intermediaries that European officials could rely on in their commercial, diplomatic, and military dealings. As slave owners, signares provided access to labor for the mercantile company and European officers, who rented slaves to do public work and to serve as crew in commercial expeditions on the Senegal. Signare households instilled European tastes and values in their children but also reinforced the link between coastal people and African societies of the mainland. In so doing, they contributed to the formation of Saint Louis society as a third space— one that neither mimicked French society nor neatly corresponded to Wolof societies of the Senegal River valley.

Mariage à la mode du pays corresponded to an expectation of marriage among African people of the interior yet was transformed to meet the realities of life in the coastal towns. Marriage between a signare and a European man involved obligations of marital exchange and a public ceremony deemed acceptable to the urban community. Typically, the man negotiated a marriage contract with the family of a young woman. He presented her family with gifts to seal the agreement and provided a house where his bride could establish their household.[42] Children born of the union inherited the last names of their European fathers. The marriage differed from Wolof or Soninke unions because families typically dismissed the one- or two-month obligatory courtship common among Senegalese societies of the interior. In addition, both parties understood that the marriage ended upon the death or permanent departure of the man from Senegal. This allowed signares to remarry without social stigma and European men to marry legally in their home country or return to their spouses in the metropole without consequence.

In late eighteenth-century Saint Louis, marriage among the Christian habitant population (métis and grumets) had more in common with marriage practices of Wolof society than the Western European ideal. After courtship, a young man and his relatives met her family at her father's house. The relatives formed a circle around the *arbre du conseil*, where the young man's father made an offer of slaves, horses, cattle, merchandise, and gold to the parents of the woman he hoped to marry. Once they reached an agreement, the marriage ceremony proceeded immediately or the following day. Priests rarely officiated because of the lack of permanent clergy, although the mayor may have performed the ceremony. Then the bride's father brought her to the groom's home, "her head covered in white cloth that she wove herself."[43] After verifying her virginity, a festival of eight days ensued. Musicians and young people of the town came to celebrate with palm wine and *eau de vie* (spirits) for the men and a punch made of muscat wine for the women. The marriage ceremony, perhaps ideally described by observers, shows conformity to notions of marriage common in Wolof society but also reveals the incorporation of practices consistent with life in this Atlantic port.[44]

As spouses of European men, signares obtained access to trade goods as well as gifts of slaves, real estate, and gold. Signares used their ties to the mercantile company and the trade systems of the island to acquire gold and slaves from upriver expeditions. They commonly sent household slaves, rented to the company for trade expeditions, to acquire gold. Signare dress styles served as visible markers of cosmopolitain consumption. They wore the *grande pagne* (wraparound cloth) of African women with a chemise of fine fabric, Moroccan shoes, and imported cloth from India (guinées) as a head wrap. Signares obtained gold from Galam on the upper Senegal that Moor goldsmiths designed into filigree bracelets, rings, and earrings. The wealthiest women maintained a goldsmith in their homes to produce jewelry exclusively for them.[45] An entourage of slave women added to the demonstration of wealth, propriety, and social esteem that signares exhibited as the wives of European men.

For European soldiers and merchants, marriage to a signare facilitated their need for an acceptable domestic life outside of the ill-constructed fortress. Signare households provided the proper nutrition, hygiene, and medical services for strangers of the severe climate who were susceptible to fatal diseases such as malaria and yellow fever. In the first half of the eighteenth century, company policy forbade cohabitation with African women yet prohibited French women from joining their husbands in the colony. The company did not believe a French woman could survive the harsh environment.[46] In 1758, when the British took control of Gorée, authorities disliked cohabitation but considered it a practical necessity. By the late eighteenth century, French observers considered the practice a feature of everyday life in the coastal towns. European officials viewed these unions as an unseemly but necessary fact of life in the West African commercial port. Town residents, however, saw mariage à la mode du pays as legitimate marital unions.

In establishing Afro-European households, signares played central roles in shaping the cultural traditions necessary for developing a class of intermediaries for African societies of the mainland and Europeans on the coast. Grumets and free African and Muslim residents shared equally in forming the cultural environment of the towns, but signares produced métis children who could also rely on their kinship with European men to act as cross-cultural brokers. By the late eighteenth century, signares expressed their attachment to the Catholic Church.[47] Habitants (métis and grumet) who carved out their niche as intermediaries in the provision trade and export trade in the river trade posts also identified with the Church, despite the lack of a permanent clerical presence. Adherence to a monotheistic tradition played an important role in defining trade relations between Saint Louis residents and traders in the Senegal River valley. Like Muslim traders along the north and south banks of the Senegal, the habitants of Saint Louis shared a belief in a religion of the book. At the same time, Christianity distinguished habitants from Muslims and shored up their affiliation with Europe. Identification with Christianity served a similar purpose for habitants establishing their reputation as intermediaries in Atlantic networks as Islam solidified trade relations among Muslim merchants operating on the Saharan side.[48]

Signares facilitated the development of a practice of religious pluralism in Saint Louis. Town residents recognized the various religious traditions of the people of Ndar and participated in Muslim and Christian rituals. Christian habitants attended mass, baptized their children, and celebrated Easter. They also carried gris-gris (talismans), circumcised their children, and celebrated Tabaski (the Muslim festival, Eid) with their neighbors. Lamiral observed that among habitants "there are some who after having been to mass still do the Salam."[49] Habitants baptized their children according to the teachings of the Church but practiced the Wolof tradition of naming children on the eighth day and celebrating with Wolof song. European observers attributed this religious syncretism to a "lack of education" that stemmed from the lax attitude toward religion at home. Signares, in particular, incorporated aspects of Islam and Wolof belief systems into Catholic mass and baptism. In doing so, these women fostered a dual cultural outlook that distinguished them and their children as Catholic maintaining their ties to Muslim and Wolof peoples of the towns and the interior.

Like religion, language served as another marker of métis identity. Linguistic dexterity was essential. The ability to speak French and Wolof allowed métis habitants to emphasize their connection to European society at certain times or evoke their relationship to the people of the Senegal River valley at others. Although Luso-Africans along the southern Senegambian coast spoke Portuguese Creole, Wolof became the language of daily communication in Saint Louis.[50] European men living in the towns developed minor proficiency in the language incorporating key words and phrases in their observations of town life. Signares likely spoke Wolof, not French, in the home, exposing their spouses to the language. According to one observer, the "blacks of Saint Louis" were like the Wolof of the Jolof kingdom.[51] Urban Wolof functioned as the language of the household, the market, and daily conversation because of the interaction among signares, their children, spouses, workers, and female slaves in the home.

French developed as the language of colonial administration. The bureaucratic systems relied on French literacy. Some men provided French education for their métis sons by hiring a tutor from among the European personnel in the town. Maitres des langues became proficient in French by serving as interpreters for French officials. Grumets also developed proficiency in spoken French by working as ship captains and key personnel for European traders. Reading and writing, however, remained the domain of a privileged few among the habitant elite.[52] The sons of European men had the greatest possibility for formal training. The ability to employ French in some circumstances and Wolof in others allowed the habitant elite to move easily between African and European societies.

Signares occupied a position of high social standing in Senegal's coastal towns. The establishment of new households that linked European men to

Senegal through their paternity of children born from African women served as the foundation for the development of métis society and identity. Some of the names of the African women who established the first wave of métis lineages are known. Others remain anonymous or lost to history. Signares who became wealthy women of high social standing embodied the cultural flexibility inherent in the residents of Senegal's coastal towns. Signares, their métis offspring, grumets, free African workers, and slaves developed the cultural elasticity that Atlantic Creoles who inhabited similar port towns needed to operate in societies shaped by geopolitical conflict and the flow of capital across the Atlantic. At the same time, the Saint Louis community maintained key continuities with the Wolof people of the lower Senegal. Signares played an essential role in establishing the systems and structures needed to facilitate trade and reproduce colonial society. These conditions gave rise to a self-conscious métis population with the ability to organize and make claims for political power and representation. The growth and empowerment of the Saint Louis community in this era provided a foundation for establishing interdependent relations among French authorities, metropolitan export merchants, and town residents that had unforeseen implications when imperialism expanded in the nineteenth century.

2

Métis Society and Transformations in the Colonial Economy (1820–70)

Whereas a self-conscious métis population emerged in the second half of the eighteenth century, the social, economic, and demographic conditions that allowed for the consolidation of métis identity occurred in the early nineteenth century. By the 1820s, métis habitants constituted a veritable oligarchy. They obtained a level of economic success that set them apart from Muslim traders and grumets. Métis habitants were chosen to serve on the governor's advisory council, as mayor of the town, and also in the General Council, a short-lived electoral body established in the 1830s. In 1848, métis habitant Durand Valantin represented Senegal in Paris when the Second Republic established a seat.[1] Signares continued to play key roles as property owners and labor recruiters in the towns, but the economic foundations of métis society increasingly centered on male-headed trade houses that controlled the gum trade in the ports on the north bank of the Senegal River. People of mixed race used their access to metropolitan capital, their familiarity with French industry, and their knowledge of the landscape and customs of Senegal's interior to establish the most highly capitalized trade houses among Saint Louis residents before 1850.

When France regained Senegal from British control in 1817, it marked the beginning of a new era of colonialism. French authorities relied on the Saint Louis elite to facilitate their relations with neighboring kingdoms. They considered the Catholics who owned property in the island town natural partners for spreading French economic, cultural, and political ideas. Despite these common ties, tensions existed between metropolitan interests and those of the habitant elite. The economic crisis of the 1840s revealed the nature of habitant dependency on metropolitan capital and raised questions about the viability of the coastal elite as metropolitan merchants sought to establish a new cash crop economy in Senegal's peanut basin. Métis families experienced the reality of French imperialism, which supported the development of an intermediary class of capitalist traders at one moment yet restructured the colonial economy in ways that threatened their status as property-owning commercial elites at another.[2] Like other free people of color in nineteenth-century Atlantic ports, the métis had to contend with their dependency on the capitalist structures of the colonial economy while seeking to maintain their autonomy in economic and political affairs.

The transition from the Atlantic slave trade to legitimate trade in West Africa created a "crisis of adaptability" for coastal middlemen, who excelled in the slave trade but struggled to adapt to the demands for exports of raw materials by European merchants.[3] For some historians, the development of the gum trade represented the last phase in the penetration of foreign capital into African economies and the ultimate dismantling of an African middle class. Others have emphasized resiliency over dependence. Métis habitants reached their heyday in the gum trade in the 1830s, but experienced dramatic financial losses in the 1840s. At the same time, Muslim habitants benefited from the loosening of protectionist policies for trade in the river ports. In the 1840s, Muslim traders established their own trade houses and served as agents for metropolitan firms in the interior. The consolidation of French rule at the turn of the twentieth century, however, corresponded with the elimination of Saint Louis traders as middlemen in the colonial economy because the rise of monopoly corporations eliminated the need for coastal elites to facilitate the import-export trade.[4]

Although recent studies have documented the resiliency of Muslim traders, few have examined the strategies that métis traders used to adapt to the changing economy. In light of new evidence about the strength of Saint Louis trade networks, it seems premature to conclude that the gum crisis of the 1840s resulted in the immediate economic collapse of métis habitants. Although métis families suffered financial losses, they did not disappear from trade and commerce. Rather, their connection to the commercial economy remained a central aspect of their identity and claim to political power. Closer examination of métis responses to transformations in Senegal's colonial economy after 1850 further illustrates the resiliency of Saint Louis traders as a whole. Métis habitants, in particular, responded to the crisis by consolidating their wealth through intermarriage, operating on the frontiers of the colonial economy, and mobilizing their kin and client networks in support of their interests.

The Economic Foundations of Métis Society

The economic foundations of métis society originated in the late eighteenth century, when people of mixed race emerged as the dominant property owners in the towns and occupied the highest rank of the commercial hierarchy. Signares accumulated wealth in houses, riverboats, slaves, and gold. Their sons and daughters inherited material wealth from their African mothers and European fathers. In the nineteenth century, a new group of metropolitan merchants from Bordeaux and Marseille arrived, seeking to escape the effects of revolutionary conflict at home, to build fortunes by entering the export trade, or to seek adventure. They established private export houses by tapping into the existing social network. The end of the mercantile company's monopoly on exports from Senegal gave rise to an era of free trade in which individuals, working on their own, organized the import and export trade between Senegal and France. The expansion of independent merchants, moreover, strengthened the socioeconomic status of the métis population, who carved out a niche as the most effective middlemen in the gum trade and as property owners.

The consolidation of wealth and power for métis habitants relied on their connection to the Atlantic commercial system. The changing environment of French imperialism provided new economic and political advantages. Because Napoleon largely ignored French interests in Senegal, Governor François Blanchot ran the colony with little support from Paris. In July 1807, shortly after Blanchot's death, Saint Louis fell to the British. Governor Charles William Maxwell administered Saint Louis from British headquarters in Gambia. In 1816, when the restored Bourbon monarchy regained control, Paris devised a plan to turn Senegal into an agricultural colony.[5] Seeking to mitigate the loss of Saint Domingue and the end of the transatlantic slave trade, Louis XVIII used African labor to produce cotton, indigo, and sugar cane in the floodplains of the lower Senegal River. Governor Julien Schmaltz (1819–20) devised a plan for agricultural colonization as the cornerstone of the restoration monarchy's interest in Senegal, gained approval from the regime, and negotiated treaties for territory from the Brak (king) of Walo.

From 1819 to 1831, the naval ministry charged Senegal's governors with implementing the plantation scheme.[6] Governor Jean François Baron Roger (1821–27), Schmaltz's successor, established a town called Richard Toll on the south bank of the lower Senegal as the site for the agricultural estates. After ten years, French officials abandoned the project because of the high cost of production, poor soil quality and cop yields, and the difficulty of ensuring adequate labor. They blamed the failure of the plantation scheme on the "idleness" of African workers, who preferred to grow millet for their own consumption rather than cotton or indigo for export.[7] The farmers of Walo, Cayor, and Fouta had little interest in cotton cultivation. At the same time, Saint Louis traders ignored official plans to develop agricultural exports because their lives were intimately tied to the Senegal River trade and Atlantic commerce.

Habitant prosperity depended on the success of the gum trade. Gum fever swept Saint Louis. The class of *négociants* (wholesale merchants) increased sharply after 1816. The demise of the mercantile company opened up trade to habitants in river ports, known as *escales,* on the lower and middle Senegal.[8] The number of licensed habitant traders increased from 40 in 1818 to 150 in 1837. The number of riverboats owned and operated by Saint Louis traders also increased, and the population of free African workers from the countryside who were hired to work in the gum trade grew steadily. In 1835, the Saint Louis population numbered 12,000 permanent residents. By 1830, at least 3,000 people were making their living from the gum trade.[9] Traders used their knowledge of the land and their relationship with Moors on the Senegal's north bank, where the gum trade took place, to assert their control over trade upriver.

The Trarza and Brakna had long specialized in tapping gum from acacia trees and transporting it to the river trade markets. In exchange for gum, Moor traders demanded guinées, a blue cloth manufactured in India and imported by French merchants. Habitants acquired trade goods from wholesale merchants in Saint Louis on credit. They assumed the risk of transporting guinées and other trade goods to the escales and paid the costs of conducting the trade. Saint Louis traders paid taxes and customs duties to the emirs, who controlled trade in the escales and negotiated the price of gum with caravan leaders who brought the gum harvest to the upriver depots for sale. The activity in the upriver markets during the trade season resembled the bustling nature of a European town on market day.[10] The Moors, Gaspard Mollien observed, arrived with their slaves and camels to meet Saint Louis traders with their fleet of riverboats and African crew (slave and free) to negotiate the price of gum. The king of the Trarza, Mollien wrote, visited the market unarmed to observe the activity and receive customary tribute.

The gum trade had existed since the early seventeenth century, but it became the primary export from Senegal in the late eighteenth century. In the era of the mercantile company, employees acquired gum from Moors on the north bank and gold and slaves from Wolof and Soninke on the south bank (map 3). Rivalry between the French, British, and Dutch intensified competition over the gum trade until France dominated the Senegal River markets.[11] In the 1780s, French observers wrote of the substantial profit margins earned from the gum-for-guinée trade with Senegal, but also noted the problem of sharp fluctuations in the price of gum on European markets. The volume of the gum trade between Europe and Senegal increased from 500–600 tons per year in the first half of the eighteenth century to nearly double that amount in the late eighteenth century.[12]

Trarza and Brakna as well as the Wolof, Soninke, and Fulbe peoples of the sahel used the edible gum in cooking and medicines. European industries preferred Senegal's gum, which they considered far superior in quality to Arabia's, for use in the manufacture of calico print textiles, pharmaceuticals, book binding, and preserves. In the Senegal River valley, guinées replaced locally woven cloth that Saharan consumers previously had acquired from West Africans in the savanna. Trarza and Brakna emirs distributed the highly sought-after blue cloth to their clients or used it to trade for grain with the Wolof along the Senegal's south bank.

The gum-for-guinée trade defined legitimate commerce between France and Senegal. Saint Louis's emergence as a flourishing Atlantic port further solidified French dominance over gum exports in the first half of the nineteenth century. The trading season revolved around the minor harvest, called the *petite traite*, which opened in November and closed in January, and the major harvest season, called the *grande traite*. The *grande traite* began in early February and lasted until the end of July. The trade took place in three ports of call located in the lower and middle Senegal. The Trarza emir, who had close relations with the Wolof of Walo, controlled the Escale du Desert and the Escale des Dramancours on the lower Senegal. The Brakna emir with cooperation from the Tukulor minister of Fouta Toro controlled the Escale du Coq on the middle Senegal. The Trarza and

Brakna rulers charged traders a tax on the volume of gum traded (one piece of guinée per half ton of gum) and expected gifts and customs duties.[13]

The upriver trade relied on inhabitants of Saint Louis who could raise capital and assume the costs of transportation and labor. Traders who specialized in the exchange of gum for guinées held the highest rank. Métis habitants, grumets, and Muslim residents of Saint Louis all participated in commerce, but métis traders had the advantage of having close ties to French wholesalers on the coast and Trarza and Brakna Moors on the river's north bank. Since the end of monopoly protections in the 1790s, métis habitants succeeded in dominating the middleman sector of the gum trade. In the late 1820s, a new wave of Wolof speakers, fleeing civil war in Walo, settled in Saint Louis and established themselves as petty traders.[14] They specialized in the trade of hides, beeswax, and ivory for export to coastal markets as well as in grain, which had a lucrative market among Moors on the north bank and was also needed for local consumption in Saint Louis. A small number of grumets and métis participated in petty trade, but Muslim town residents made up the vast majority.

Métis habitants operated as the best-capitalized middlemen in the gum-for-guinée trade. They owned riverboats to reach the escales. They traveled to the upriver markets when the trade season opened and lived in these locations for weeks or months until the gum caravans arrived. They paid maitres des langues to intercept the caravans with the best harvest and hosted the Moors in the escales, courting the emirs and the heads of trade caravans with gifts and favors to secure the best gum harvests of the season. Métis habitants played key roles in the political conflicts of the Trarza and used their ties to Walo and Trarza lineages to mediate conflict in the region.[15] Trade relied on trust, reliability, security, and skilled negotiation. The success of the métis in the gum trade depended on their knowledge of the land and their familiarity with the customs of people in the interior. Their ability to draw upon kin and client ties with Europeans and Africans strengthened their credibility with metropolitan merchants as well as African rulers and traders in the interior.

Métis traders also capitalized on their distinct advantages with French wholesale merchants and retailers in the coastal port. In the early 1800s, a new generation of Frenchmen arrived in Senegal to take advantage of the end of the monopoly by mercantile companies. Hubert Prom, the brothers Justin and Bruno Devès, Pierre Delile Jay, and Auguste Teisseire were among the new arrivals who established retail or wholesale firms in Saint Louis.[16] They did not all come from Bordeaux, but most passed through it. Some began as agents for trade houses in Bordeaux, but almost all established the headquarters of their import-export firms in France's southwestern port. The majority began commerce in Senegal as young men. In 1822, Hubert Prom arrived in Senegal at age 15 and established a wholesale company six years later. In 1831, Prom created an association with his cousin Hilaire Maurel. The new company, Maurel and Prom, transferred its headquarters to Bordeaux, but emerged as the most powerful French firm in Saint Louis in the 1830s and 1840s. In 1837, Hubert Prom served on Senegal's appeal court and as secretary of Senegal's short-lived General Council.[17]

In 1807, Justin Devès left Bordeaux after his family faced bankruptcy. He traveled as far as Philadelphia as a sailor aboard an American ship, then embarked for Senegal. In 1810, at age 21, Devès arrived on Gorée Island aboard a slave ship. He entered the export trade, formed a trade house, and then built an import-export firm with his brothers Bruno and Edouard, who later joined him in Senegal.[18] Auguste Teisseire began selling birds and ostrich feathers and earned enough capital to establish his own import-export house. The commercial firm Buhan and Teisseire resulted from the merger of his métis son's trade house and his Bordeaux father-in-law's firm. The Bordeaux merchants operated wholesale firms that supplied guinées to the Senegal market and gum to Europe. All of these men participated in the political life of the colony thanks to their close associations with the minister of the navy and the military officials in Saint Louis. The Bordeaux merchants literally shaped colonial policy in the 1840s and 1850s.[19]

French merchants who came to Senegal followed the same practice of mariage à la mode du pays established in the eighteenth century. They married signares or daughters of métis families and often sent their children to Bordeaux to study. Three children of one Bordeaux merchant reportedly spoke only Wolof up to age 7, when they first arrived in France for schooling.[20] These familial relationships facilitated métis access to the upper strata of the commercial hierarchy, but also created unexpected tensions. Some métis men entered trade as the sons of Bordeaux merchants. Others came from métis families of an earlier generation but still benefited from access to capital and relations of trust because of their position. Some worked closely with their Bordeaux relatives, while others were excluded from the metropolitan side of their family's business.

Métis family firms patterned themselves after the Bordeaux model, forming trade houses based on associations between brothers, cousins, fathers, sons, and in-laws. The Durand brothers, the Pellegrin family, Louis and George Alsace, and Charles Floissac (both the father and the son) formed business associations based on family ties. While these firms resembled the businesses of Bordeaux merchants, they differed in one respect. The title of *négociant* was reserved for individuals who operated highly capitalized wholesale firms that specialized in importing goods from overseas. Négociants held a monopoly on the import of guinées to Senegal and controlled the merchandising of European trade goods in the colony. Metropolitan Frenchmen dominated this level of the commercial system, as only a few métis traders reached the status of wholesale merchants.

In addition to trade, property ownership played a central role in consolidating métis identity. Property owners held honorable rank in the town and were listed among notable habitants in official documents. Property ownership also bore a direct relationship to participation in political life. In early nineteenth-century France, property ownership conveyed a set of political rights denied to individuals who did not have access to capital. The expansion of political rights for the metropolitain bourgeoisie corresponded to policies that extended limited voting rights in the colonies. In the 1830s and 1840s, officials appointed notable habitants to serve on advisory councils and local assemblies because of their status as property owners. In Senegal, métis notables gained access to positions of power, in part, because of their control of real estate and capital assets.

Property ownership also served as a visible marker of identity for habitant women. Signares gained high social standing and influence based on their wealth in gold, homes, trade goods, and slaves. In the mid- and late eighteenth century, signares owned the majority of buildings, small sailing craft, riverboats, and warehouses on the island. European merchants and officials commonly rented homes, buildings, and boats from signares. Their métis children inherited their wealth, bolstering their position as the town's main property owners.[21] By the 1820s, Saint Louis residents depended on the capitalist economy of Atlantic networks rather than on agricultural production for their livelihood. Property had legally recognized value in the flow of global capital that structured the local economies of the towns and became an essential component for free town residents in establishing their socioeconomic status as part of the bourgeoisie.

Slave ownership was central to habitant production while also demonstrating wealth and social standing. By the mid-eighteenth century, Saint Louis had adopted the characteristics of an urban slave society.[22] Slavery developed as a result of the town's connection to the transatlantic slave trade, but it corresponded to notions of slavery that existed in the Wolof societies of the mainland. In the seventeenth century, the Wolof kingdoms developed a system in which the state controlled the slave trade and profited from it.[23] Relying on slave labor for intensive agricultural production allowed the Wolof nobility to increase surpluses and satisfy the rising demand for millet by coastal inhabitants, crew of slave ships, and the enslaved at the coast. Wolof systems of slavery recognized different status categories. One group within the slave hierarchy included a titled class of slave warriors created by the nobility and known as *ceedo*. Perhaps initially recruited from among slave laborers or captives of neighboring territories, ceedo conducted warfare, collected taxes, and did not experience the same handicaps as common slaves. *Jaam juddu* (domestic slaves) also retained a special status as members of the family. Associated with royal lineages or the lineages of free peasants, jaam juudu were integrated into their masters' households over generations and could not be sold or killed. *Jaam sayor*, however, were considered trade slaves. Acquired through war, kidnapping, or purchase, trade slaves cultivated millet and other surplus agriculture on the royal estates of the nobility and could be sold at a moment's notice.

As slavery for agricultural production intensified among the Wolof, slavery in households became an essential element of the town's labor regime. By the late eighteenth century, slaves formed the majority of the town's population and constituted its primary labor force until France outlawed slavery in 1848.[24] In addition, French policy introduced a system of indentured labor in the colony. On 28 July 1828, the administration issued a decree declaring all captives in the colony, and those born to slave parents in the colony, as captives for life. Any captives entering the colony after the decree were considered *engages á temps* (indentured servants) until age 21.[25] In Saint Louis, the labor system included slaves, indentured servants, and free wage laborers. Free and slave workers commonly performed the same tasks, and both could earn wages. Workers in the town did manual labor, domestic work, and craft production. They cultivated habitant gardens on the island and its environs and could be hired out to do any work needed by the administration or trade houses.

Female slaves remained in high demand throughout the nineteenth century.[26] Women and girls served as laundresses and *pileuses* or grain pounders. They prepared millet, the staple grain of local dishes, for town residents. Female slaves carried out all of the household work for their owners from cleaning, cooking, and tending gardens to taking care of children and the sick. Signares hired out slave women to prepare food for river expeditions during the trading season. Whether as concubines of their masters or wives to slave men in the household, slave women generally had no claim to their children, who automatically became part of the slave labor population even though they likely lived in the same household as their mothers. Occasionally, slave women became the "country wives" of habitant men through mariage à la mode du pays. The nature of slavery in this commercial society, however, meant a variety of arrangements for slave women. Some became petty traders and even earned enough to purchase their own slaves.[27]

Male workers fulfilled a variety of tasks for habitants and the French administration. They provided the labor for the government's construction projects on the island, repaired boats, and worked in the warehouses of European merchants. The majority of male workers also provided the labor needed to conduct trade along the Senegal River. In the eighteenth century, a class of sailors called *laptots* emerged as a specialized group in the Senegal River trade network. Laptot work, as François Manchuelle describes it, was not a slave occupation that was carried out by free men but rather a wage labor occupation often filled by slaves.[28] Laptots served as crew for commercial voyages. They hauled shipping vessels up and down the river and conducted commercial transactions with Africans in the trading posts. During the trading season, laptots traveled the river as navigators, riverboat captains, pilots, masons, blacksmiths, porters, interpreters, trade agents, and security for the captain. These sailors received wages for their work in currency or trade goods. Slave ownership varied in habitant households. The average family owned at least ten, but the wealthiest owned between fifty and one hundred.[29] The habitant elite considered slaves essential to household production but also relied on them to carry out trade in the escales.

In addition to material benefits, slave ownership had a symbolic value for the inhabitants of Saint Louis. Signares maintained an entourage of slave women to accompany them on public outings. For elite women, owning slaves served as a tangible form of wealth and a conspicuous marker of their status. Slave ownership symbolized the wealth and prosperity of the household. Slaves of habitant households, in many cases, became incorporated into the kinship networks of their owners. Eighteenth-century observers wrote that domestic slaves lived in the same house as their owners and intermarried within the slave population of their master's house. In the era of the Atlantic slave trade, slaves of habitant households were distinguished from slaves who "circulated like commerce." Household slaves, according to a local priest, were treated like members of the house and never sold into the export trade. Saint Louis's habitants rarely baptized slaves, believing that "keeping Christian slaves was not allowed," whereas habitants on Gorée baptized slaves.[30] As a result, the majority of slaves and former captives in Saint Louis practiced Islam.

Métis families measured wealth not only in terms of slave ownership but also according to the material possessions that translated into capital assets. Notarized documents and inventories for inheritance settlements include real estate, furnishings, boats, retail merchandise, currency, credit (owed to them), and jewelry among their assets. Métis wealth resembled the same level of material wealth for members of the Parisian middle class in the 1840s. Real estate constituted a third of the assets that male and female spouses declared in their marriage contracts. Slaves constituted between 7 and 9 percent of the husband's net worth but provided between 17 and 27 percent of the assets that women brought into a marriage.[31] Signares and their métis daughters owned the vast majority of slaves in Saint Louis and contributed these assets to male-headed households when they married habitant men.

Women acquired substantial assets in gold. Signares developed a reputation for their taste in gold filigree worked by local goldsmiths. Métis women possessed wealth in gold jewelry and could use it as a tangible asset in building capital for their husband's business ventures. Nicholas d'Erneville, for example, owed his wife, Adélaïde Crespin, 300 *gros* (wholesale value) in gold for investing in his trading business. In 1847, Charles d'Erneville entered his marriage to the daughter of a notable habitant with a credit of 6,000 francs, a box of silver, and five captives, while his wife possessed a house, furniture, gold, jewelry, and forty-seven captives.[32] The habitant tradition of providing their daughters with impressive dowries enabled the transfer of wealth between families through marriage. Conformity to French law for marital property and inheritances, however, gave husbands primary control over the use of these assets to support their economic ventures.

The métis consolidated their position as the dominant propertied class of Senegal's coastal towns in the first half of the nineteenth century. The livelihood of the people of Saint Louis depended on trade networks that linked the produce of the Senegal River valley to European and Atlantic world markets. Despite French attempts to turn Senegal into a plantation colony, the gum trade prevailed because the Saint Louis community considered it the cornerstone of their economic survival. Grumets, signares, Muslim habitants, laptots, and slaves all played key roles in the growth and development of Senegal's export trade, but métis habitants controlled the middleman niche of the gum trade. Métis men relied on their intimate knowledge of the social environment of the Senegal River valley and their access to capital from Bordeaux merchants. Personal and familial relations among métis families, Bordeaux merchants, and African ruling elites in the lower and middle Senegal further cemented their position as the most effective and skilled intermediaries in the gum trade. The transition from the Atlantic slave trade to legitimate trade corresponded to a transformation from signare-headed households to male-headed trade houses. The establishment of formal French control over Senegal's coastal towns and the development of male public space also contributed to the formation of the métis bourgeoisie, but the economic crisis of the 1840s threatened to disrupt their hold on power and revealed tensions in the relationship between the interests of metropolitan merchants and the role of coastal intermediaries in the colonial economy.

Economic Crisis and Métis Losses (1837–52)

While the 1830s were boom years for habitant traders, the 1840s brought economic depression and severe financial losses for the Saint Louis elite. French officials vacillated between free trade, semiprotectionist practices, and monopoly in an effort to control the fluctuating price of gum in the escales. In the 1840s, the administration eased restrictions on the licensing system that opened the gum trade in the escales to Muslim habitants. The 1848 declaration that prohibited slavery on French soil caused further economic insecurity for Muslim and Catholic habitants. Signares, especially, lost significant material assets as well as the symbolic capital that slave ownership afforded them. Finally, Bordeaux merchants introduced peanut cultivation in Senegal, which led to a restructuring of the colonial economy to satisfy French demand for the commodity. By 1850, colonial authorities and the Bordeaux lobby succeeded in reorienting the export economy to the burgeoning peanut basin south of the Senegal River. These changes raised concerns about the future of the métis population as the dominant middlemen in the colonial economy and the primary propertied class within the urban community.

Wild fluctuation in the price of gum for quantities of guinées and rampant speculation by coastal merchants and Moors had long plagued the gum trade.[33] By the 1820s, demand for guinées increased among the Trarza but also among the Wolof of Walo and Cayor and the Pulaar of Fouta Toro. Problems plagued the supply of guinées as the textiles were manufactured in French factories in India and had to be ordered a year or two in advance. The supply of gum harvests also posed inherent risks. The unpredictability of wind and rainfall led to good harvests in some years and poor harvests in others. In addition, political conflict between Walo, Trarza, and Saint Louis heightened anxieties over the ability to conduct trade in the escales during periods of tension. Nevertheless, the balance between the export of gum from the Senegal River valley and the import of guinées by négociants on the coast remained stable and profitable. In the late 1830s, however, a series of events contributed to the end of the boom cycle of gum prosperity and led to a sharp decline in the trade's profitability for habitant middlemen.

At the start of the 1837 trading season, Bordeaux merchants ordered a larger quantity of guinées than usual. Euphoria over a number of good harvests and speculation over rising demand fuelled enthusiasm. Technological innovation also led to an increase in the production of guinées in French-controlled factories. Senegal absorbed 50,000 guinées per year on average. At the opening of the 1837 trading season, 138,000 guinées arrived in merchant warehouses.[34] The flood of guinées caused the price of the textile to drop dramatically. Saint Louis traders who had already taken supplies of guinées with the promise to repay their debts in gum could not acquire enough gum in the escales to satisfy their obligations.

Négociants took advantage of the situation by hiring traders to take guinées to the escales for sale directly to buyers. The importers loaned the first 100,000 to independent gum traders at the regular exchange rate and then sold the surplus directly to Moors in the trade posts for 50 percent less than the rates offered by the middlemen.[35] This practice continued through the 1840 trading season. Métis traders took on high levels of debt as they operated the majority of independent trade houses for gum. Individuals who became agents for French firms faired a bit better. Négociants, as the most highly capitalized of the Saint Louis merchants, absorbed losses with little cost to their enterprises.[36] Métis traders operating in the escales lost money on the exchange of guinées, while their French creditors were able to undercut their prices and sell the goods directly to buyers along the Senegal River.

Colonial authorities in Saint Louis responded to the economic crisis by implementing new measures to regulate the price of guinées in the escales and by reorganizing the trading system. Competition at the escales caused inflation in the interior and a seemingly insurmountable debt burden for Saint Louis traders. In 1839, French officials attempted to create a gum association to regulate the trade by setting a limit on the bottom price for guinées in the escales. In 1842, the administration launched plans for another association aimed at the grande traite by giving négociants, retailers, and traders an incentive to buy shares in the association and split the profits. In this arrangement, creditors received 75 percent of the profit of trader debtors.[37] The associations alleviated the problem of price fluctuation, but did little to address the debt of the Saint Louis traders.

A royal ordinance of 15 November 1842 further regulated the gum trade. The order stated that trade in the posts could only be carried out by traders commissioned by the government. The criteria for registration included that of a free person born in Saint Louis who was not a négociant and had traded in the escales since 1836.[38] Since petty traders from Saint Louis already operated in the secondary markets of the upriver trade depots, this legislation lifted restrictions on their entry into the gum trade. The ordinance also prohibited traders from paying customs to the Moors on the north bank, a practice that métis habitants had long specialized in. While competition in the gum trade increased, supplies of gum remained about the same. As a result, Saint Louis traders made less profit from the once lucrative gum trade. New commercial policy combined with escalating habitant debt, moreover, resulted in unrecoverable losses to métis family firms.

Faced with increasing debt and the inability to obtain merchandise on credit from the wholesalers, some of the wealthiest members of the métis were forced to declare bankruptcy. In the late 1830s, the administration calculated the debt of the intermediary traders at between three and four

million francs.[39] While French officials attempted to put measures in place
to relieve habitant debt and reform trade practices, collectively habitant
traders still owed approximately two million francs to their creditors in
1849. As a result, a number of traders found it nearly impossible to remain
in business. In 1843, 50 percent of registered traders worked for their own
account. By 1852, only 25 percent were independent, and by the end of the
decade, only six or eight habitants held their position as négociants. Métis
merchants sold or mortgaged their properties in order to avoid bankruptcy
and thus had to dissolve the family trade houses that they had established
early in the century. In the 1820s and early 1830s, a few métis firms earned
enough capital to achieve the rank of négociant. After 1850, métis men
found it virtually impossible to compete with metropolitan merchants.
Métis habitants Louis Alsace, Adolphe Beynis, Blaise Dumont, and John
Sleight, who achieved the rank of licensed négociant, no longer held the
most highly capitalized trade houses in the colony.[40]

In addition to the local economic crisis, Saint Louis residents faced
changes brought about to the regime of slavery and slave ownership in the
towns as a result of reforms implemented under the Second Republic. The
1848 revolution brought forth new ideologies concerning the rights of workers
and their inclusion as full citizens in the nation. The revolution also brought
the issue of slavery to the forefront of national discourse. Intent on solving
the problem of slavery in the Caribbean's plantation colonies, the new regime
declared an end to slavery in French territories. The law, however, struck a
severe blow to slave owners in Saint Louis and Gorée.[41] Métis families depended on their ability to recruit slave labor to work in the Senegal River trade
as well as in their households. For signares, the end of slavery had significant
implications for the demonstration of their wealth and social standing.

French antislavery policies focused on the legal implications of loss of
property. Paris provided indemnity payments for slave owners in Senegal,
but lawmakers offered low compensation to Senegal slave owners by paying
a portion in currency and a portion in stock certificates issued by the newly
established Bank of Senegal.[42] Because speculation remained high, most habitants sold their stock shares or converted their indemnity payments into
debt repayment. Typically, former slave owners (signares especially) lost
money while French merchants who operated wholesale firms profited.
Maurel and Prom bought the largest amount of indemnity payments from
signares and habitant families in financial distress by offering higher prices

than the remuneration paid by the bank.[43] For the métis population, these changes meant that they could no longer depend on slave ownership or compensation from the state as a viable form of financial security.

The short-lived reforms instituted under the Second Republic (1848–51) strengthened the principle of free trade in the colonies. In 1849, new laws opened the gum trade to members of the entire indigenous population in Senegal, eliminating the system that restricted access only to individuals who paid the licensing fee.[44] Metropolitan proponents of France's new imperialist agenda argued that only the introduction of free trade in the colonies would eradicate the practice of slavery and bring the values of civilization to their unenlightened subjects. According to Frederic Carrère and Paul Holle, two members of the administrative service in Senegal, free trade would instill western notions of hard work, discipline, and capitalism that would make Saint Louis traders "good agents of French civilization."[45] In their view, encouraging free trade went along with spreading Christianity, eradicating slavery, and eliminating the supposed tyranny of African rulers as a rationale for colonial expansion.

Métis priest David Boilat summed up his impressions of the waning days of "gum fever" and the declining fortunes of the habitants. He lamented the end of earlier times when "this trade was like an inexhaustible source" that allowed habitants to easily make "colossal fortunes." Habitant prosperity, he wrote, exemplified the future of civilization and westernization for Senegal. In the boom years of the gum trade, habitants lived well. "Gold sparkled around the neck, ears and arms, of the wives and daughters" and their many servants. Boilat decried the trend he witnessed in which the number of traders increased markedly. Boilat wrote, "All, even the marabouts [Muslim clerics], go into trade and the quantity of gum that enriched a small number cannot suffice for so many traders. . . the return of the trade is no longer a subject of joy for the families but one of chagrin and sadness."[46] During the 1851 trade season, the upriver posts did not even open for trade, and by 1853 the administration abolished the last of its protectionist policies. The gum trade continued, but the decline of habitant prosperity meant that métis traders no longer held a monopoly on the intermediary niche of the colonial economy.

Métis Responses to Economic Change

Contemporary observers predicted that the crisis in the gum trade combined with the abolition of slavery would lead to the ruin of the habitant elite. In their view, the consequences of these transformations threatened the growth of the class of elite town dwellers most closely identified with French culture and customs. Transformations in Senegal's colonial economy had disastrous effects for the entire Saint Louis elite, but métis families faced added competition in the middleman trade and the inability to compete with metropolitan firms at the highest levels of the commercial system. The economic crisis of the 1840s laid the foundation for the merger of Bordeaux trade houses into corporations that sought to open new markets in regions of the interior beyond the escales. The development of cash crop agriculture in peanuts thus added to the climate of economic instability for the Saint Louis elite. In the 1850s, French military penetration into strategic regions of the interior shifted the momentum further in the direction of the aims of metropolitan capitalist firms.

These events, some have argued, resulted in the suppression of Senegal's coastal elites and the domination of monopoly corporations over all stages of the colonial economy in the second half of the nineteenth century. This view overlooks the resiliency of the Saint Louis trading community, in general, and the métis, in particular.[47] Bordeaux firms continued to rely on Saint Louis traders after 1850. Muslim traders gained importance in the escales during the heyday of the gum trade. They took advantage of the changing economic environment to become the primary middlemen in peanut exports. Métis habitants suffered significant financial losses that prevented the majority from competing with metropolitan wholesalers, yet they continued to play influential roles in commerce. A few achieved a level of economic success that afforded them independence from metropolitan interests. Moreover, recent research on urban land tenure in Saint Louis suggests that signares and métis women owned most of the town's real estate until the late nineteenth century.[48] The 1850s and 1860s presented challenges for the economic viability of métis habitants, but it did not result in their disappearance from the colony's economy.

The decline in the gum trade corresponded to the introduction of cash crop production of groundnuts for export to French markets. The expansion of peanut agriculture in the south and east drew the center of the colonial economy away from the escales of the Senegal River basin and toward the agricultural producers of the region's interior. Aided by the Bordeaux Chamber of Commerce, Bordeaux merchants lobbied Paris to support peanut exports from Senegal as a reliable source for Marseille soap makers and as a less expensive alternative to olive oil for cooking.[49] In the 1850s, French firms introduced peanut culture along the coast, then in the river ports, and finally in the Sine, Saloum, Casamance, and Gambia River valleys. The development of peanuts as the primary cash crop from Senegal fuelled the growth of peanut oil manufacturing facilities. Devés and Chaumet and Maurel and Prom established the first *huileries* to produce peanut oil in Bordeaux. In a 1908 meeting with members of the Bordeaux Chamber of Commerce, William Ponty, the governor general of French West Africa, acknowledged the role of industrialists from the French port in the colony's economy, stating that "Senegal of the peanut was created by the Bordelais."[50]

Métis merchants who operated independent trade houses developed strategies to avoid direct competition with Muslim traders and maintain access to flows of merchant capital coming into the country. Métis traders operated on the frontiers of the expanding colonial economy by using their knowledge of the interior and establishing kin and client ties with ruling elites in the Senegal River valley. A number of the most successful métis traders became creditors for rulers in the interior whom they supplied with guns, ammunition, and other trade goods in return for gum, peanuts, or cattle. The métis also established businesses that employed town residents.

In the 1850s, Gaspard Devès, the son of Bordeaux merchant Bruno Devès and a Fulbe woman named Coumbel Ardo Ka, took over John Sleight's contract to supply the administration in Saint Louis with grain.[51] When Devès's first wife died in childbirth, he managed the fortune that his infant daughter inherited from his wife, who was the only child of the successful gum trader Guillaume Foy. Devès became the most successful métis entrepreneur in late nineteenth-century Senegal. He capitalized on his mother's ties in the middle Senegal, developed networks among the Trarza, and entered the gum trade by importing guinées directly to Senegal as an agent for a French firm in Pondicherry, India, which manufactured the textiles. He entered the peanut export market by establishing operations on the Mellacorie River at the Sierra Leone frontier and becoming a creditor for Wolof rulers in the interior. He employed workers in his brick factory on the outskirts of Saint Louis. Devès operated on the frontiers of French expansion and mobilized family and client networks to compete with Bordeaux merchants. This afforded him an extraordinary level of autonomy from the interests of metropolitan commercial firms and the colonial administration.

Louis Descemet began in administrative service as the secretary of General Faidherbe when he assumed the post in December 1852. Descemet left the colonial bureaucracy a short time later. He went on to establish a trade house with métis habitant Auguste "Omer" Teisseire, the son of Bordeaux négociant Auguste Teisseire and Marie-Anne d'Erneville.[52] In 1869, his brother Albert married the daughter of Bordeaux merchant Joseph Buhan. Albert Teisseire and his father-in-law merged their firms to create the company Buhan and Teisseire, which stood among the five primary corporations that pushed peanut agriculture and controlled peanut exports from Senegal. The trade house Descemet and O. Teisseire held a contract to supply the administration in Dakar and Gorée with fresh beef. Descemet's maternal kin ties extended to the pastoral region of Fouta Toro, strengthening his contacts among suppliers of cattle and allowing him to act as creditor for rulers in the region.

Devès and Descemet stand out as successful businessmen who operated independent trade houses after 1850. Their success afforded them a certain degree of independence in commercial affairs while financial losses in the gum trade pushed other métis to seek work in administrative service. Saint Louis traders, however, experienced resurgence between 1850 and 1880. Muslim habitants capitalized on the middleman trade, making significant profits in the escales and in Senegal's peanut basin.[53] Traders continued to operate independent trade houses by working as agents for Bordeaux firms in the escales and trade depots under French control on the Saloum, Gambia, and Southern Rivers region, as far south as Mellacourie on the border with Sierra Leone (map 4). Since metropolitan firms did not have warehouses and retail stores in these locations, they relied on Saint Louis agents to conduct business on their behalf. Saint Louis traders facilitated the export of peanuts for their French backers but also traded on their own account, which allowed them to establish control over cash crops and secondary markets for millet, rice, beef, and retail trade goods.

Muslim traders took advantage of these arrangements and carved out their niche in commerce by the 1850s. Several métis men also continued to operate their own businesses this way. Theophile Turpin, a métis trader from Gorée, became wealthy by starting out as an agent for Maurel and Prom in the town of Foundiougne on the Saloum. Hippolyte d'Erneville, a *commerçant,* traded in Sine and Boké on the Rio Nunez in the Southern Rivers region.[54] Antoine Guillabert specialized in the peanut trade and developed a network in Louga, a growing town on the railway corridor. When metropolitan firms did not have a presence in the interior trade depots, Saint Louis traders filled those positions. Métis and Muslim habitants carried out trade in these remote locations with the help of their laptots, former slaves/apprentices, and domestic workers. Métis traders sponsored young men raised in their homes who left for trade in Rio Nunez and Sierra Leone.[55] After 1850, the focus of commerce shifted to regions of Senegal's interior, and métis and Muslim habitants preceded metropolitan merchants in establishing markets in these areas.

Any understanding of métis responses to changes in the colonial economy must take into account the effect of antislavery legislation in Senegal's coastal towns. Saint Louis and Gorée emerged in relationship to the transatlantic slave trade, but slavery functioned in particular ways to support a household's production, in carrying out commercial operations, and for public works while demonstrating prestige and social standing for signares and their métis daughters. The 1848 declaration that ended slavery in the French plantation colonies also applied to Senegal, Gorée, and a few river posts under French control. Although France viewed antislavery as a primary objective of colonial expansion in West Africa, officials in Saint Louis expressed ambivalence about applying antislavery measures outside of the coastal enclaves. Any attempts to close slave markets in the interior, officials feared, would disrupt trade relations and unite African rulers against French military forces on the coast.[56]

General Louis Faidherbe introduced antislavery policies to eliminate the practice in the colonial towns. An 1855 decree specified that "subjects" who lived outside of the jurisdiction of French law could own slaves while town "citizens" could not. In 1857, Faidherbe issued a circular that clarified Saint Louis's position on liberating slaves entering the towns from the interior. According to this policy, slaves fleeing states at war with France could seek liberation in the capital, but slaves fleeing states at peace with France would be considered "vagabonds" and returned to their masters.[57] The same year, Faidherbe reformed the wardship system that sought to deal with the problem of slave children in the towns by placing minors with families or assigning them to apprenticeship programs. Although this policy was enacted in 1849, Saint Louis residents bought children in the river posts. Faidherbe allowed habitants to buy children from the river posts on the condition that they be freed and registered as soon as they arrived in Saint Louis. Slave boys or girls younger than eighteen, called apprentices, were supervised by a committee that placed them with respectable families, whereas those older than eighteen automatically received a certificate of emancipation.

The wardship program provided an opening for urban elites to recruit household labor by buying back young people in slave markets. The committee responsible for supervising children placed in the program, called the *conseil de tutelle*, was notoriously lax. French administrators stayed in the colony for short periods, leaving the elite responsible for dealing with the problem of escaped slaves and unsupervised children. Traffic in children between the interior and Saint Louis continued until the governor general of French West Africa enacted sweeping antislavery laws in 1904.[58]

Young girls constituted the vast majority of liberations under this system. An 1862 report found that females made up 70 percent of 433 slaves liberated since 1856. This data affirms the civil registry of birth for Saint Louis that indicates that *pileuses* (grain pounders) gave birth to children in the homes of Saint Louis residents.[59] Catholic and Muslim habitant families sought young girls to fulfill the demand for domestic labor. Female labor played a key role in Saint Louis's domestic economy as the habits and systems for acquiring household labor persisted well after the 1848 decree. One informant recalled the existence of household slavery in her mother's time, suggesting the practice remained part of Saint Louis life in the early 1900s. The wardship system that placed freed slave girls under the supervision of habitants perpetuated sexual and domestic relations. Habitant families, moreover, circumvented laws prohibiting citizens from owning slaves by moving slave workers to villages in their country farms on the suburb of Sor where they could use them to cultivate gardens. While métis families officially held only a small number of individuals liberated under the wardship program, they were part of a wider practice in the urban community that relied on apprenticeship and buying back slaves from interior markets to reestablish household labor and workers for trade after slavery formally ended in the coastal towns.[60]

In the first half of the nineteenth century, the métis derived their elite status from their position as property owners and their ability to exercise control over the intermediary niche of the gum-for-guinée trade. Signares and their métis offspring relied on exclusive access to metropolitan capital to become the primary traders in the escales. In addition, métis habitants had an advantage over Bordeaux merchants because of their knowledge of the land and their connections to Trarza emirs and caravan traders on the Senegal's north bank. Inheritances of gold, real estate, and slaves further strengthened métis prosperity. These conditions gave rise to the growth of male-headed habitant trade houses that resembled metropolitan merchant firms. Signares remained a vital part of Saint Louis society, but female entrepreneurship, a key mechanism of the town's economy in the eighteenth century, gave way to masculine relations of power.

In the 1850s, the outcome of the economic crisis left métis families vulnerable to financial ruin and the loss of political influence in the colony. The gum trade served as the central mechanism for gaining wealth and making claims to political rights in the colony. The financial ruin that contemporary observers predicted and future historians surmised did not result in a "crisis of adaptability" for the habitant elite. After 1850, Saint Louis traders adapted to the changes in the colonial economy. Muslim traders played more influential roles in the intermediary trade by taking advantage of Bordeaux merchants' lack of knowledge of the landscape and customs of Senegal's interior. Métis merchants also proved resilient to economic change by establishing new trade interests on the frontiers of colonial expansion, relying on kin and client ties with African rulers, and collaborating with Bordeaux commercial houses.

Shifting economic interests and the expansion of French colonial rule in Senegal impacted the economic life of the urban community. Métis habitants bore the brunt of gum fever's end because of the extent of their investments in the gum trade. The abolition of slavery in the colonies led to greater financial insecurity for signares, widows, and métis women who held a large number of the domestic slaves. The ambiguous nature of French antislavery laws, however, provided an opening for elite households in the Saint Louis community to maintain a network of dependents who met their labor demands and also enhanced their social networks. Laptots, pileuses, and apprentices continued to play integral roles as "people of the house" in Saint Louis society in a similar way that households in Wolof societies of the mainland included extended kin and clients.

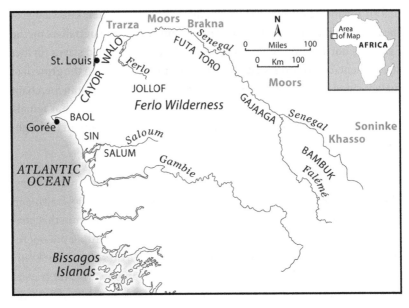

MAP 1. Eighteenth-century Senegal

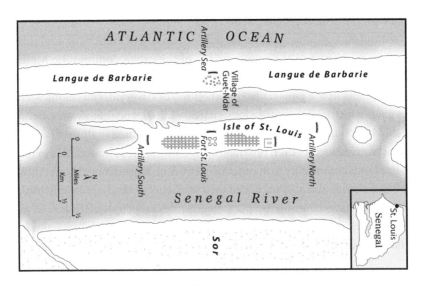

MAP 2. Saint Louis in the late eighteenth century

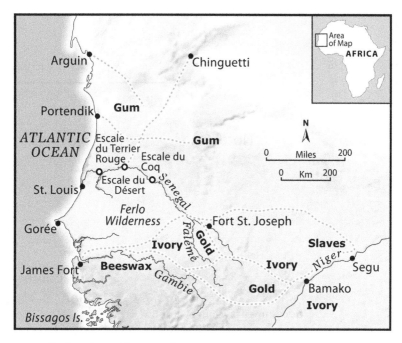

MAP 3. Trade in Senegal (1750–1850)

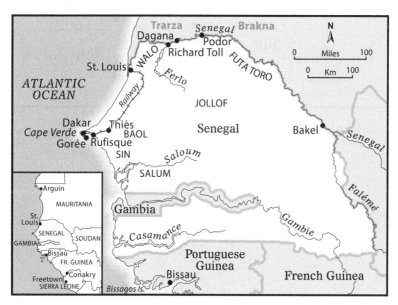

MAP 4. Senegal (1870–1920)

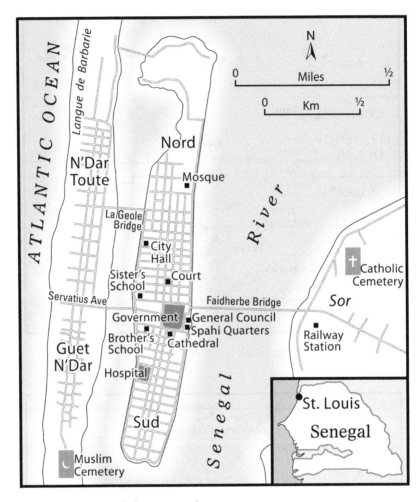

MAP 5. Saint Louis in the late nineteenth century

Signar ou Femme de couleur du Sénégal.

FIGURE 1. "Signar or femme de couleur du Sénégal."

FIGURE 2. *Facing.* Louise Crespin, wife of Jules Berteloot.
Used by permission from Georges Crespin.

FIGURE 3. *Above.* Hannah Isaacs and her daughter, Madeleine.
Used by permission from Georges Crespin.

FIGURE 4. Jules Berteloot.
*Used by permission from
Georges Crespin.*

FIGURE 5. *Below.* Justin Devès
and his daughter Elizabeth,
c. 1905. *Used by permission
from the Senegal Archives.*

FIGURE 6. Typical residence in Quartier Kretien (Sud) Saint Louis.

FIGURE 7. Madame Gaspard Devès, born Fatima Daba Densira and called Madeleine Tamba. *Used by permission from the Senegal Archives.*

FIGURE 8. Justin Devès and associates. From left to right, Piecentin, Durand
Valantin, Ka, and François Devès. *Used by permission from the Senegal Archives.*

FIGURE 9. Members of the Conseil Colonial, Inauguration 1920.
Used by permission from Christian Valantin.

3

Religion, Marriage, and Material Culture

On Saturday, 22 June 1889, at nine in the morning, Mayor Charles Molinet pronounced Hyacinthe Devès and Charlotte Crespin married at the town hall in Saint Louis. The marriage act read:

> Sir Jean Lazare Hyacinthe Devès, *licensed in law, commercial agent, and General Councilor* [author's emphasis], age 29 years and a half and born in Saint Louis, Senegal on the 13th of November 1858, living here as the adult and legitimate son of Pierre Gaspard Devès, *wholesale merchant and property-owner* and Dame Madeleine Fatma (Tamba) Daba Daguissery, *without profession* both residing in Saint Louis presents and consents to the marriage of their son, of one part and demoiselle Charlotte Louise Crespin, *without profession,* age 25, born on the island of Matacong (Sierra Leone) on March 3, 1864 and residing in Saint Louis as the single adult and legitimate daughter of Jean Jacques Crespin, *conseil commissionné, General Councilor* and Dame Hannah Isaacs, *without profession,* presents and consents to the marriage of their daughter on the other part.[1]

The civil marriage between Hyacinthe Devès and Charlotte Crespin legitimized their union in the eyes of the French state. It confirmed their adherence to the legal and cultural expectations of French marriage, family, and religion. A closer reading suggests that families who opted for unions that conformed to French law and the teachings of the Church rather than marriage à la mode du pays understood the official act in other ways. Declaring one's marriage in the civil registry strengthened claims to citizenship and conveyed respectability on the individuals and their families. Marriage, moreover, had a direct bearing on the field of electoral politics. The Devès-Crespin marriage occurred at a key moment in the formation of a political alliance between Jean Jacques Crespin and Gaspard Devès. Madeleine and Gaspard Devès made their mariage à la mode du pays official less than a month before the wedding of their son to Charlotte Crespin, perhaps in an effort to assert the influence of their household by conforming to European expectations.[2]

The expansion of French rule in Senegal operated as much through the private sphere of marriage and family as it did through military force. Church teachings and the establishment of civil law in the colonies served as a means of articulating notions of bourgeois respectability and republican womanhood. Colonial officials, missionaries, and members of the colonial judiciary considered the Church, the school, and the court system tools for instilling colonialism's culture. Strategies to secure European rule, as Ann Stoler suggests, pushed away from "ambiguous racial genres and open domestic arrangements" while clarifying European standards.[3] Missionaries and colonial officials attacked mariage à la mode du pays, promoted orthodoxy over syncretism, and elevated metropolitan notions of family, womanhood, and domestic consumption in order to rule through fixed categories of race and class. French authorities, however, walked a fine line in imposing their cultural ideals. Seeking not to antagonize Muslims of the town and along the Senegal, they turned to grumets, signares, and the métis to instill the cultural aims of French rule.

Scholarship on the culture of colonialism has advanced our understanding of how colonial hegemony operated through culture yet does not fully consider how people who lived in close proximity to colonial powers interpreted the discourse of colonialism to their advantage. Marriage and inheritance served as mechanisms for reproducing wealth and power among commercial elites in Saint Louis as they did for ruling elites in metropolitan France.[4] Habits of dress and taste conveyed the image of respectable, middle-class households that enabled certain town residents to assume the role of power broker in colonial affairs. For men, honor came from the public sphere of law, trade, and politics, whereas respectability for women derived from the private sphere of family and home. Being named as a "woman without profession" signified a woman's middle-class status, separating her from women of the working class.

For Christian habitants in Senegal, adhering to the teachings of the Church, conforming to French civil law, and adopting French tastes created the appropriate image of morally upstanding town residents. For Muslim habitants, marriage according to Islamic law officiated by the tamsir (judge) of the Muslim tribunal and recorded in its registry strengthened their status as pious and respectable.[5] Muslim habitants rejected cultural assimilation yet claimed their status as French citizens, whereas métis habitants articulated their claim to citizenship by strengthening their cultural ties to French authorities. For all town residents, adherence to religious orthodoxy played a key role in establishing group identity and shoring up their influence with colonial officials.

Despite the emergence of a self-conscious métis population at the end of the eighteenth century, transformations in métis identity and society took shape over the course of the next century. Individuals and groups within the town used the cultural symbols of colonialism to redefine themselves in relation to the changing political landscape of French expansion in the Senegal River valley. Métis men and women staked out their position as a group equal to the ruling elites by presenting themselves as Catholics who followed the expectations of middle-class marriage, lived in square concrete dwellings, and adorned themselves in the latest fashions of metropolitan France. Christianity, French civil law, and bourgeois taste served as visible markers of identity that distinguished well-born métis from others in the Saint Louis community. The métis conformed to the cultural expectations imposed by French rule. Adopting strategies of cultural assimilation fostered métis distinctiveness and exclusivity. At the same time, articulating their affiliation to colonial power in cultural terms strengthened their influence as relevant intermediaries in commerce and colonial affairs.

Transformations in Religion (1820–50)

Religion had long played a role in defining group identities within the Saint Louis community, but the expansion of French imperialism and the rise of Islamic revolution in the middle Senegal changed the meaning of religion. The institutionalization of Christianity and Islam in the coastal towns encouraged adherence to orthodox teachings of both religions. The consternation that the Catholic clergy expressed over what they described as the moral laxity of the town's inhabitants speaks to the depth of their anxiety over interracial mixing in marriage and sexuality. Sister Rosalie Javouhey decried the scandalous practice of mariage à la mode du pays, which she regarded as concubinage. Parish priests sought to root out "vestiges of superstition" among signares in an effort to enforce religious purity and establish French culture.[6] They singled out signares, grumet women, and slave girls as the focus of their evangelical mission.

Officials in the colonial office of the naval ministry considered Christianity an essential aspect of colonization. The minister of the navy charged Governor Julien Schmaltz with instilling respect for the Catholic Church in the colony, which in his view served as a means of measuring the progress of the civilizing mission. Schmaltz soon recognized the danger of aggressive evangelism. He cautioned the ministry not to act prematurely by proselytizing among "*indigenes*" of the lower Senegal. Instead, he suggested encouraging free work and elementary instruction. The ministry agreed to focus missionary efforts on the inhabitants of Saint Louis who had "ties of family and friendship" that could help to introduce Christianity to Africa.[7] Officials welcomed Christian orders to the colony but relegated them to the coastal towns for fear that evangelism in the interior could incite war with their neighbors and disrupt trade relations in the escales. French officials, moreover, considered it essential that the clergy regularize interracial unions and cultivate the growing population of children born from these unions into an acceptable class of middle-class men and women.

The Congregation of Saint-Esprit had an exclusive agreement with the naval ministry to provide clergy for France's overseas colonies and coordinate missionary activities.[8] The order sent a representative to Senegal with the delegation that reestablished French control in 1817. The first parish priest left, discouraged, after a few months because the majority of inhabitants did not speak French, no chapel existed in the town, and the building housing the rectory had fallen into disrepair during British occupation. In addition, he had received little financial support from the administration. The fact that the governor retained financial control as well as the power to relieve appointed clerics of their duties at any time created tension between subsequent priests and officials in Saint Louis. In the 1820s, the difficulty of living in the *sahelian* climate and obstacles to conversion resulted in a rapid turnover of priests. Still local practices of Catholicism predominated.

Métis and grumets welcomed the arrival of the clergy. The institutionalization of the Church solidified the relationship between the métis elite and the clergy. Faced with inadequate housing and a lack of facilities to conduct worship services, the clergy mobilized métis habitants to build a church as well as housing for the religious orders. Abbé Baradère requested land from the administration to build a permanent facility. He encouraged métis and grumet families to contribute to the Church's construction by providing financial support or donating their labor. On 4 November 1828, the church opened in the *quartier Kretien* on the south side where signares, métis, and grumets resided.[9] The building served as a material symbol of métis influence and of their affiliation with the Catholic Church.

Missionaries cast their work in gendered terms. In southern Africa, wives joined their husbands in heading Protestant mission enterprises. In Senegal, the Sisters of Saint Joseph de Cluny had the greatest impact on shaping urban life for Catholic residents of Saint Louis and Gorée. Métis families held the order in high esteem and considered the presence of the nuns essential to the development of family and social life.[10]

Founded in 1807, the Sisters of Saint Joseph de Cluny ministered to the sick and taught poor girls and orphans the discipline of work in rural France. The renewed emphasis on colonization under the restored monarchy opened new fields for missionary work overseas. In 1817, Mother Anne-Marie Javouhey, the founder of the order, sent a group to Bourbon (Réunion) to provide medical services at the request of the minister of the interior. The minister turned again to Mother Javouhey to support the hospital in Saint Louis and provide religious instruction for young girls in the town. On 19 March 1819, seven nuns (accompanied by Mother Javouhey's brother) arrived in Saint Louis.[11]

The first class of twelve signares began in 1819. Three years later, the nuns reopened the school aimed at providing religious and moral instruction as well as French language instruction to young *demoiselles* of notable habitant families. Forty-eight signares and the daughters of signares attended the first class of the new school. In 1826, the governor authorized the establishment of *l'école de jeunes négresses,* explicitly for the education of free girls, indentured servants, or orphans.[12] He charged the nuns of Saint Joseph de Cluny with teaching "poor and abandoned" girls the habits of industriousness, discipline for work, and proper Christian morals. Girls of métis families, for example, had to be orphans to attend the school. The plan devised by the governor and implemented by the nuns separated poor girls from the young girls in the burgeoning middle class. In so doing, the religious orders instilled in their pupils new class and gender expectations that sought to order Saint Louis society according to metropolitan ideals.

At the same time, French clergy and officials recognized that the success of evangelism in Senegal depended on the development of an African clergy that could minister the local population in local languages. Mother Javouhey maintained that an African clergy who could survive the hinterland

climate, had familiarity with the population, and could speak Wolof provided the best opportunity for the Catholic orders to reach the people of
the interior. With approval from Baron Roger and the congregation of
Beauvais in L'Oise, Mother Javouhey established a seminary for African
children in the town of Baileul. In spring 1825, a group of seven boys and
three girls arrived. The following year, another group of ten arrived. This
group included Amand Mamdou Sy, son of the king of Bondu, Charles
Arsène Fridoil, the son of a British father and a signare, Jean Pierre Moussa,
son of a grumet, and David Boilat, son of a Frenchman and a signare. Florence, a young Pulaar girl from Fouta Toro, also joined the group. Liberated
from captivity aboard a slave ship, Florence was assigned to a French family
in Saint Louis. When the family returned to France, Mother Javouhey took
charge of Florence, who became her interpreter and then accompanied
Mother Javouhey when she returned to France.[13]

　　Few of the young African seminarians survived the unfamiliar climate.
Ten died of tuberculosis, and others returned to Senegal complaining of
homesickness. Moussa, Fridoil, and Boilat finished their studies at the
Seminary of Saint-Esprit in Paris and were ordained. They also became
objects of fascination for the French nobility, who invited them to celebrate
mass in the presence of King Louis-Philippe and Queen Marie-Amelie at
Fontainebleau. African priests were regarded as exotic, but they also represented the future promise of French imperialism in Africa.[14]

　　After completing their studies, the three men sailed to Senegal to
serve as priests and instructors. Moussa became the interim priest for
Saint Louis when the appointed priest returned abruptly to France. Governor Louis Édouard Bouët-Willaumez (1843–44) established a secondary
school to train free African boys and slaves. In addition to educating African town residents, the governor considered the institution necessary
for preparing slaves for emancipation. Bouët-Willaumez named Boilat as
director of this school and inspector for public instruction. Fridoil served
as rector for Gorée and later succeeded Boilat. Despite their efforts, the
Senegalese priests faced resistance from Muslim habitants who disagreed
with the clergy's plans for evangelism. Their superiors and French officials
complained of school mismanagement and accused them of usurping
power from authorities in the colony.[15] While some of these claims may
have had merit, it is clear that the idea of creating an African clergy to
proselytize in the colony was at odds with the power struggles between

metropolitan clergy and African priests that stemmed from attitudes about race and class.

The work of the African clergy lasted less than a decade. In 1851, Rome and Paris agreed to give exclusive jurisdiction for propagation in Senegal to the Congregation of Saint-Esprit. With the assurance that regular clergy would serve in Senegal, administrators questioned the value and necessity of developing an African clergy. Moussa turned his attention to ministering to former slaves in Saint Louis, Gorée, and Bathurst (Gambia). He ended his career in Haiti, where he was called by Emperor Soulouque to serve as a parish priest in Port-au-Prince. Moussa died in Haiti on 23 July 1860. Granted a sabbatical from the Spiritains, Boilat traveled through Senegal's countryside for a year. He lived in Sierra Leone with his sister Anne, the wife of métis merchant and habitant François Pellegrin, before accepting reassignment to a parish in France. Fridoil died during his return voyage to France in 1853.[16]

The Catholic clergy did not record who or how many members of the urban community converted to Catholicism. The fact that they sought to reform beliefs and practices among signares and grumets who already claimed to be Catholic complicated any effort to measure progress in spreading Christianity. The clergy did define success according to their ability to eliminate practices they considered immoral or irrational. In 1824, Abbé Fournier wrote to his superiors to report a mass where the sig- nares of Gorée relinquished their gris-gris by bringing them to church and throwing them into the sea. Boilat admonished signares to rid their homes of gris-gris because they amounted to irrational superstition.[17]

Mariage à la mode du pays came under intense scrutiny by the clergy, who considered it an immoral practice that encouraged extramarital sexual relations between African women and European men. "Legitimate mar- riage," Boilat wrote, remained "the most difficult to enforce and the most essential for Christian morality and civilization."[18] He advised signares and grumets to abandon mariage à la mode du pays for Christian marriage. Colonial authorities objected to unions that occurred outside of French civil law and the moral teachings of the Church, but they also sought to control sexual relations between European men and African women in order to maintain distinct boundaries between colonized and colonizer.

Women became the objects of the clergy's reform efforts, and church marriages for Christian habitants served as a sign of evangelism's progress.

In 1827, the clergy recorded just one marriage for Saint Louis and Gorée. Between 1830 and 1840, there were five marriages for Gorée and thirty-two for Saint Louis.[19] By 1850, the clergy succeeded in making church marriage a regular practice among métis elites and some grumets, although they made fewer inroads in eliminating mariage à la mode du pays completely.

The intensification of Christian orthodoxy in Saint Louis paralleled the growth of Islam there. Governor Bouët-Willaumez expressed concern about the growth of "fanatical" Islam in the Senegal River valley because Futanke reformer Al-Hajj Umar Tal established a Tijani community in the middle Senegal. Having established the Sufi order in the middle Senegal, Tal waged war to the east in order to defeat the "pagan" Bamana states of Segou and Karta on the Niger. Intent on achieving "social distance" from Saint Louis, Tal engaged in several "skirmishes," as Robinson calls them, with French officials. The last confrontation, resulting in the 1857 attack on the fort at Médine, led French officials to describe Tal and his supporters as fanatics.[20] Umar's expansionist aims specifically threatened French supremacy on the coast and in the river trade depots. By 1852, when Louis Faidherbe arrived in Senegal, the French and the Umarians were engaged in a struggle for control of the middle and upper Senegal.

Umar recruited supporters from among the Saint Louis trading community. Muslim traders who operated in posts along the middle and upper Senegal acted as his key suppliers of trade goods and ammunition.[21] Umar implored the faithful "children of Ndar" not to join the infidel (French). Tijani clerics established a presence in Saint Louis strengthening the town's reputation as a center of Tijani teaching. Umar, moreover, relied on his connections with traders and interpreters who lived in the commercial and administrative centers along the Senegal for information about the French.[22]

Bouët-Willaumez sought to deal with the expansion of Islam and its perceived threat by developing a policy that centered on cultivating allies and possible interlocutors among the Muslim population. The administration created a Muslim tribunal and appointed a tamsir (head of the Muslim community) to serve as judge. In 1844, the administration began building a mosque.[23] Three years later, a neogothic French interpretation of a mosque, complete with a clock on the minaret tower, stood on the north side of the island. In December 1854, when Faidherbe became governor, he bolstered Saint Louis's reputation as a friendly power to Muslim societies by strengthening Bouët-Willaumez's policy. Shoring up the loyalty of the

Muslim community became a vital component of Faidherbe's strategy to maintain security for French commerce in the Senegal River valley.

After 1850, métis and grumets confronted a new reality in which religious affiliation held political significance. The clash between the Umarians and Faidherbe for control of the middle Senegal signaled the end of the Senegal colony as an economic satellite of France and the beginning of wars of conquest. Bordeaux merchants complained of the need to suppress Umar's forces in order to secure their economic interests. Frédéric Carrère, a member of the judiciary, and Paul Holle, a métis trader and commandant of Bakel, complained of the "dangerous fanaticism" of certain Muslim marabouts and decried a "Muslim invasion" of Saint Louis.[24] The habitant authors used this new threat to advocate for more aggressive French military expansion and the suppression of Umar Tal's Tijani followers. In addition, Carrère and Holle called for the Catholics to counter Tal's forces by demonstrating their faith and the advantages of French civilization.

While colonial officials sounded alarms over the spread of Islam, it is doubtful that the Saint Louis community viewed this conflict in the same way. The history of cooperation between Muslims and Christians and the nature of commercial relations mitigated religious conflict. Yet affiliation to Islam and Christianity gained new meaning in a time of imperialist expansion. The institutionalization of the church and the establishment of a permanent clergy that ministered specifically to the town's Catholic population strengthened métis identification with the Church. For métis habitants, adherence to the teachings of the Catholic Church, particularly with regard to marriage and family, became one means of maintaining their distinctiveness.

Becoming Métis: Marriage and Métis Identity

As religion took on new significance, the meaning of marriage also changed. By the end of the nineteenth century, the most advantageous marriage involved a union between two individuals of equal or greater social standing that conformed to French civil law and the teachings of the Church. Making a public pronouncement of intent to marry at the town hall and marrying in the Church with a priest officiating conferred respectability on the couple and their families. Conforming to bourgeois expectations of marriage also strengthened a family's symbolic capital, which in turn bolstered the family's claim to power in colonial society.[25] For métis families,

mariage à la mode du pays gradually gave way to marriage practices considered legitimate under French law and morally acceptable to the Church.
These changing notions heightened the métis tendency toward marriage
with individuals of similar social standing and outlook. Endogamous marriage limited the boundaries of inclusion, thus creating a tight-knit group
of families.

Although Senegal's métis population moved toward marriage arrangements that conformed to the expectations of the Church and the French
state, mariage à la mode du pays continued. Bordeaux merchants who arrived in Saint Louis and Gorée in the early nineteenth century formed
unions with signares. Officials and bureaucrats who arrived after 1820 also
entered into customary marital arrangements with African women. Métis
men married in the Church but also wed signares according to the tradition
of the towns.[26] Metropolitan merchants and bureaucrats understood that
marriage into the métis elite afforded access to influence in business, politics, and society in the colony. Consequently, French bureaucrats and merchants sometimes opted to marry métis women in weddings sanctioned by
the Church and considered legal under French law.

For the métis, the ability to trace one's ancestry to an eighteenth-century signare and a European company employee or official gave particular
families long-standing claims to habitant status. Individuals with British
or Irish surnames signified métissage that extended to periods of British
occupation. In the 1800s, new lineages emerged as a result of bureaucrats,
soldiers, and merchants who arrived during the Napoleonic wars and after
the restoration monarchy regained control of Saint Louis and Gorée.
Names such as Guillabert, Devès, Provost, Floissac, Berteloot, Foy, Angrand, Teisseire, and Carrère appeared in contrast to Thevenot, Pellegrin,
Sleight, Crespin, Valantin, d'Erneville, Alain, and André, whose origins
dated to the eighteenth century.[27] By the late nineteenth century, the self-
identified métis population consisted of individuals who could trace their
ancestry to a signare and a European merchant, soldier, or colonial official
who had arrived in the colony in the eighteenth century or the first half of
the nineteenth century.

The growth of legally recognized "mulatto" children, who were accorded the same civil status as Frenchmen, created problems for officials
who sought to control the growth of an indeterminate class that fit into
neither category of native subject nor French citizen. Instilling proper

marital customs served as a way to shape the métis population into an acceptable class of French men and women. The ideal arrangement for habitants, as Boilat described it, involved a union between two families of equal standing. In his view, courtship, betrothal, and marriage combined elements of Saint Louis society with the expectations of marriage among the French bourgeoisie. The process, he wrote, began when a young man assembled his family, friends, allies, and "notable habitants" to present his intentions to the family of the young woman he hoped to marry. His representative negotiated their courtship and engagement. With her family's approval, the young man arranged to visit the young woman under the supervision of her parents for a period lasting from one to four years.

At the end of the courtship, a chosen group of distinguished habitants presented her family with the young man's request for marriage and offered a symbolic gift on his behalf. The *demandeur*, Boilat reported, carried a sum of 1,000 francs. He distributed between 10 and 100 francs to the "companies of signares," while the rest went to his new bride. The signares "responded with compliments in favor of the intended husband," set the date the bride would be taken to her husband's house, and busied themselves with invitations for the wedding celebration. The next stage in the process required a verbal agreement to acknowledge the material assets that each spouse brought to the marriage.

According to Boilat, the ceremony involved demonstrations of loyalty, affinity, and patronage by the couple's relatives and friends:

> Each one also furnishes their part in the celebration because outside of the guests, one must send dishes of food to the companies of gourmets, the old signares and griots who will sing praises to the couple for eight hours. . . . The day of the celebration the bride is adorned with all the pompe africaine that is to say her ears and neck are encircled with gold; she is dressed in white, surrounded by parents and followed by a multitude of domestics all luxuriously dressed and with their heads covered with Louis d'or gold coins pierced in a manner to imitate a true headpiece. She is followed by all of the guests and all of the Christians of the place. The mahometans themselves are not absent, in the hope of receiving some gifts.[28]

In contrast to mariage à la mode du pays, Boilat's view of a proper habitant marriage consisted of a long courtship, family approval, a formal declaration of property rights, and even a white wedding dress. Christian habitants, he argued, should aspire to these symbols of bourgeois respectability.

A young woman's dowry served as a means of ensuring the groom's social status and asserting the bride's social standing.[29]

Marital exchange for habitant families, as for commercial elites in Lagos and Bordeaux, combined the transfer of economic capital with the demonstration of a family's reputation as upstanding members of the community. The ceremony provided an occasion to mobilize kin and clients—signares, *griots* (praise-singers), servants, Christians, and Muslims—to assert the honor, prestige, and influence of notable families. Boilat's description sets forth a model to which he believed habitant families should aspire, although whether grumets and métis met these criteria is difficult to ascertain. At the same time that the Church imposed stricter guidelines for marriage, the colonial administration used French law to rationalize the civil status of people of mixed-racial ancestry who benefited from paternal recognition by having the surnames of their fathers.

The institution of marriage and the family became the focus of highly contested issues dealing with women's rights, adultery, and inheritance. Revolutionary laws sought to suppress a father's authority over his sons and established new rights for women in marriage, including the right to divorce.[30] Subsequent struggles upheld the authority of husbands over wives and reinforced patriarchy over the rights of women. Social anxieties over female adultery, children born out of wedlock, and sexual immorality became a source of public debate among writers, thinkers, legislators, and artists. The public obsession over private morality directly affected metropolitan attitudes toward interracial sexuality. These debates contributed to the intense scrutiny of sexual relations in the colonies and help to explain why French officials placed greater emphasis on regularizing the status of people of the métis in Senegal's coastal towns.[31] Metropolitan discourse about family, marriage, and sexuality shaped how colonial administrators articulated France's civilizing mission by defining the heterogeneous nature of the urban community according to proscribed notions of race, class, and religion.

The application of French civil law in Senegal's colonial capital sought to unify colonial and metropolitan legal systems, on the one hand, while accommodating cultural difference in the colonial capital, on the other. Promulgated on 1 March 1804, the civil code created the first coherent system of law pertaining to property, family, and individual rights of French subjects. The civil code brought together canonic laws, regional customs, and revolutionary statutes under a uniform legal code that separated the private sphere of marriage, family, and property from the public sphere. On 5 November 1830, Paris extended application of the civil code to Senegal. The decree specified that all adult men born free and living in Senegal could enjoy the same rights as those granted to French citizens by the civil code, but specified that those rights could only be exercised in the colony and not in metropolitan France.[32]

In Senegal, French civil law not only resolved disputes but also served as the foundation for the urban community's claim to citizenship. The law prohibited polygamy, gave instructions for civil marriage ceremonies, distinguished between legitimate and illegitimate children, and specified the rules of inheritance.[33] The bureaucratization of marriage involved establishing an officer of the civil state in each commune to keep a registry of marriages, births, and deaths and to officiate in legal ceremonies. In Saint Louis, the mayor typically performed this role. Publication of intent to marry had to be made at the town hall eight days before the ceremony so that an announcement could be posted on the town hall gates. Each party had to produce birth certificates. Their witnesses presented a request to the Tribunal of First Instance, on behalf of the couple, before going before the civil officer at city hall for an official pronouncement of marriage.

For marriages and for births, the state required listing the Christian names of the parties involved, their ages, professions, and residences as well as the names and professions of their witnesses. In addition, the state recognized dowries as the only acceptable forms of marital exchange. Whereas previously both parties entered into a verbal contract, the state required written, notarized matrimonial agreements as part of the marriage contract. City hall and the officer of the civil state became as important as the parish priest in sanctioning marriage. Recording marriages and births in the civil registry, moreover, guaranteed the legitimacy of the children who were born of legal unions and established the rules for family inheritance. The métis regularly recorded their marriages and the births of their children in the civil registries of the municipalities.[34]

Civil law thus became part of a civilizing discourse that emphasized monogamy over polygamy, dowry over bride wealth, and bourgeois respectability over the perceived primitiveness of African society. Muslim habitants rejected conformity to French culture and argued for their right to be both Muslim and citizen. They could, however, seek redress for civil disputes through the town's Muslim tribunal. In contrast, the law afforded métis habitants the same civil status as Frenchmen when their fathers claimed paternity for children born to African women. The fact that the métis population appeared to conform to French religious and cultural expectations further substantiated their claim to equal citizenship.

The codification of French civil law in the Napoleonic era created a new legal and bureaucratic system that redefined the meaning of marriage, family, inheritance, and rules of paternity. It also stimulated debate over what constituted appropriate expressions of marriage, love, and sexuality. Enlightenment thinkers upheld the notion that compassionate marriage between individuals should take the place of arranged marriages, but the rise of the nuclear family in metropolitan France also cast open marital arrangements favored by the aristocracy in terms of immorality.[35] The civil code criminalized adultery, suppressed the right of illegitimate children to claim an inheritance, and imposed strict rules for investigating paternity. Fathers could recognize a child born out of wedlock as an *enfant naturel,* but the child had no right to claim direct inheritance.[36] Because French society perceived adultery as a social problem, metropolitan attitudes about French men claiming paternity over children born to African women provoked anxieties over arrangements such as mariage à la mode du pays.

Colonial authorities, beginning with Baron Roger, explicitly discouraged mariage à la mode du pays. Faidherbe cautioned soldiers against pursuing the daughters of mulatto families. He suggested they look instead to women of the countryside to accommodate their sexual desires without the complications of a formal union. Ironically, Faidherbe and Nkounda Siadibi, a Sarakole woman, lived together in a union that resembled mariage à la mode du pays and produced a son.[37] In 1858, when the governor left for a brief sabbatical in France, the two separated. Faidherbe returned to Senegal with his new wife, Angele. Faidherbe's "marriage" to Nkounda Siadibi concerned the clergy, who condemned it, yet his relationship to Siadibi continued the same practice followed by high officials from the Chevalier de Boufflers and Blanchot, Bordeaux merchants, and some of the métis elite. Powerful men of the towns understood that marrying signares accorded them influence with the African population and could expand their network of clients.

Although the idea of marriage and family underwent a transformation in the first half of the nineteenth century, métis men and women and their families made decisions about whom to marry, when to marry, and if they should marry for practical reasons. Economic and political considerations factored into their decisions. Social standing mattered in making a good match, but so did individual choice. In Senegal's towns, marriage served as a means for commercial elites to consolidate wealth and form political alliances. For métis families, making the right match created an intangible bond of "immediately recognizable affinity."[38] Strategic marriage alliances could also strengthen kin and client networks with the ruling elites in the Senegal River valley or the Senegambian coast as well as bolster ties with Bordeaux merchants and metropolitan lawmakers.

The métis sought marriage partners among other métis families or European men and women. First marriages, in particular, followed this trend, although marriage and birth registries show that it was not uncommon for métis men to marry African women in second marriages. The generation born in the second half of the nineteenth century opted for marriage to other métis, metropolitan French men (occasionally French women), or individuals of similar background from the Caribbean colonies or elsewhere in the French Empire. A sample of thirty-two marriages recorded in the civil registry for Saint Louis between 1885 and 1890 shows that seventeen occurred between métis families, eleven between a métis and a European, and four between habitants and African women.[39]

By the late nineteenth century, virtually all of the métis were related by marriage. The tendency toward marriage within the group led to population stagnation and decline. According to one observer, the métis population of Saint Louis and Gorée peaked at 1,600 in 1860 and remained virtually unchanged in 1909.[40] A 1916 administrative report on the population for French West Africa counted the mulatto population of Senegal's towns at approximately 1,620 individuals. One reason for intergroup marriage involved financial security. Métis habitants who experienced financial loss in the gum trade sought advantageous marriages for their daughters with men who could rebuild family wealth. Louis Descemet married Adelaide Duchesne, the daughter of a métis family that traced its ancestry to the eighteenth century. Jean Charles Descemet married Josephine Sleight, the daughter of a métis gum merchant. Métis habitant Guillaume Foy, a notable gum merchant, married off his daughter Catherine to Gaspard Devès.[41] These marriages consolidated wealth but also bolstered the reputation of both families because male spouses benefited from the social status that accompanied marriage to a woman from a highly respectable family.

French shopkeepers, lawyers, and clerks who settled in the colony occasionally married daughters of the métis elite.[42] This class, known as *petit
colons,* began arriving in the 1880s and 1890s. For them, marriage into a prominent Saint Louis family elevated their social standing and bolstered their
influence in electoral politics. Sons of the métis elite, however, faced fewer
options for marrying European women. Few single European women settled
in Senegal until the turn of the twentieth century. Some métis men who traveled to France for their studies or spent part of the year there met and married
French women.[43] After 1850, métis men and women typically sought partners
among métis families of the coastal towns or among similar groups in French
and British commercial and administrative territories from the Saloum to the
Gambia. Anna Isaacs of Bathurst, the daughter of British explorer and trader
Nathaniel Isaacs and Madeleine Diole, married Jean Jacques Crespin of Saint
Louis and gave birth to their children in Mellacorie, Sierra Leone.[44] As the
French Empire expanded, other métis sought unions with individuals of simi-
lar background from Teneriffe to Martinique.

Marriage within the group concentrated wealth and influence among
a small population but also reflected the ambiguity of people of mixed-
racial ancestry. The métis became a closed society, and as Idowu put it,
"they more readily accepted themselves than they were accepted either by
the French or by the Africans."[45] Signatures of witnesses on marriage and
birth registries as well as naming practices reflected their interconnected
nature. Parents typically gave their children multiple first names, usually
indicating a connection to a deceased relative, the family matriarch, godparents, or allies among Bordeaux merchants or French administrators.[46]
The names Jean Jacques, Alain, and Adolphe are found repeatedly in the
Crespin family, whereas Augustin, Antoine, Henri, and Eudoxie are associated with the Guillabert family.

The Wolof tradition called *turando* recognizes the special relationship
that exists between a child and his or her namesake. Métis men and women
commonly served as godparents for grumet children.[47] Names could indicate
patron-client relations but they also revealed hidden kin ties often relegated
to memory. In coastal towns where patrilineal descent predominated, the
names of African women were not officially recognized in legal documents.
Naming practices could operate to assert maternal kin ties absent from the
official record.[48] Coumbel Ardo Ka, for example, took the name Silvie Bruno
to signify her union with Bruno Devès. While knowledge of one's maternal

lineage could be erased by the French bureaucracy, this information remained part of the collective memory. Métis men and women, accordingly, evoked either European or African kin ties at key moments to support their political, economic, and social interests.

Changing attitudes about marriage, family, and sexuality contributed to a new social order in the towns. The expansion of cultural imperialism rendered some women acceptable for marriage and others suitable only for extramarital relations. While European women occupied a position of superiority as examples of true and respectable womanhood, African women, particularly women of the countryside, were considered unsuitable for marriage. In Senegal, métis and grumet women navigated this hierarchy by constructing an image of themselves as pious wives and mothers. Although it is not altogether clear that wives of métis men lived a total life of leisure, as the moniker "without profession" implies, they certainly cultivated the same image as middle-class women in metropolitan society. While marital and family ties bound métis men and women more tightly as a group, material culture served as a key element in constructing their public image as upstanding and respectable citizens.

Visible Markers of Métis Identity

The consumption of material goods provides a view of the daily habits of métis men and women, their choices as consumers, and the public images of themselves that they sought to promote. The clothes they wore, the portraits they sat for, the food they ate, and the dwellings they inhabited offer clues about self-representation and group identification. Everyday material objects functioned as visible markers of identity in urban life. Dress styles, furnishings, and eating habits of the métis suggest a cohesive sense of identification with French taste and style yet hint at hidden paradoxes. West African port towns became locations for articulating new tastes and habits because transatlantic commerce made foreign objects easily available and adaptable to people in the coastal towns.[49] The history of Africans as producers for Atlantic capitalist markets is well known, yet the history of urban Africans as consumers in the global economy is less so.

Taste and style are essential for understanding how and why the métis of Senegal emphasized identification with French material culture in the late nineteenth century. The state used taste as a means of imposing power in metropolitan society and the colonies. In France, the idea of remaking society by educating the public about new standards of taste became a cornerstone of republican power. The same idea operated in colonial society where the French idea of imperialism included spreading what they perceived as superior cultural tastes to unenlightened Africa. Whether in the colonies or the metropole, individuals used material objects to generate their own subjectivities and express their own sense of personal style that may or may not have been what the state envisioned. Although material culture functions in the realm of everyday habits and individual choices, it is not beyond the reach of politics. Métis men and women dressed in formal western attire for photographs, but what did they eat or wear in the comfort of their own homes? Does the public appearance of an African in western dress epitomize colonial hegemony, or does it indicate a subversion of the colonial order?

Between 1830 and 1880, a new cadre of taste professionals introduced a "bourgeois-style regime" in metropolitan France.[50] Dress and furniture making no longer served as symbols of aristocratic political power as they had during the ancien régime and the Restoration monarchy. A new ideology grounded in republican ideals emphasized the development of aesthetic taste as a means of class distinction. Dress and furnishings provided a way to distinguish between middle and working classes while shoring up bourgeois social power.[51] Writers, artists, philosophers, and lawmakers viewed the education in taste as a way to transform society by instilling the ideals of republican citizenship among the middle class. These taste professionals considered the domestic realm as the most important arena for cultivating values of virtue, practicality, sincerity, and civility. Women, in this conception, occupied a central role in the family's consumption habits. By purchasing goods for the household, arranging furniture, and dressing themselves and the family, middle-class women were expected to express a sense of refinement, propriety, and modest luxury. Wives and mothers educated the family in the appropriate taste and style for their class, as they represented the family's social identity to the wider community.

The close proximity of the métis to metropolitan trade houses and French merchants and officials gave this group exclusive access to European fabrics, furnishings, food products, and other manufactured goods. By the mid-nineteenth century, regular steamship transportation and increasing opportunities for travel to metropolitan France for business and education increased the métis population's exposure to the latest trends and fashions. A few European tailors came to Saint Louis, but Protestant missions also began training former slaves in skilled trades such as watchmaking, shoemaking, and tailoring.[52] By the 1870s, the métis had regular access to European dress and tailors who could fashion garments to their liking.

The dress and comportment of the métis reflected the ideal characteristics of well-educated, virtuous middle-class men and women. Photographs of métis taken in the last quarter of the nineteenth century depict the formal yet dignified image expected of the bourgeoisie.[53] Women imported the latest taffeta fabrics from Europe and fashioned them into fitted gowns with intricate bustles and corsets embellished with lace or even fur garniture. They abandoned the conical head ties worn by their signare foremothers in favor of uncovered, European-style coiffures with ribbons or hairnets (figs. 2 and 3). By the 1920s, women typically wore western hats to Sunday mass, and young girls tied ribbons in their hair rather than the head ties commonly worn by Wolof, Pulaar, or Soninke women.[54] For Catholic women in the towns, adopting specific adornments signified their position in colonial society as pious girls and mothers of respectable families.

Métis men are depicted in photographs in a similar reserved yet sophisticated image. They typically wore tailored suits with jackets, vests, pocket watches, and European neckties. The men had elegant, neatly trimmed moustaches and sideburns or the goatee popular among the educated French elite. They wore their hair closely cut and parted on the side in a style appropriate for refined gentlemen (figs. 4 and 5).[55] Their physical appearance distinguished them from Muslim town residents, who preferred long, flowing robes, Moroccan slippers, and a fez, turban, or traditional headdress befitting their status. The dress of métis men also linked them to the colonial administration in Saint Louis, which undoubtedly strengthened their position when conducting trade or serving as soldiers or bureaucrats in the interior.

Writing in the 1840s, Boilat commented that habitant men dress "entirely à la française," whereas signares are only beginning to "put luxury in their costume" by buying European embroidered shirts and wearing them with wraparound skirts called *pagnes* made by local weavers in the cloth of the country. Women, according to Boilat, still acquired *beaux madras* that they wrapped around their head in the form of *ndioumbeul* or a hairstyle known in French as *pain de sucre*. Although Boilat sought to illustrate progress and modernization in Senegal through local adaptation to dress, his reflections offer a means of visualizing the gradual shift in aesthetic choices from the

African dress of signares to the mixture of styles in the habitant era and European clothes favored by the métis. It is also not surprising that women of the towns were slower to adopt European dress than men, who operated in the public arena of politics and trade by emphasizing their affiliation with the colonial regime. Women had greater flexibility in the private spaces of their homes and courtyards to wear a variety of dress styles.

While for many the choice of garments, hairstyles, and accessories illustrated an acceptance of the civilizing discourse imposed by the colonial regime, others may have used material culture in ambiguous or possibly oppositional ways. One Saint Louis resident recalled how appearance and material possessions reflected the multifaceted cultural identity of the métis. The child of a métis father and an African woman, François Parsine converted to Islam by joining the Muridiyya, a Sufi order founded by cleric Cheikh Amadou Bamba, and adopted the name Farah. He is commonly remembered as the man who dressed in a long, flowing boubou and who rode through the streets of Saint Louis astride a beautiful white horse.[56] Parsine did not fit neatly into the expectation of the westernized métis class that French officials expected. Other signifiers, such as the consumption of Senegalese dishes prepared by African women domestics, the wearing of clothes more suitable for the sahelian climate, or métis collections of filigree jewelry made by local goldsmiths, fall outside of the idealized notion of cultural assimilation and consequently do not appear in photographs and writings.[57]

On the whole, the wardrobes of métis men and women advanced their position as republican citizens. In adopting the styles of the French ruling classes, métis men asserted their role as influential power brokers, and métis women cultivated respectability and high moral standing for the family. While the colonial regime sought to impose a certain standard of taste, métis men and women understood the role of fashion for the modern citizen. By sitting for portraits that depicted them in the simple but elegant styles deemed appropriate for the French middle class, the métis could assert their own sense of equality with the captains of industry and rulers of empire.

Proponents of colonialism considered the imposition of new building styles as an important sign of progress and modernization in Senegal. In the early nineteenth century, the municipal government imposed laws to encourage town residents to build in brick and abandon mud dwellings with thatch roofs. French writers insisted that the adoption of square windows and doors as well as the acquisition of European furnishings by town residents constituted positive signs of European influence.[58] By the 1840s, the majority of métis families lived in brick homes rather than the square adobe dwellings that housed the majority of the African working-class populations of the town. Two-story square houses lined the wide avenues where métis families lived. Stylized door and window frames with wrought-iron balconies imported from Europe became a sign of progress and modernity, but the interior quarters indicated continuity with African form and function. The *rez de chaussée* (ground floor) contained courtyards for household workers, a ground floor shop or storehouse, and servant quarters. Winding staircases led to the second floor, which opened up onto a number of rooms for the family's living space.[59] Small balconies adorned second-story windows, reportedly to allow women to discreetly observe the street scene below without being seen (fig. 6).

As in metropolitan France, the salon became the center of domestic life. The public image that métis men and women sought to create of their families and home life reflected the characteristics most valued by the bourgeoisie. In the 1880s, professional photographers staged sittings in the homes of elite residents that corresponded to the idea of the virtuous and well-fashioned life of the modern citizen.[60] Typically, photographs depicted people of mixed-racial heritage in a salon-like setting and posed next to or seated in ornate, high-backed Victorian chairs. The 1889 photograph of Madeleine Tamba, taken on the same day as her son's marriage to Charlotte Crespin, shows her standing next to a stuffed chair with what appears to be needlepoint on the seat—an appropriate hobby for respectable wives and mothers (fig.7). A 1905 photograph of Justin Devès and his daughter Elizabeth shows the father seated on a bench with her standing close to him in front of what appears to be a backdrop of palm trees and the top of a conical thatch roof (fig.5). By the turn of the century, scenes of African life became part of the image that the photographer and his client wished to convey. These subtle touches show the changing realities of urban life in which western-educated African town residents held greater power in politics and trade and sought avenues to depict themselves at the center of life in the colonies.

Photographs provide only a limited view of the interior lives of individuals. They do not tell us what foods they ate on a daily basis, what type of bed they slept on, or what sorts of garments they wore in their most private moments. However, they do offer an indication of the image that men and women sought to convey to others. The many photographs kept in private family collections demonstrate the importance that Métis families placed on conveying an image of themselves as republican citizens. Wives and daughters served as powerful vehicles in which to communicate the impression of a respectable household. And yet photographs reveal disruptions in the typical image associated with the métis elite. In keeping with the style set by signares, African women continued to wear their hair wrapped in cloth. Madeleine Tamba appears with hair covered yet adorned in contemporary French fashion.

The homes of métis families and the choices that women made in furnishings conveyed a sense of modest luxury considered appropriate for the middle class. The salon or adjacent office provided a space to entertain clients or friends and to hold important meetings. The bottom floor often served as a warehouse, retail space, or place of domestic work. The physical structure of the house and the interior décor signified the authority, honor, and prestige associated with the family and bolstered the influence of the male head of household. These visible markers conveyed important meanings in politics, business, and society. Aesthetic choices brought the private realm of family and domesticity squarely into the public realm of political power.

Between 1820 and 1870, urban society changed in significant ways. France initiated a new phase of imperialism in West Africa by seeking to spread the virtues of French civilization through evangelism, education, and the imposition of new laws and customs. Muslim traders gained greater influence in colonial affairs, and Islam took on greater significance within the urban community. Métis habitants responded to these changes by emphasizing their distinctiveness as a group with strong ties to French religious and cultural values. Adherence to the orthodox teachings of the Catholic Church, conformity to metropolitan expectations for marriage and family, and the adoption of French dress, habits, and tastes bolstered the métis as a politically influential class.

In 1820, when control was reestablished over its territories in Senegal, France envisioned Saint Louis as the place for implementing the cultural objectives of French imperialism. The establishment of religious orders in the colony along with the development of an African clergy helped to establish new expectations about private life and sought to control sexual relations that crossed the color line. Métis endogamy did not occur by happenstance. The clergy and French officials attacked the problem of social and sexual contact between African women and European men with the goal of eliminating the flexible domestic relations that dominated town life in the period of mercantile commerce and containing the growth of métis offspring from these unions. One consequence of these efforts was the decline of signares in establishing new Afro-European households in the coastal towns. In cultivating pious young women, according to the bourgeois notions of respectability, Catholic clergy and French officials sought to ensure the reproduction of colonial society. The métis daughters and granddaughters of signares became the models of respectable womanhood.

These transformations, nevertheless, occurred gradually. Despite the cultural objectives of French rule, officials in Saint Louis opted for accommodating local practices rather than imposing cultural hegemony by force. Accommodation fostered relations of cooperation needed to advance the political and economic aims of French rule in Senegal. The perpetuation of mariage à la mode du pays , the creation of a mosque on the north side of the island, and the cultivation of ties with Muslim clerics and traders in the urban community show the malleability of French cultural objectives when faced with local realities.

Métis men and women identified with the values, lifestyle, and culture of metropolitan France, but they were also products of an African environment. They maintained a social network that kept them firmly connected to the societies of Senegal's interior. The métis of Saint Louis observed urban Wolof customs. They spoke Wolof, interacted with Muslims in the town, maintained relations with Muslim clerics in the interior, and recognized kin ties with Africans of the town and countryside. These actions defined them as *doomu Ndar* (sons and daughters of Saint Louis) like Muslim and grumet inhabitants of the town. Their responses to the culture of colonial rule varied, but affiliation with French tastes worked to promote a public image of themselves as a group closely associated with French power. While in the long term, their cultural choices distanced them from the majority African population, in the short term this outlook positioned the métis to assert their right to equal access to political power with metropolitan Frenchmen when the Third Republic came to power in the 1870s.

4

Education, Association, and an Independent Press

Colonial cultures were never direct translations of European society
planted in the colonies, but unique cultural configurations, homespun
creations in which European food, dress, housing and morality were given
new political meanings in the particular social order of colonial rule.

—*Ann Laura Stoler, "Rethinking Colonial Categories:
European Communities and the Boundaries of Rule."*

In the late nineteenth century, as France engaged in wars of conquest and
consolidated control over the states of the Senegal River valley and the peanut basin, some within the métis population joined the Alliance Française,
an organization founded to protect and support the spread of French language and culture. Others joined the Masonic lodge and founded newspapers with an anticlerical point of view. They espoused the virtues of the
republic in their newspapers, celebrated Bastille Day, joined rifle clubs, and
held annual regattas on the Senegal River. Although the métis attended
French schools, adopted French dress, and identified closely with the ideals
espoused by the Third Republic, they also transformed these cultural idioms
to serve their purposes. They solidified their role as the predominant
French-educated and professional elite of Senegal's colonial capital.

The notion of a unified, monolithic colonizer conquering and permanently altering the kinship structures, political economy, and daily life of
the heterogeneous African masses is no longer tenable. Anthropologists
have turned the lens back on European communities in the colonies to

show that they brought the class, regional, and gender distinctions of metropolitan societies with them as they established new communities in overseas territories. Colonial projects, as Ann Laura Stoler points out, were aimed at not only remaking African or Asian people but also maintaining social distinctions among themselves while keeping European subordinates and potential subversives in line. The cultural idioms imposed through colonial policies centered on education, sexuality, civil law, food, dress, and national celebration brought about a new construction of Europeanness.[1]

As the descendants of European men and African women, the métis population in Senegal blurred the boundaries of colonial rule. A settler community only emerged in Senegal after World War I and then on a fairly small scale. The ministry of the navy governed the Senegal colony until a civilian administration replaced the military in the 1880s. Between 1850 and 1900, the majority of European personnel in Senegal consisted of military officers, members of the judiciary, bureaucrats, and representatives of French commercial firms. Mainly young men, Europeans in the colony rarely remained in the country for long. As France began to launch wars of conquest in Senegal's interior, the métis represented the primary group of French-educated town residents who had close ties to French culture and society but also possessed intimate knowledge of the local situation. Colonial officials and capitalist firms needed the métis as partners in their imperialist aims.

In the wake of the gum crisis of the 1840s, the métis increasingly looked to the liberal professions for socioeconomic mobility. Colonial policies supported advanced education for the métis in order to affirm their identification with French culture and values and to develop this class of intermediaries who could facilitate French policies in the colony. For the métis, pursuing higher education afforded them the same qualifications for leadership as French military officers or bureaucrats. Becoming lawyers and joining associations such as the chamber of commerce strengthened métis networks with ruling elites in metropolitan France. French education sought to make young girls into pious wives and respectable mothers, but schooling also allowed métis women to enter public discourse as the voice of morality for the urban community. Schools and associations provided an institutional framework for the métis population to engage with republican ideas and enter into metropolitan debates, creating new fields of interaction between Africans and Europeans in the urban community.

The emergence of an independent press provided an avenue for certain individuals within the métis community to articulate their ideas and contest colonial practices. The métis adopted the tools espoused under the Third Republic for expanding political discourse and democratic rights for French citizens and used it to their own advantage. In their newspapers and public speeches, they grappled with the same contradictions inherent in French colonialism. They argued against the abuse of colonial power but considered conquest necessary for progress. They decried the exploitation of workers but held personal investments in the perpetuation of slave markets in the interior and the colonial labor regime.

The development of schools, associations, and an independent press fostered civic participation and provided an institutional basis for cooperation between the métis elite and colonial authorities. At the same time, the liberal reforms enacted facilitated the exchange of ideas between Senegal's urban elite and subversives within the European community, providing new avenues for the métis to articulate their ideas and challenge French power.

Educational and Professional Choices

Schools, like law and dress, provided colonial regimes with tools for transforming African people in the cities into individuals who would further the aims of empire. Schools also provided residents with important institutions for group socialization and the reproduction of elite status. French schools taught métis boys and girls the appropriate habits of republican citizenship and provided the necessary qualifications for entry into the professional and intellectual classes of metropolitan France and the empire. Possessing knowledge of French language, culture, and society also allowed individuals within the métis community to survive their declining role as middlemen in the colonial economy and reassert their relevance in political and economic affairs.

Colonial education in Senegal embodied similar class and gender divisions that structured metropolitan society. In nineteenth-century France, schools aimed to provide young men with the skills and social networks to operate in the public sphere. The education of young middle-class women sought to elevate their status by enhancing the social esteem of their future husbands and the reputation of the family. In nineteenth-century Senegal, officials viewed education in similar terms, but while they focused on educating boys to provide lower-level bureaucratic services, they placed greater emphasis on educating girls as a key to the civilizing mission. Properly educated girls turned into pious Catholic wives and mothers and culturally assimilated young women who would instill the values of French civilization and progress in future generations. French officials viewed education for the elite inhabitants of Saint Louis and Gorée as a mechanism for reproducing colonial society.

In the 1820s and 1830s, colonial officials encouraged the Sisters of Saint Joseph de Cluny to provide instruction to signares and their métis daughters to eliminate interracial sexual relations and to mold the growing mixed-race population into a French-identified group. In 1854, the Sisters of Saint Joseph received a subsidy from the administration to broaden their educational program in the colony. They used part of the subsidy to open an orphanage in the coastal fishing village of Ndar Toute. The school followed one program for habitant demoiselles that focused on subjects appropriate for young middle-class ladies and another program for jeunes négresses that emphasized practical education such as laundering, sewing, and cooking—skills they considered appropriate for young girls destined to become domestics.[2]

Educational reform in Senegal's colonial towns followed reforms in metropolitan France. Between 1815 and 1850, religious orders held primary responsibility for providing education for girls. The upper class sent their daughters to convents or private boarding schools. The Falloux Law of 15 March 1850 introduced national reforms to education for boys but also called for the establishment of public education for girls.[3] While religious orders continued to run public schools, the new program of elementary education for girls focused on teaching them an elaborate view of women's domestic roles in society. Girls' schools taught subjects suitable for their "feminine nature" and appropriate for their class. Middle-class girls learned the *arts d'agrément,* including music, dance, and sewing—subjects believed to make them more pleasing to their educated husbands and families. The religious orders continued to hold a monopoly on schools for young girls as instruction remained tied to instilling Catholic teachings and ideas of morality.

The schools run by the Sisters of Saint Joseph de Cluny in Saint Louis and Gorée provided a popular option for métis parents seeking to attain the same religious and academic training for their daughters as that expected for middle-class French girls. Most of the students enrolled came from families of the métis elite. In 1881, Anna Dumont, Rose d'Erneville, Suzanne Descemet, Amélie Molinet, and Constance Pécarrère attended. In the 1890s, young women who attended the sisters' school in Gorée were *habitants de la commune* but came from regions further south in the second arrondissement or from new port towns like Rufisque or as far as Gambia and Sierra Leone.[4] When métis and grumet families left Saint Louis for the peanut basin to work as traders, commercial agents, or employees of the administration, they placed a high priority on the education of their daughters by sending them back to the towns for schooling.

In the 1880s, the curriculum of the order's schools in Senegal expanded to include subjects promoted by the Third Republic. The curriculum consisted of five classes or levels of instruction. The youngest group began with instruction in reading, catechism, and fables. The more advanced classes followed courses in French grammar, religious history, ecclesiastical history, French and African history, European and African geography, and arithmetic.[5] Students also learned civic instruction, reading, recitation of fables, poetry, writing, grammar, spelling, arithmetic, history, geography, and basic physical and natural science. In addition, their lessons included training in home economics, singing, sewing, and design. Young girls devoted considerable time to pursuing hobbies like piano and needlework that were popular among the bourgeoisie in metropolitan France. Girls' education taught specific academic skills and required instruction in leisure activities appropriate for middle-class ladies.

Although the education of young women held great importance for métis society, that education did not exist outside of the gendered realm of colonial power and policy. Colonial officials believed women obstructed the effort to make French rather than Wolof the language of the capital. The clergy focused on teaching signares and their daughters to speak French because they considered women the key to instilling the habit of communicating in French for future generations. In a speech for the annual prize ceremony to graduates of the Gorée school, David Boilat urged men to facilitate their children "in the path of progress" by speaking to them in French and demanding that "they never speak any other language in your house." Boilat considered speaking French to be absolutely necessary for cultivating "educated youth, virtuous daughters, and civilized persons."[6]

Métis and grumet households, however, did not operate outside of African society. Wolof was spoken in the courtyards, kitchens, and warehouses that formed part of the family's living quarters. It remained the primary language spoken in the town and an essential for daily activities, even as métis families viewed their role in spreading the French language as essential to promoting modern life in Senegal. Accordingly, in 1864 métis habitant Louis Descemet published his own Wolof-French phrase book aimed specifically at teaching French to Wolof speakers. In his view, African town residents did not easily master spoken French because metropolitan instructors used the same method of rote memorization to teach Africans as that used in metropolitan schools. Instead Descemet devised a system to teach Wolof speakers French by providing translations of key French phrases and terms in Wolof, as understood by residents of the towns.[7]

The administration instituted an annual prize ceremony to recognize the educational achievements of habitant students. Representatives of the administration used the event to confirm the importance of French education for colonial objectives. A commission of civil servants and notable town residents named by the governor administered annual examinations. At the end of the examination period, the commission awarded prizes and primary school certificates in a formal ceremony attended by students, parents, teachers, and members of the administration. The mayor or a prominent member of the community presided over the ceremony and delivered a speech to honor the occasion. Traditionally, the governor held a dinner for the laureates and their families at the governor's palace. The sisters' schools were consistently commended for providing excellent academic instruction, and the prize commission routinely recognized female students for exemplifying high standards of academic achievement. In an 1895 address at the annual prize ceremony for the Gorée school, métis notable Leopold Angrand extolled the "brilliant success" of the student Clotilde Dolly and reminded young women to remain modest despite their success. He also cautioned the "mothers of families" to "keep a firm hand so that their children do not miss even an entire hour of their studies."[8]

From the standpoint of the colonial administration, the education of young women played an important role in reproducing and modernizing colonial society. For métis habitants, education placed their daughters on an equal footing with middle-class women of metropolitan France as respectable wives and mothers. Colonial education unintentionally created a cadre of western-educated women who, like their French counterparts, broke the gender barrier in the professions. In the 1880s, a few métis women took advantage of metropolitan reforms addressed at providing them with equal access to higher education by offering scholarships to pursue secondary education in France. The realities of financial loss in the wake of the gum crisis affected widows and single women differently from men. The administration made special provisions for financial support to widows. In the late nineteenth and early twentieth centuries, women found employment in Senegal's capital as librarians, midwives, piano teachers, or secretaries in the colonial administration. Others worked behind the scenes helping to manage the family business.[9] Despite their training as proper middle-class women, the lives of métis women did not necessarily correspond neatly to the ideal life of leisure expected of women in their class.

The educational aspirations for young men differed sharply from the expectations set for young women. From the period of company government, colonial officials needed to train interpreters and lower-level bureaucrats to make up for the lack of personnel and knowledge about political, economic, and social relations with Africans in the interior. Bordeaux merchants also needed agents on the ground who could read and write French and keep financial records. In the early nineteenth century, wholesale merchants hired European personnel in the settlement as tutors for their sons while others sent their male children to France for education.[10] In the 1840s, the administration invested in the development of French schools in Saint Louis precisely to develop skilled workers and to regularize the growing métis population of the towns. For métis habitants, the schools provided an important avenue for preserving their socioeconomic status as they faced increased competition with Muslim habitants.

The educational system established in the colony reflected the same tensions that characterized colonial expansion in Senegal. Officials in Saint Louis sought to implement their vision of colonialism by instituting French schools in the capital while also recognizing the importance of accommodating Muslim residents. In addition, as the French military increasingly sought to subjugate ruling elites in the Senegal River valley, colonial officials viewed schools as another institution that could be used to enforce colonial domination. In the 1820s, treaties between African rulers and French officials required that a chief's son be taken to Saint Louis and entrusted to the care of the first French school founded in the colony, called the mutual school. In 1856, Faidherbe institutionalized this practice by creating the School for Hostages to develop allies for the French with ruling elites in the interior. Prior to establishing this school, a school run by the Brothers of Ploërmel served the dual purpose of educating men of the habitant elite and the so-called sons of chiefs placed under French authority.[11]

French education in the colonial towns operated according to one program for Christian and Muslim habitants and another for Saint Louis's working class. Faidherbe introduced schools in Saint Louis and the French posts along the Senegal River as part of this Islamic policy. These schools offered courses in French and arithmetic with limited Islamic education.[12] Faidherbe also imposed regulations on popular Koranic schools and required the religious orders to permit voluntary enrollment of Muslim students. In 1857, the Brothers of Ploërmel opened night classes for adult Muslims. In 1876, the instructors opened regular day classes to Muslims. The classes offered by the brothers appealed to the children of Muslim traders and employees of the administration whose parents found it advantageous for their children to learn French and mathematics and to become more familiar with the systems of French rule.[13] Muslims who attended the night classes at the brothers' school did so irregularly. In a sign of resistance to French schooling among the majority Muslim population of Saint Louis, the schools established under Faidherbe's Islamic policy closed because of declining enrollment and lack of funding.

Despite colonial objectives, the métis looked to the French schools as a strategy for socioeconomic advancement. In November 1837, the Brothers of Ploërmel (also known as the Brothers for Christian Instruction) agreed to a request by the naval ministry to send six members of the order to Senegal.[14] The brothers opened two schools, one in Saint Louis and the other in Gorée. Unlike metropolitan schools, students in Senegal did not pay enrollment fees, and the administration furnished school supplies. A close relationship developed between the métis and the order during its sixty-three years in the colony (1841–1904). Métis habitants used their influence as advisers to the administration and as elected officials to push for financial support for the school. In 1870, a métis habitant leased his own building to the government explicitly for the purpose of providing space for the school and its instructors.

The Brothers of Ploërmel sought to instill in their pupils greater adherence to Church doctrine through religious and moral instruction while providing the academic training required by the state. Students followed four classes according to age and academic level. The youngest students took courses in catechism and reading. As they advanced, boys received instruction in writing, grammar, arithmetic, religious history, French history, linear design, ancient history, and Roman history. Out of five hours of class time, an hour and a half was devoted to Catholic instruction. In 1882 and 1884, when the Third Republic introduced educational reforms, the curriculum of the school expanded to fulfill the new regime's requirement for civic education. Students took courses in civics, French language, reading, writing, arithmetic, history, geography, basic agriculture, and linear design.[15]

The sons of the métis, grumets, and Muslim traders attended the school along with sons of French merchants or bureaucrats living in the colony. Between 1843 and 1850, Germain Benjamin Crespin, Jean Jacques Crespin, Louis Guillabert, Alfred d'Erneville, and Louis Descemet attended regular day classes. Grumet students François Demba, Gabriel Medor, and Mathurin Chimer were also enrolled. In addition, four boys came to the school through their affiliation with habitant families. Jean Aly, born near the coast in 1833 and raised "chez M. Valantin," entered the school in 1846, received baptism in 1849, and left for Rio Nunez on 16 April 1854. Former slaves, indentured servants, or wards, these men probably became apprentices to habitant families with trade interests on the Saloum and in the southern rivers. The first group of students found employment in the administration or military after finishing their studies. By the end of the 1850s, métis students received scholarships from the administration to pursue secondary education in France.[16]

The school contained a cross section of the urban elite, but also cut across class and regional lines. Children of métis, grumets, and Muslim traders sat in classrooms with children of the aristocracy, who came from interior regions of the country, and future interpreters for the Muslim tribunal.[17] It constituted a new type of community, one that embodied new ideas of what it might mean to be "Senegalese," but at the same time it reflected the hierarchies and tensions produced by the expansion of colonial rule. Métis students generally followed a path that led them to employment in the administration or the military or higher education in France. Sons of Muslim traders and grumets followed their fathers into commerce. In the 1880s, Abdoulaye Seck and Jules Demba left the brothers' school for France, perhaps as scholarship recipients. Generally, schools in Senegal operated according to expectations that people of mixed racial ancestry were the best suited to pursue higher education in France while African students should receive only enough education for working in trade or as clerks and interpreters for the administration.

Access to French education allowed métis men entry into metropolitan French society and facilitated their ability to influence colonial affairs. The Second Empire of Louis Napoleon introduced educational reforms that made public education at the secondary level more widely available to the public, and yet education perpetuated exclusivity.[18] Specific schools granted access to the machinery that controlled industry and politics, and métis families competed for access to these institutions. Colonial officials, concerned only with educating a class of clerks and trade agents, did not consider secondary or higher education necessary for Africans in the urban community. The métis, however, argued for access to the same level of public education available in metropolitan France. They demanded instruction in Latin for students in Senegal's primary schools because it remained the language of instruction in universities. Secondary education opened up the liberal professions to the métis and provided a needed pathway to social and economic mobility.[19] Higher education allowed métis families to make the transition from a primarily commercial elite to the dominant population of French-educated elite in Senegal.

Following the close of Boilat's college in 1849, the inspector for schools decided that creating a scholarship program for habitants to attend lycée or university in France presented a more efficient and less costly option than creating secondary schools in the colony. The administration instituted a scholarship program for qualified and needy male students who completed primary studies under the Brothers of Ploërmel. In the 1850s and 1860s, the administration awarded scholarships to five students chosen by French officials from among children of the European and métis population who had provided important services to the administration or whom officials held in high esteem.[20] Roger Descemet received an award in 1853 for military training at the College de l'Orient. He went on to attend military school at Saint Cyr and returned to Senegal as sub-lieutenant. In the 1850s, colonial officials rewarded a select number of individuals with scholarships in an effort to encourage members of the habitant elite to become high-ranking military officers or assume positions in the colonial bureaucracy.

In 1879, the scholarship program expanded when the Third Republic reinstituted the General Council and gave responsibility for awarding grants and allocating budgetary expenses for public education to members of the local assembly. Métis habitants made up the majority of members elected to the assembly and placed a high priority on the scholarship program. In the council's first meeting, its members voted to raise the number of half-scholarships to three and increase the funds allocated to cover the cost of students returning to Senegal after completing their studies. The 1880 budget increased the amount dedicated for scholarship funding from 15,000 to 18,000 francs.[21] The funds allocated for scholarship increased each year until 1887, when the total expense for metropolitan scholarships reached 125,000 francs distributed to 125 scholarship students.

In the first General Council session, members agreed to name two representatives to the permanent commission of civil servants and notables appointed by the governor. The commission ranked students according to their examination results, their family background, history of service to the administration, and their financial situation. The program required that students take an examination in spelling, grammar, religious history, geography, and basic Latin.[22] The scholarships provided support for five years or until the student reached age 18. Recipients had the option of extending the grant for two additional years.

When the administration first implemented the program, the governor's council in charge of administering scholarships stipulated that awards only covered room and board. The General Council expanded the award to include travel expenses. Students could apply the award to study at any lycée, college, or trade school in France. In 1882, the General Council granted additional subsidies for university studies. These awards went primarily to students for studies in law, medicine, or colonial administration at the newly founded École Coloniale.[23] The commission awarded a few scholarships to young women in keeping with metropolitan reforms that opened secondary education to women. Métis representatives placed such importance on the scholarship program that even when faced with budgetary constraints, pressure from the director of the interior to end the program, and the creation of a secondary school in Senegal, métis councilors preferred to eliminate other expenditures rather than reduce the budget for metropolitan scholarships.[24]

Although records of the General Council's deliberations on public education illustrate the important role this program played in the métis community, little is known about Senegalese students in nineteenth-century France, the schools they attended, the subjects they studied, or the nature of their successes or failures.[25] The history of Senegalese scholarship recipients in France raises intriguing questions about what it meant to be an enfant du pays in the school environment and how people of mixed race from the colonies were perceived in France. Writings of nobility regarding African servants in France exist for the eighteenth century, and the study of race in France in the twentieth century has yielded important insights. Still gaps remain in understanding how people of African descent operated in late nineteenth-century France.

The enrollment register for Lycée Michel Montaigne in Bordeaux offers a rare glimpse into the educational experience of a particular cohort of Senegalese scholarship recipients in France from 1875 to 1881. At least twenty young men from Senegal enrolled in the lycée as boarding students during this period. The Devès brothers (Justin, Hyacinthe, and Francois), the Carpot brothers (Charles, Francois, and Ernest), and three members of the Valantin family appear in the register.[26] In addition, a few children of colonial administrators and French merchants residing in Senegal attended the school. Most scholarship recipients returned to Senegal after their studies or brief apprenticeships in their new professions, although some may have remained in France. This group of Senegalese scholarship recipients may have returned to the colony because of the limits of upward mobility in France, or their decision to return may have been because the métis considered themselves to have the most appropriate qualifications for guiding the imperial project and introducing westernization in the colony.

Children of widows also attended the school because the General Council emphasized awarding scholarships to needy children, especially those who suffered financial loss as a result of the father's death. The métis relied on their social networks with Bordeaux commercial agents, administrators, and French branches of their family to sponsor children from Saint Louis or Gorée who attended the schools in France. Hubler, an employee of the post and telegraph department, represented the Carpot children. Bordeaux merchant Maurel served as liaison for all three Valantins.[27] The close proximity of the métis population to French merchants and bureaucrats residing in the colonies likely facilitated their entry into schools in Bordeaux, where leaders of metropolitan industry and commerce had established ties to Senegal.

Lycée Michel Montaigne attracted students of the French upper classes as well as children of the European elite residing throughout the French

Empire and in major commercial ports of North and South America. Strategically located in a central port city on the Atlantic coast of southwest France, the enrollment registry suggests that the school accommodated children of diplomats, leaders of international commerce, and civil and military officials stationed throughout the French Empire. Boarders from Senegal lived and studied with classmates whose parents lived in Martinique, Guadeloupe, Réunion, and Algeria as well as key mercantile ports like Buenos Aires, Liverpool, New Orleans, and San Francisco.[28] They also attended school with children of Bordeaux merchants—Maurel and Prom, Rabaud, Buhan and Teisseire, and Devès and Chaumet. While there may or may not have been tensions between Senegalese and French branches of the same family, young métis men shared a similar social formation with young men of the French bourgeoisie. The school served as a field of interaction between sons of the métis elite and sons of the Bordeaux merchant lobby (who they may have been related to) as well as individuals who could become future leaders in politics, industry, and law.

Lycée Michel Montaigne can be understood as a microcosm of European bourgeois society but one that included children of color raised in the colonies. Colonial education policies not only transformed urban life in the colonies but also impacted metropolitan education. The school provided an institutional basis for young men to establish social networks that could be useful in the future. It also acted as a training ground in the habits of republican citizenship. Students followed courses in civic participation and the history of the republic while learning advanced skills in writing, mathematics, science, rhetoric, and oratory. Studying in France prepared young métis men to enter the liberal professions and develop the skills needed to serve as potential leaders in the political life of the colony. Their educational experiences created informal networks of socialization that proved useful to métis men as they sought to carve out a new niche for themselves in colonial Senegal.

Associations and Urban Life in the late Nineteenth Century

The generation of métis who studied with the religious orders in the 1860s traveled to France for their studies in the 1870s and returned to Senegal in the 1880s. They witnessed the renewal of democratic thought and practice in metropolitan France as Louis-Napoleon Bonaparte's regime gave way to the Third Republic. During this period, France experienced the expansion of democratic institutions and public debate over issues from equal rights for women to the role of secularism in the new republic. A new middle class, consisting of businessmen and professionals, championed its qualifications to replace the landed aristocracy as rulers of France. Unions expanded political rights for working men who did not own property. Voluntary associations played a key role in stabilizing democratic institutions and advancing ideas such as human rights, anticlericalism, and business enterprise. Traditional institutions like the Church or the bar association and radical associations like the Freemasons played key roles in shaping public opinion, developing "the electoral arts," and articulating oppositional views capable of challenging state control.[29]

Associations also influenced public life in Senegal's colonial towns in the last quarter of the nineteenth century. In the 1870s and 1880s, residents of the capital participated in a variety of organizations. Alliance Française explicitly sought to promote the spread of French language and culture in the colony. Métis and French members of Alliance Française financed French schools in interior towns that had recently come under French control. The Masonic lodge, the bar association, and a women's group called the Mothers of Families brought together various interests in the urban community that provided a vocal and, at times, oppositional element in public discourse.

In the mid- and late 1880s, a handful of *cercles* founded by young people appeared in Saint Louis. The administration authorized meetings of the cercle des habitants notables du pays and the cercle de la fraternité.[30] Official publications offer little information on the content of these meetings or their membership, but we can glean ideas about their purpose from their names. The majority of organizations listed emphasized youth and civic behavior. Their titles correspond to similar civic clubs that emerged in France to educate young people about the meaning of the republic and the value of electoral and civic participation. In Senegal as in France, these organizations tended also to focus on youth participation. The civic clubs of the 1880s may have served as a model for the Jeunes Sénégalais, an association founded in 1912 by African youth of the towns to break the color barrier by promoting African participation in electoral politics.

In the 1870s and 1880s, town residents and Europeans in the colonies participated in these associations. Association choices indicated different ideological viewpoints but also reflected different social networks. For elite women, membership elevated their position as respectable wives and mothers. The Mothers of Families originated among women of Saint Louis who belonged to the Church. In 1867, sixty to seventy métis and European women founded the group to bring together "naturally married women or widows," but also admitted "honorable people not having been married due to age or situation."[31] Madame Legros, Madame François Crespin, Madame Jean Jacques Crespin, Madame Floissac, Madame Octave Armstrong, Madame Jules Andre, and Widow Charles Carpot were among the organization's members.

In addition to celebrating particular religious festivals, women contributed 1.50 francs monthly that went to helping the poor. Also a mutual aid society, the group distributed a portion of the contributions among two or three women at each meeting. The Mothers of Families demonstrated its piety through charity and acts of goodwill in the community. The association also provided a platform for the leading women of the communes to express their role as guardians of morality and decency in public life. On 15 March 1887, the Mothers of Families wrote to the governor objecting to articles printed in one of the newly founded independent newspapers called *Le Réveil du Senegal*. The group of women who signed the petition objected to the scandalous tone of the journal and its defamatory attacks on certain "Senegalese" families. The women called on the governor to alert the minister of the navy, Jean-Bernard Jauréguiberry, whom they knew from his time serving as the governor of Senegal, and demanded that the ministry intervene in the conflict.[32]

Membership also served as a means for individuals to embrace new ideas and articulate their own positions about the major debates shaping metropolitan and colonial society. Freemasons stood at the forefront of the debate over the role of the Church in matters of the state. Arguing for secularism, the Masons attracted liberal members of government, the military, commerce, and industry. Funeral ceremonies, like civil marriages, became occasions for anticlerical demonstrations. Members of the Masonic lodges opted for civil burial as a means of proclaiming their belief in secularism and liberal ideologies such as freedom of religion and association.[33] In the 1870s, solemn funeral professions commonly erupted into violent confrontations between the police and average citizens. The Masons established civil burial societies, substituting their rituals for the rites of the Church and replacing the priest with Masons who offered speeches in honor of their brother.

Members of the Masonic lodge in Senegal's capital participated in this debate. The constitution of the Union Sénégalaise required that in the case of a member's death, the entire lodge would attend the funeral regardless of the wishes of the family or the state.[34] Associations that espoused radical and oppositional ideas had the potential to disrupt state power. In Senegal, the presence of anticlerical Masons became a bone of contention with colonial authorities. In June 1874, Governor Valière authorized the opening of the Union Sénégalaise, a lodge affiliated with the Grand Orient in Paris.[35] It is unclear if Gaspard Devès joined the lodge, but he and his allies had the ability to support an institution at odds with the administration because of their economic and political influence. As mayor of Saint Louis, Gaspard Devès recommended its establishment and hosted the first meeting at his residence. The lodge attracted French and métis merchants and their representatives as well as soldiers and civil servants. In March 1875, the lodge inducted métis lawyer Jean Jacques "J. J." Crespin into the Union Sénégalais. He achieved the rank of master in October of the same year.[36] Crespin's and Devès's affiliation with the lodge conformed with their position as individuals who took positions that opposed the Church and the administration.

Two years after the lodge opened, the governor called for its dissolution in response to a public scandal over the burial of a colonial official. The head of the Catholic congregation in Saint Louis claimed that the director of the bridges and highways department had received last rites by a priest and asked for a Christian burial in the final moments before his death. The clergy accused the Masons of interfering with the Catholic ceremony by placing Masonic insignia on the coffin during the funeral procession and performing their own rites during the ceremony. The Church called the act a "grave insult to the deceased and all Catholics in the capital." Members of the lodge claimed innocence, stating that they simply accompanied their brother to his last resting place and that they were "struggling now more than ever against the attacks of a fanatical and ignorant clergy."[37] On 30 March 1876, Governor Valière ordered the suspension of the lodge in a clear demonstration of the administration's support of the Church over the Freemasons and a willingness to suppress potentially subversive ideologies.

Despite this setback, clandestine initiations continued among Freemasons in the late 1870s, and members lobbied their brothers in Bordeaux to intercede with the governor and colonial ministry on their behalf. On 20 December 1880, Governor Brière de l'Isle announced the reinstatement of the lodge in response to a request from the Municipal Council, headed by Mayor Gaspard Devès and Deputy Mayor J. J. Crespin.

In the 1880s, the Union Sénégalaise turned to "humanitarian and civilizing questions" to bolster its reputation. The Union proposed to develop a school for "apprentices, *hommes de couleur,* and former slaves" and sought to counter the influence of Muslim marabouts by training Africans to be "good French workers."[38] Directing their attack against clericalism away from the Catholic clergy by targeting Islam brought their actions in line with colonial priorities rather than antagonizing French authorities.

The Union Sénégalaise survived the scandal of the 1870s. It continued to attract métis habitants, French merchants, and civil servants with radical viewpoints. Members included Pastor Taylor, the Sierra Leonean head of the Protestant Church who ran a mission for runaway slaves, French entrepreneur Albert Laplène, Bordeaux merchant Victor Pronnier, Adolphe Crespin, and François Valantin. Biram Sady, a Saint Louis trader, Mamdou Racine, captain in the colonial army called the *tirailleurs,* and Mademba Seye, an employee of the telegraph office, also received diplomas of initiation in the lodge.[39]

Despite their ardent support of republican ideals, métis members of the lodge held contradictory positions when it came to questions of forced labor and antislavery policies in Senegal's interior. Like other members of the urban elite, Bordeaux merchants, and colonial administrations who relied on labor regimes that stimulated the colonial economy, members of the Masonic lodge had to reconcile republican ideals with the realities of their class.[40] Members included pastors and civilian administrators, some of whom held antislavery views, as well as entrepreneurs and merchants who had practical investments in maintaining capitalist relations of production. Despite these conflicts, membership in the lodge strengthened ties between the métis, Africans, and Europeans with individuals in metropolitan France who played key roles in economic and political affairs in the colony.

The last association that deserves mention concerns membership in the most venerable of professional organizations in late nineteenth-century France: the association of barristers. Known alternatively as the Republic of Laws, the Third Republic developed a reputation as a government dominated by lawyers.[41] Specifically, a group of young energetic men trained at the Paris Bar sought to counter the authoritarian practices of Napoleon Bonaparte through the rule of law and their professional code of ethics. The Paris Bar was seen as the ideal training ground for developing the qualities required to lead a virtuous life of public service by mastering skills of independent thinking, cultivating morality and ethics, and instilling the discipline needed for self-government. For instance, lawyers Leon Gambetta and Jules Ferry studied at the Paris Bar before becoming lawmakers overseeing democratic transition in France and pushing the Republic to expand its imperial interests.

In the 1870s and 1880s, the field of law attracted métis men of Saint Louis for many of the same reasons that young men in France gravitated toward the legal profession. The Devès brothers all completed studies at the law school of Bordeaux. François Carpot graduated from the law school in Paris, the most prestigious in the country, and completed an apprenticeship in law before returning to Senegal in the 1880s. J. J. Crespin earned a reputation as a master barrister who argued unpopular and also controversial positions despite never having studied law in France. Crespin began his career in the colonial bureaucracy but left the administration to pursue law in the late 1860s. He did not train formally in France but read for the law as an apprentice to French lawyers in Saint Louis. As conseil commissionné, a term reserved for local lawyers, Crespin developed a reputation as a skilled orator in Senegal's court system who fought tirelessly on behalf of his clients.[42]

Speeches pronounced upon Crespin's untimely death on 2 January 1895 by his peers and associates in law and administration illustrate the importance of professional affiliation, the close relationship between law and politics, and the ways in which lawyers used their professional position to advocate for controversial and often contentious issues in politics and government. Crespin died early in his term as mayor of Saint Louis. His fellow elected officials characterized him as a passionate advocate and skilled administrator who often "walked against his countrymen" to defend causes he believed in and to fight in the interests of his country. Governor Clement-Thomas referred to Crespin as the most remarkable representative of the "Senegalese spirit," even though they held sharp disagreements. Fellow members of the bar emphasized his qualities as an ideal jurist: independent, in love with truth and justice, and a true confrère. The Lawyer Sazie described Crespin as "a lawyer of business informed better than all others in the habits of this country . . . he was also an orator of lofty ideas, of vast conceptions."[43]

These pronouncements necessarily carry the reverence and esteem for an influential member of the community recently deceased. However, they also reveal the extent to which professional affiliation shaped the lives of métis men, particularly in their role as lawyers, businessmen, and elected officials. A member of the bar of Saint Louis, Crespin belonged to a select group of professionals who sought to live a virtuous life of public service. As lawyers, métis men felt they held a sacred obligation to uphold democratic principles and challenge state officials. The notable figures who eulogized Crespin all said that he fought for the interests of "Senegal" and in the "Senegalese spirit," thus emphasizing a distinction between the Senegal colony as the administration understood it and local interests as articulated by Crespin. Associational life bound métis men and women to French society in new ways, but it also created an avenue for entering into public discourse and articulating views that differed from that of the administration or merchant capital.

Origins of an Independent Press

In late nineteenth-century France, struggles over freedom of the press defined the transition from state control over the circulation of ideas to liberalization of the public sphere. In Senegal, the question of freedom of the press became an issue of colonial control and the subversive potential embodied in independent journalism.[44] Unlike Freetown or Lagos in the same period, Senegal did not produce an extensive press with multiple publications and authors. Yet two key newspapers appeared in the colony and played an important role in shaping public discourse.

In May 1868, the Second Empire introduced reforms eliminating censorship of the press. This resulted in an increase in the number of journalists and publications in metropolitan France. A ministerial dispatch of 16 February 1880 extended freedom of the press to the colonies.[45] The first newspaper appeared in July 1885, three months before the date scheduled for Senegal's legislative election. Calling itself a "political, literary, commercial, and financial journal appearing every Sunday," *Le Réveil du Sénégal* focused primarily on politics.[46] J. J. Crespin and Gaspard Devès founded the journal to support Crespin's candidacy for the 1885 legislative elections. The newspaper launched fierce attacks on Alfred Gasconi, Crespin's opponent in the race and longtime occupant of Senegal's seat in the Chamber of Deputies. The newspaper also supported what Devès termed "Senegalese interests." The newspaper sought to restrict the power of Bordeaux merchant firms to monopolize all segments of Senegal's export economy and argued that the administration should provide more opportunity for

African residents of the towns to participate in politics. While some viewed this as a ploy for votes, the journal represented Devès and Crespin's view that the urban elite should play a more dominant role in governing the colony than metropolitan administrators or French commerce.[47]

A second journal, *Le Petit Sénégalais,* appeared in Saint Louis in August 1886. The weekly publication sought to advance the political agenda of the Devès/Crespin group, but adopted an aggressive anticlerical position. The masthead of the newspaper read "journal republican" and included the paper's slogan: "Le Cléricalisme, Voila l'Ennemi!"[48] The paper opined on topics such as divorce and the right to civil marriage, the activities of Freemasons in the French empire, progress in public education, freedom of the press, and women's rights. *Le Petit Sénégalais* vehemently criticized members of the colonial government (the governor, judiciary, mayor, city council, members of the General Council) for attending Catholic festivals and associating with the Church. The editors decried this mixing of religion and government in Senegal as "a poor example of our democratic morals."[49] In addition, the paper reported on events of interest in France and throughout the empire, including a vote in the Chamber of Deputies that defeated a measure for the secularization of primary schools. Its editors supported legislation addressing equal rights for women and the freedom of Freemasons in Réunion to celebrate openly without reprisal.

Le Petit Sénégalais circulated among the urban elite as well as among French merchants and officials in the colony. Toward the end of its run, the newspaper attempted to reach the Muslim population in the towns by announcing its intention to begin printing some articles in Arabic on politics in Senegal. The journal also circulated in Bordeaux, as one issue advised readers that they could find the publication at the Grand Café Dumon, Allées de Tourny. By the late 1880s, regular steamship service between Saint Louis and the French port facilitated communication and the exchange of ideas between metropole and colony by making newspapers available in both locations.[50] Its editors aimed for supporters who read French, but may have seen an opportunity to reach interpreters and Saint Louis traders and clerics who had close links to Muslim clerics and ruling elites in the interior.

Both publications caused intense debate within the Saint Louis community. Devès, Crespin, and their supporters solidified their coalition in the electoral institutions and used these publications to advocate their position. The newspapers advanced their coalition as a group concerned with

"Senegalese" interests rather than metropolitan interests and did not spare members of the métis community closely linked to French merchants, the Catholic clergy, or colonial officials. The approach of the publications raised new concerns among administrative officials over the threat that an independent press posed for maintaining colonial control. Colonial officials became more suspicious of members of the métis population who were behind the creation of the journals and who they perceived as hostile to the administration.

In October 1886, Governor Genouille wrote to Paris asking for permission to close down the journals. An October 10 article in *Le Réveil du Senegal* concerning the killing of the Damel of Cayor as part of France's pacification campaign pushed the governor to take action. The editors criticized the administration's characterization of the military campaign in the official bulletin as "an act of punishment for the insolent provocation of the Damel" and a "glorious day for France." *Le Réveil du Sénégal* titled its article "The Execution of Samba Laobé."[51] Despite Genouille's request, republican principles prevailed. The colonial ministry denied the governor permission to interfere with the law granting freedom of the press in the colonies. Stockholders in the paper, however, dissolved their interest a few months later, claiming disappointment over the tone taken. In early 1887, *Le Petit Sénégalais* disappeared after a series of attacks waged by the journal on the governor and leading families of Saint Louis resulted in a lawsuit for defamation against the paper. A guilty verdict led to bankruptcy and the paper's closure shortly thereafter.

This did not end official concern over the reappearance of an independent press in the colony or lessen their suspicions of certain town residents that openly opposed the administration. Henri de Lamothe wrote of his fear over the revival of the press in the colony during his tenure as governor of Senegal (1891–95). After de Lamothe's departure, several newspapers critical of the administration and its economic policies appeared in Senegal. This time the journals focused on issues affecting the colony as a whole, not simply the colonial towns, and they adopted an even stronger stance as a watchdog over French commercial interests and their exploitation of Senegalese workers.[52] The new publications turned their attention to the peanut basin and the relationship between capitalist export firms and peasants in the countryside at the same time that French officials launched a concerted attack on the power of Saint Louis representatives in the local assemblies.

Ann Laura Stoler observes that colonial cultures could never exactly replicate metropolitan society but instead took on new meanings, revealing the paradoxes, tensions, and contradictions of colonial rule. This rings true when we examine how the métis community understood and responded to French republicanism in Senegal. French schools provided a central component for the imposition of cultural imperialism. While many Muslim town residents rejected cultural assimilation through French education, for métis families schools provided a pathway for maintaining and strengthening their elite status. French schools in the colony and in metropolitan France also granted young métis of the 1870s and 1880s with knowledge of French society and access to networks of power. Entering into the liberal professions helped to stabilize this group at a critical moment and facilitated their transition from the dominant commercial elite to the primary Senegalese French educated class of this era.

Educational strategies, professional choices, and associational affiliations solidified a sense of common group identification between members of the métis population. These institutions and organizations provided a framework for developing partnerships with colonial officials and representatives of merchant capital in the colony, but they also enlarged their social networks to include leaders of industry, religious organizations, antislavery activists, lawmakers, and government officials in metropolitan France. Exposure to the debates shaping Third Republic France and the expansion of French imperialism overseas informed their outlook on political life in Senegal. While their associational choices show that métis men and women held divergent viewpoints, they emerged as an active and engaged citizenry. The short-lived but influential independent press of the 1880s illustrates the tensions over opposition and cooperation that existed among the métis elite. It also offers important clues about organization and articulation of democratic political culture in the colonial towns at the same time that France sought to impose colonial order over Senegal's interior.

5

From Outpost to Empire

In March 1887, the Mothers of Families sent a letter to the governor of Senegal followed by a second letter to Jean Jauréguiberry, the naval minister and former governor of the colony. The women wrote to inform the governor that "public peace and good order have been put at peril" by the only political newspaper in the colony, *Le Réveil du Senegal*. The women complained about the newspaper's attack on key members of the political elite and expressed their concern that the newspaper, "guided uniquely by hatred, jealousy and lowly rancor," took advantage of the lack of competition from any other newspaper. They continued:

> This sheet wrapping itself in the cloak of republicanism, crowds odiously on the feet of all the principles that made the glory of the Government of the Republic . . . it has dragged in the mud our best intentioned administrators, our judges and the most integral, you yourself, Mr. Governor, despite all your devotion to the colony, have not been saved. Today it is all the Senegalese families that it attacks and that it looks to dishonor by slander, scandal and lies. In the name of the protection that honest people have the right to expect from their government, in the name of grossly insulted and violated republican principles, we ask you to make the Minister of the Marine cognizant of the situation. We ask you to call upon his old memories of Senegal where his memory remains still popular in our colonies still under the regime of decree. We wish from the bottom of our heart that he would bring an energetic remedy to this intolerable situation.[1]

As upstanding wives, mothers, and widows, the women who authored these letters relied on their moral authority within the European community to demand action in the public sphere despite the fact that they could not vote or hold public office.

This letter appeared at a critical moment in Senegal's history when French forces embarked on the final phase of conquest in Sin and Saloum and among the Futanke of the middle Senegal. Electoral politics in the colonial towns reached a fever pitch as métis men gained influence in the local assemblies. The debate in electoral campaigns increasingly revealed conflict between Bordeaux merchants and their allies, on the one hand, and those who subscribed to Senegalese interests, on the other. The history of colonial expansion and the rise of modern politics in Senegal are often told through the masculine lens of soldiers, commandants, businessmen, and political authorities. The story of colonial hegemony and the competition for power that it entailed does not consider women's participation in public life because evidence rarely exists in the official record.

The Mothers of Families entered public discourse as members of the educated elite with close ties to French power. They called upon their personal relationships with the minister of the navy and argued for government action in ways appropriate for women of their class in the late nineteenth century. The Mothers of Families objected to freedom of the press when the newspapers maligned the reputations of the women's husbands, fathers, and representatives of the state. They understood the strict division in nineteenth-century politics between the private sphere where women operated and the public sphere of government and politics. Although women could not vote or hold public office, in France or Senegal, the act of writing letters and petitioning colonial officials on behalf of morality and decency shows the mechanism of civil society at work in Senegal's colonial capital.[2]

The idea of civil society has gained popularity over the past several decades as a means of analyzing politics and the state in Africa today, yet the concept poses certain problems for understanding how democratic institutions functioned in the context of colonial rule.[3] Rooted in a particular history of western democracy, Enlightenment thinkers who embraced the concept in the eighteenth century saw Africa as the antithesis of civil society. In their view, civil society meant rational, civilized government rather than the irrational, prehistoric, and uncivilized state of "man in nature" that Africa represented. The revival of the idea in the twentieth century, however, has a great deal to do with understanding how moral communities and organic intellectuals reacted to the totalitarian pressures of communist rule and the growth of state capitalism in ways not unlike colonialism.[4]

More often when the term *civil society* is applied to Africa today, it is used to invoke the weakness of a bifurcated colonial state or the failure of the postcolonial state to modernize and provide sufficient socioeconomic development for its citizens.[5] Some focus on its absence. Others see the emergence of civil society in contemporary Africa as a means of combating elite self-interested state actors who practice what Jean François Bayart termed "politics of the belly."[6] While colonial rule operated through authoritarian practices and limited the development of civil society to a handful of urban elites with access to electoral institutions, the expansion of democratic rights at home and the elaboration of colonial control overseas created a situation in Senegal where the urban community, a group with long-standing ties to French power, could make claims to political participation and influence the decision-making apparatus of the colonial regime by organizing as groups of civil society. In the late nineteenth century, the métis strengthened their influence in colonial affairs by dominating the republican institutions that formed the nexus of political power for the urban community.

Conquest and Colonial Administration

Political society took shape in Senegal through military conquest, the suppression of African resistance, and the imposition of French power through a bureaucratic system that sought to rationalize French control. The expansion of French rule occurred as a result of the aggressive actions of military commanders on the ground rather than through cohesive directives from Paris. Credited with expanding French control beyond the towns and the escales to strategic areas of the middle and upper Senegal, Louis Faidherbe's governorship marked the first phase of colonial expansion. In 1852, Faidherbe arrived in Senegal as a captain in the engineering corps. His first assignment involved constructing a fort at Podor, on the middle Senegal, to eliminate the escales and solidify French control over the trade on the Senegal. Having served in Algeria, Faidherbe knew Arabic and was familiar with Islam. This experience, coupled with support from Bordeaux merchants who lobbied officials in Paris on his behalf, secured Faidherbe's promotion to governor of the colony in 1854.[7]

Faidherbe developed a dual administrative system that served as the foundation of colonial policy and practice in Senegal. He elaborated on the Islamic policy put in place by Bouët-Willaumez that strengthened Saint Louis's reputation as a foreign power friendly to Muslim societies.[8] He shored up the institutional presence of Islam in the capital by completing construction of a mosque, establishing a Muslim tribunal, and financing education for

Muslim students in French schools. In Faidherbe's view, building strong institutional support for Islam in the towns cultivated key allies among the Saint Louis Muslim population that were essential for gathering information about Islamic expansion and the ruling elites in the interior. After 1850, colonial authorities sought cooperative relationships with Muslim clerics, interpreters, and traders in Saint Louis, rather than with the métis elite to advance French political goals in the middle and upper Senegal.

During Faidherbe's governorship, Bordeaux merchants implemented plans to eliminate competition from habitants in the escales and to restructure the export economy for peanut production. Faidherbe enjoyed the backing of Maurel and Prom, one of the most highly capitalized merchant houses in the colony, who led the introduction of peanut culture in Senegal.[9] Faidherbe aided French merchants on the Senegal who complained of being overtaxed by the monopoly that the Trarza held over the gum trade in Walo. In 1855, Faidherbe launched a campaign in Walo that resulted in the final defeat of the aristocracy after two decades of Saint Louis's interference in the kingdom's affairs. Faidherbe's defeat of Walo established French rule in the lower Senegal and paved the way for establishing peanut cultivation on the river's south bank.

After gaining control over the trade centers of the lower and middle Senegal, Faidherbe turned his attention to the upper Senegal. He ordered the construction of a fort at Médine to serve as a gateway for French control over strategic resources in the Niger River valley.[10] In 1857, Al-Hajj Umar Tal's army seized the fort. Faidherbe sent a military command headed by métis habitant Roger Descemet to liberate the fort.[11] Descemet suffered a fatal gunshot wound at the battle of Médine at age 24. The three-month conflict pushed Tal's forces out of the Senegal River valley and east along the Niger, but it also prevented French forces from moving beyond the head waters of the Senegal into the Niger River valley, stymieing their plans to build the Saint Louis–Niger railroad for another thirty years.

This conflict established Senegal's northern border and redirected French forces beyond the mainland corridor along the coast to inland territory between the Senegal and Gambia Rivers that became Senegal's peanut basin. Faidherbe initiated diplomatic relations with Cayor during his first term (1854–61) and continued these negotiations during his second term (1863–65) to establish French commercial posts in the Atlantic corridor between Saint Louis and Gorée.[12] Pinet-Laprade, the commandant of Gorée, launched violent campaigns in Senegal's Cap Vert peninsula to further establish control over key areas. In 1857, French forces erected a fort at Dakar and brought the sovereign territory of the Lebu chiefs under French control. Faidherbe's governorship signaled an end to informal imperialism in which France considered Senegal a distant economic satellite. By the 1860s, France no longer ruled over the coastal enclaves but also occupied strategic interior locations that extended French capital along the southern frontier in the competition for commercial supremacy with British interests along the Gambia River and in Sierra Leone.

French conquest operated through violent military campaigns and displays of force, but it also worked by exploiting rivalries between and within African states and by destabilizing populations in the countryside by burning crops or seizing villages. With Faidherbe's departure, Paris called for a halt to military action and a period of "pacification" to follow the violent and destabilizing effects of the previous decade's military campaigns. Preoccupied with the Franco-Prussian War and the rise of a new regime in Paris, the French shifted from military conquest to affairs at home. Officials in Saint Louis turned their attention to competition with Britain for control of peanut exports along the Gambia and in the Southern Rivers region.[13] New French forts at Boké on the Rio Nunez and at Benty on the Mellacourie created a foothold for the expansion of commerce as far south as the border with Sierra Leone.

On 18 June 1876, Colonel Louis Alexandre Brière de l'Isle (1876–81) began his term as governor and embarked on a new phase of territorial expansion. An imposing military figure, Brière de l'Isle was concerned with maintaining security and stabilizing the economy.[14] He reinforced French authority in the Southern Rivers region, suppressed pockets of resistance in Futa Toro, and established additional military posts on the upper Senegal. Brière de l'Isle pushed French rule further east by launching new campaigns on the lower Niger.[15]

Brière de l'Isle's aggressive style coincided with increasing fervor among proponents of the French Empire in metropolitan France who were eager to extend French power in sub-Saharan Africa.[16] Paris supported his initiatives and sought parliamentary approval to finance the first phase of the construction for the Senegal–Niger railway line. As governor, Brière de l'Isle brought to the forefront the inherent contradictions between French republican ideals as a principle of overseas expansion and the reality of colonial conquest. Convinced that the military should have ultimate authority to establish colonial policy, Brière de l'Isle eliminated all civilian administrators in the colony. His conflict with politically influential members of the Saint Louis community, representatives of Bordeaux merchants, and certain members of the métis elite led to his removal.[17] On 16 November 1882, Paris named Rene Servatius as the first civilian governor of the colony, signaling a transition from military to civilian administration.

In 1885, when European powers officially sanctioned the scramble for Africa at the Berlin Conference, France had already elaborated on the system of colonial administration adopted by Faidherbe to bring its imperial objectives in line with republican principles. In keeping with Faidherbe's distinction between the towns and the countryside, Paris instituted a regime of laws for permanent residents of the colonial towns and established a protectorate regime for states of the countryside that submitted to "treaties of protection" with the French. This distinction separated town from countryside, in the bureaucratic logic of French officials, but it also created a host of legal and political ambiguities in applying two systems for populations that fell somewhere between French citizens and African subjects.

The bureaucratic structure of the colony had a governor who served as head of the administration. An advisory council—consisting of the head of the judiciary, commander of the armed forces, an archival secretary, and two habitants from each jurisdiction (Saint Louis and Gorée)—served as a consultative body for the governor.[18] By decree of 1 September 1869, Paris established a separate department of the interior. The director of the interior was responsible for accounting and budgetary matters, the police force, and surveillance of the protectorate. The protectorate regime imposed heavy taxation and could conscript Africans for work projects or to serve in the colonial army. In civil matters, inhabitants of the protectorate had the right to seek redress under Islamic or customary law, but because the protectorate regime existed outside of republican laws, responsibility for hearing criminal complaints remained with the regional officers. The administration sanctioned the use of arbitrary fines and punishment in cases decided by officials.[19] In contrast to residents of the towns, inhabitants of the interior had no political rights under the protectorate regime.

In the first half of the nineteenth century, France adhered to the notion of assimilation in Senegal, which sought to unify the laws, tax regime, and political institutions of overseas territories with metropolitan systems, but did so in a limited, inconsistent fashion. Permanent residents of Saint Louis and Gorée lived under the same laws and had access to the same legal and political institutions as commune residents in metropolitan France. On 10 August 1872, Paris granted Saint Louis and Gorée the same legal status as communes in France. The municipal decree organized Senegal's communes according to the basic unit of city government. In 1880, Paris extended commune status to Rufisqsue. Dakar received commune status seven years later. Senegal's Four Communes existed as enclaves of republican rights. Saint Louis represented the old colonial capital, centered on commerce along the Senegal. Rufisque and Dakar gained importance as modern ports that were connected to the railway. The French corporations established warehouses to store peanuts and invested in new infrastructure to facilitate the transportation of peanuts to oil processing factories in Bordeaux. In addition, Gorée regained importance as the headquarters for French commandants charged with overseeing administrative centers in Sin and Saloum, the Casamance, and the Southern Rivers (map 4).

An additional administrative district created by French authorities further redefined the boundary between town and country in the late nineteenth century. The district, known as the territories of direct administration, brought together the pockets of French authority (primarily river trade depots, railway towns, and administrative centers) in the interior. Saint Louis administered the territories of direct administration for the first arrondissement, which included the escales, forts, and annexed territories under French control on the Senegal River. The territories of direct administration for the second arrondissement, administered from Gorée-Dakar, included territories annexed by France in the peanut basin and the Petit Côte as well as the Casamance River and the Southern Rivers region.[20]

The governor held ultimate authority over these territories, but the elected General Council controlled decisions regarding the budget for territories under direct administration.[21] These interior towns served as bases for French military and commercial expansion, but they also complicated distinctions between what constituted urban and rural. The Saint Louis trading community lived and worked in these regions. Métis men, by virtue of their position on the General Council, held budgetary authority that influenced political and economic affairs in these territories.

Conquest and the establishment of new administrative structures transformed the nature of power relations for the ruling elite in the interior as well as for urban residents in the coastal towns. French officials sought to develop avenues of cooperation with Muslims of the towns to enhance colonial power and prestige with ruling elites in the interior. They also depended on the métis, who had long-standing kinship and client networks. Métis occupied key positions in the military and in administration of the territories as French rule expanded. In an effort to satisfy republican principles and maintain colonial control, French officials elaborated on the system of one set of laws and institutions for "citizens" in the towns and another for "natives" in the countryside. The Saint Louis community, however, had extensive social, commercial, and political networks with inhabitants of the interior that blurred these administrative lines. The existence of republican institutions in Saint Louis meant that colonial authorities had to deal with a population of town residents who had contacts and interests in the interior as well as access to power through the republican institutions of the capital.

Republican Institutions in Senegal's Colonial Capital

The 1870s witnessed a new phase in the development of democratic institutions in metropolitan France. The liberalization of politics had direct implications for political life in Senegal's colonial towns. The decade began with Napoleon III suffering defeat in the Franco-Prussian War. In early 1871, a working-class uprising in the Paris commune signaled an imminent end to the second Napoleonic era. In 1875, Paris created a new constitution based on republican laws, and by the end of the decade republicans held a majority in both chambers of the National Assembly. At the same time, French military forces made gains in subjugating African rulers to French authority.

The expansion of republican institutions in Senegal created a new field for developing political networks and organizing members of the urban community. Paris lawmakers did not envision the establishment of these institutions to empower Senegal's urban community. These reforms were aimed at providing a means for metropolitan commerce and their representatives to weigh in on major political and economic decisions affecting the colony. French authorities did not anticipate that the urban community would use electoral politics to assert its own interests.

A democratic tradition in city governance had existed in Senegal's coastal towns since the mid-eighteenth century. Saint Louis and Gorée residents developed a practice of selecting a mayor from among notable town residents. In the 1820s, Paris established limited representation for residents of Saint Louis after granting the Antilles and Réunion a local assembly patterned after the General Council, a revered departmental assembly in metropolitan France. The naval ministry considered granting Senegal a similar council, but instead it established the Conseil Privé (Governor's Advisory Council) owing to Senegal's status as *comptoir*, or commercial outpost, rather than one of the Grandes Colonies. The governor named one habitant and one notable from Saint Louis to join seven French officials on the council, which informed him about local affairs and offered opinions on relevant economic questions.

In September 1840, Paris established a General Council for Senegal by royal ordinance.[22] The decree called for forty to sixty habitants and notables of Saint Louis to elect ten delegates—eight wholesale merchants and two middleman traders—to serve five-year terms. The council met annually and fulfilled the same functions as the Conseil Privé. In 1848, Paris granted Senegal a seat in the newly formed National Assembly.[23] Durand Valantin, a habitant and gum merchant, arrived in Paris to represent Senegal in constitutional negotiations following the revolution. While in Paris, French officials appointed Valantin to Senegal's legislative seat in the newly formed National Assembly. However, Napoleon III suppressed political representation for Senegal when he became emperor in 1851.

The complete extension of republican rights and laws in colonial Senegal occurred under the Third Republic. Between 1871 and 1879, a series of decrees organized the local assemblies and representation for Senegal in the National Assembly. On 1 February 1871, Paris reestablished legislative representation for Senegal; Senegal was assigned a seat in the Chamber of Deputies by decree in 1879. The municipal decree of 10 August 1872 created a city council for Saint Louis and Gorée that was elected by universal male suffrage charged with "regulating by their mandates the interests of the commune."[24] After the Third Republic reinstituted a General Council for Martinique and Guadeloupe in the West Indies, Bordeaux merchants and their métis allies petitioned Paris to establish a similar institution for Senegal. The decree of 4 February 1879 organized a General Council for Senegal composed of members elected from Gorée and Saint Louis, the only two communes at the time.

The municipal council held responsibility for matters relating to the administration of community services, commune property, and the well-being of town residents. The municipal law established a mayor, two deputy mayors, and fifteen councilors for Saint Louis, the commune with the largest population. Gorée received eleven councilors as well as the office of mayor and two deputy mayors. All male residents of the communes who had lived in the city for at least one year and were registered on the electoral list had the right to elect council members for a six-year term.[25] Candidates for election had to prove literacy in French, thereby excluding the vast majority of African town residents from running for office. Initially, the governor appointed the mayor and deputy mayors from the list of candidates that received the most votes. A decree of 28 March 1882 clarified the law by stating that the municipal council had the power to choose the mayor and deputy mayor from within the body. Ultimately, the governor retained the power to suspend the mayor and deputy mayors for at least three months but could only revoke their election by decree of the president of the republic.

The work of the municipal council included deliberating on the local tax rate, collecting communal revenues, and reviewing the annual commune budget. The mayor presented this budget to the governor for approval. The council met four times a year to decide on these issues and advise the mayor. The mayor had the added responsibility of publishing laws and rules enacted by the state, providing general safety, and serving as an officer of the *état civil* (civil registry). He established market prices, oversaw community work projects, and represented the commune in legal proceedings.[26] The mayor was also in charge of the police, local roads, local tax collection, and public health. The mayor and municipal council fulfilled a central role in the urban community because they served as spokesmen for the daily concerns and business dealings that commune residents had with French authorities.

The deputyship gave commune residents access to Paris lawmakers and representation at the highest level of legislative authority in the republic. From 1871 until 1902, French men represented Senegal in Paris. They tended to be military officers who had served in Senegal or as agents of French commercial houses. Alfred Gasconi, Senegal's representative to Paris from 1879 to 1889, may have been the son of a signare.[27] The legislative seat required the representative to carry out most of his duties in Paris. As a result, he tended to be somewhat removed from the everyday politics of the communes. In the late nineteenth century, Senegal's representative in the Chamber of Deputies did not play as central a role as the local assemblymen in negotiating issues of importance to the urban community.

The General Council, on the other hand, was the most prestigious and effective of all the republican institutions for the métis. The powerful budgetary authority of this council and the assertiveness of its members made Senegal's assembly far more important to commune residents than departmental assemblies in metropolitan France. The General Council met for a few days annually in its Saint Louis headquarters to advise the governor and approve the colony's budget. Council members deliberated on economic issues such as tax collection and assessment, customs fees, and the establishment of trade depots, markets, and fairs in areas under direct rule. In a few cases, such as the timing of road construction and public works projects or the management of public property and contributions, the council had the power to enact legislation.

The General Council's control over part of the colonial budget elevated its importance and prestige within the colony's administrative system. The colonial budget contained two categories of expenses: mandatory and optional. The governor fixed mandatory expenses that pertained to the governor's operating budget and resources for administration. The council could not alter mandatory expenses but did maintain control over optional expenses. Council members could dispute and reallocate funds for budgetary items such as the services and furnishing of offices or expenditures for books in public libraries. In addition, the General Council was responsible for managing affairs and determining the budget in the territories of direct administration, giving councilors authority in areas of commercial and political importance in the interior.[28]

Representatives to the council could serve unlimited six-year terms. The organization of the body called for a renewal of half of the assembly every three years. The council originally consisted of sixteen members. Saint Louis received ten members and Gorée six. In 1897, the law augmented the number of councilors to twenty, with ten for Saint Louis, five for Gorée-Dakar, and five for Rufisque.[29] The governor convened the council for an annual fifteen-day session in November or December at the end of the trading season, when members habitually returned to Saint Louis from the interior or from overseas. The governor could, however, call for an extraordinary session at any time. In August 1885, the governor issued a decree that formed a permanent committee of three to five members to deal with the council's continual work. Yet unlike departmental assemblies in the metropolis, the power to suspend or dissolve the elected assembly rested with the governor subject to the approval of the minister of colonies.

The inauguration of a separate building to house the assembly indicated the importance of this institution to the urban community and symbolized the central role that the Saint Louis community played. Located on the south side of the island, overlooking the mouth of the Senegal River, the building with its whitewashed concrete balconies, cast-iron window frames, majestic staircases, and great halls of deliberation provided a visible marker of Senegal's identification with republican ideals. The inauguration took place on 28 January 1888 and was followed by a ball hosted by the president and members of the General Council and attended by "a crowd of women and young girls" as well as civil and military authorities. The fanfare of the tirailleurs (African soldiers who made up the rank and file of the colonial army) animated the event.[30] The building contained a library, the customs office, and a printing press, in addition to the *salle de délibération*. Financed primarily by the métis, the building served as a reminder to officials temporarily residing in the colony of the long history of interdependence between the Saint Louis community and France, particularly in matters relating to commerce.

The opening ceremony of the annual session also communicated the importance that commune residents placed on their close relationship with the governor. Council members selected a president at the start of the session. The eldest member of the assembly held the honorary title *président doyen d'âge* and opened the session. The youngest member of the assembly held the position of secretary. A delegation of five members was then chosen to accompany the governor as he entered the conference room to give his opening speech before the entire council. After his address, the delegation escorted the governor from the conference room with the same ceremony so that the councilors could begin their work.

The issues addressed in the first session, from 24 November to 6 December 1879, included the budget proposal, the construction of the Saint Louis–Dakar railway, rules for trade along the Senegal River, and a complaint by Maurel and Prom over the cost of dues for anchoring steamships in the ports. The assembly also considered a request by the Catholic mission of St. Joseph of Ngazobil for a land concession and a certain Widow Michel's request for financial assistance for her two daughters to attend the school run by the Sisters of Saint Joseph de Cluny.[31] The General Council made decisions regarding infrastructure development, the movement of commerce, and financial allocations to individuals and groups with whom they shared close personal and social ties.

Métis men dominated representation on the General Council between 1879 and 1914. While the métis held clear advantages in education and political ties to Europeans, an individual's connection to trade and commerce also mattered. Bacre Waly Gueye, head of an influential trade house in Podor, held a seat on the council from its opening until the turn of the century.[32] The métis considered the assembly their field for negotiating with French officials largely because they constituted the majority of permanent town residents who possessed high levels of French education, interests in the exchange of capital through the colonial economy, and knowledge of the local situation. In addition, the métis benefited from their social and cultural proximity to French officials and merchants in the colony because they shared a similar habitus with the metropolitan French. At the same time, the assemblymen demonstrated a willingness to debate controversial issues and to reject protocol at key moments.[33] Their independence served as a reminder to the administration that this group took seriously their self-appointed duty as watchdogs over the administration and upholders of republican ideals.

A number of other republican institutions appeared in the capital in the second half of the nineteenth century. Courts operated as extensions of the colonial bureaucracy but also possessed autonomy from the functions of the administration. Members of the judiciary routinely arrived in Senegal, having served in the French Antilles. Key judicial officials sought to enforce antislavery measures and expressed concern over human rights abuses by administrators in the interior.[34] The legal system centered on the notion that town residents should have access to French law for civil, commercial, and criminal matters while Muslim habitants should be able to seek redress under Islamic law for civil matters.

In 1837, a royal ordinance established a high court called the Tribunal de Première Instance that administered French law in civil and criminal cases. Paris appointed professional magistrates to render decisions in the French court and the appeals court. According to ministerial decree, all adult men born free and living in Senegal enjoyed the same rights as those granted to French citizens by the civil code.[35] However, the decree specified that these rights were to be enjoyed in the colony, leaving room for debate about whether residents of the colonial town could exercise these rights in metropolitan France or other areas of the empire. In practice, the decree meant that all town residents (Muslim or Catholic; African, European, or métis) and Africans outside of the towns involved in cases against French citizens or those who voluntarily renounced their customary civil status technically could have their cases heard before the Tribunal de Première Instance.

Faidherbe created the Muslim tribunal as a cornerstone of his Islamic policy. Doing so distinguished Muslim town residents who recognized Islamic law in civil matters from those who recognized French civil law. The formation of the court served Faidherbe's political purposes, but also became recognized as an important marker of identity for Muslim Saint Louis residents in the late nineteenth century.[36] Located on the north side of the island, the court became a center of authority for Muslim scholars of the town. The administration appointed a *tamsir* to preside over the tribunal and render decisions regarding marriage, death, and inheritance. The tamsir also served as the officer of the civil registry for Muslims in Saint Louis. In 1903, the governor general of French West Africa established Muslim tribunals in Médine on the upper Senegal and in Kayes on the lower Niger as part of the judiciary's reorganization. These reforms occurred largely because Saint Louis traders protested the absence of French courts that adjudicated Muslim law in French territories of the interior. As citizens, urban African traders and interpreters argued that they had the right to be heard by the Muslim tribunal, even though they lived and operated outside of the capital.

From the administrative point of view, financial institutions facilitated the economic objectives of imperialism and maintained the flow of capital between colony and metropolis. For habitants, financial institutions provided their only means of capital liquidity to finance their entrepreneurial ventures. In 1848, the colonial ministry established banks in the Antilles to handle indemnity payments following the end of slavery. Habitants and Bordeaux merchants pushed for the creation of a colonial bank in Senegal for the same purpose. In 1851, Paris approved the formation of the Bank of Senegal. It operated as a private company with an administrative council consisting of a director named by decree, three administrators elected by shareholders, the treasurer of the colony, and two censors who surveyed the management of the bank and reported to the colonial ministry. The central colonial bank in Paris organized under the ministry of the navy acted as the intermediary between the state and the bank in Senegal.[37]

The Bank of Senegal served the financial needs of small and medium-scale traders in Saint Louis. It managed accounts, offered limited credit, and also issued bank notes in colonial francs that were printed in France but circulated only in Senegal. Bordeaux merchants rarely used the bank. Instead, they exported the capital earned in Senegal and invested it directly in metropolitan financial institutions. As a result, the Bank of Senegal frequently experienced cash shortages, causing liquidity problems for habitants. In 1901, the administration dissolved the Bank of Senegal and replaced it with the Banque de l'Afrique Occidentale, which operated from its headquarters in Paris.[38]

Bordeaux merchants and habitants also petitioned the ministry for the creation of a chamber of commerce that would defend commercial interests in the colony. In 1869, a ministerial order authorized the organization of two chambers of commerce for Saint Louis and Gorée and charged them with responding to requests for information on trade and industry and advising the administration on how to maximize profit and form better commercial legislation for Senegal.[39] Agents of Bordeaux firms and a few métis traders ran the institution and used it as a forum for presenting their interests to the administration and leaders of commerce and industry in Bordeaux and Paris. Members of the organization were elected from the list of wholesalers and traders who paid patent fees. The Saint Louis Chamber of Commerce essentially excluded Africans from membership until a series of reforms opened up the institution to African traders and artisans in 1892. African inclusion in the chamber of commerce occurred more than a decade before African commune residents broke métis and French dominance in electoral politics, perhaps because of the central role that Saint Louis traders played in the colonial economy.

Electoral institutions, courts, and financial institutions as well as the church, the mosque, schools, and the Masonic lodge created a basis for cooperation and contestation between the Saint Louis community and colonial authorities. These institutions energized political life and civic activity for town residents by conferring special legal and political rights on residents of the capital. In the late nineteenth century, the métis possessed the educational, social, and cultural credentials that allowed them to gain power and influence through the republican institutions, while the majority of African residents faced exclusion or operated at the margins of these bodies. Nevertheless, the expansion of democratic institutions in the colony worked to solidify group interests within the urban community.

Civil Society in the Late Nineteenth Century

Civil society depends upon the influence of local actors who organize to assert their interests within the democratic institutions established by liberal regimes. In a colonial context, state authority could and often effectively used violence to suppress dissent, but French officials needed cooperation from key groups of local actors to make colonial rule work in Senegal. The urban community long sustained a sense of loyalty to the French regime and saw themselves as citizens entitled to the same rights and responsibilities as French men and women of the metropolis. Saint Louis represented the center of French power. The Saint Louis community occupied a particular place within the expansion of French colonial rule and took advantage of their close proximity to French power to make demands of French authorities in exchange for their cooperation.

The expansion of electoral institutions under the Third Republic provided a new mechanism for the métis, in particular, to assert their interests and to influence decisions made regarding the budget, tariffs, customs duties, infrastructure development, and city services. All of these issues had particular relevance for the urban community. Inhabitants of Saint Louis, moreover, viewed the ensemble of republican institutions located in the capital as organizations that should serve them and facilitate their access to power. The métis capitalized on the development of electoral politics to advance their particular interest and carve out a new niche for themselves as power brokers in the colony despite the fact that they had suffered significant economic losses during the gum trade crisis and no longer dominated the middlemen sector of the colonial economy.

In the last quarter of the nineteenth century, the first arrondissement (Saint Louis) exercised more influence in the political life of the colony than residents of the second arrondissement (Gorée, Dakar, and Rufisque). Saint Louis remained the headquarters of military operations on the upper Senegal and the lower Niger. The gum trade continued to operate, and the river trade posts played key roles in the export trade in peanuts. The governor's palace, the French court, the bank, the Muslim tribunal, the school of the Brothers of Ploërmel, and the school run by the Sisters of Saint Joseph lined the avenues of the island. The cathedral, mosque, headquarters of the tirailleurs Sénégalais (also known as Spahi), the General Council, and the warehouses of French merchant firms defined urban life (map 5). Far from the remote outpost for mercantile trade, Saint Louis existed as the center of French rule in West Africa and a vibrant urban African society.

Historians have understood the struggle for political power that animated urban politics during this period as competition between three distinct groups: French merchants, the métis, and African commune residents. While electoral campaigns evolved in ways that corresponded to racial categories, the individuals who participated in electoral politics often formed alliances that were far from monolithic in their outlook. Class, religion, or ideological orientation played as important a role in shaping political alliances, but the struggle for access to power tended to follow colonialism's racial logic.

Metropolitan French men and women remained a very small segment of the commune population until the early twentieth century. After 1890, a new wave of shopkeepers and professionals arrived in Dakar and Rufisque. By 1910, the European population in Senegal amounted to 2,500. Most Europeans were employees of the governor general's office in Dakar or agents of the French merchant firms.[40] French civil servants (judiciary, engineers, etc.) and commercial agents lived in Saint Louis temporarily. European shopkeepers and professionals (called *petits colons*) began to outnumber French military and civilian officers in the colony.

Bordeaux merchants remained a powerful lobby for Senegal in the ministry of colonies in Paris and with top officials in Saint Louis. Unlike the early nineteenth century, when French men established households in Senegal, most French wholesalers operated from their headquarters in Bordeaux and appointed representatives to manage their business affairs in the colony. Steamship service from Bordeaux to Saint Louis facilitated communication between colonial officials and Bordeaux merchants. Senegal's governors commonly passed through the French port on their way to and from the colony.[41] The monopoly capital firms formed after 1850 regularly placed their allies, whether métis or metropolitan French men, in strategic positions on the local assemblies, the Conseil Privé, the governing board of the bank, and in the chamber of commerce to represent their interests.

Muslim traders, clerics, and bureaucrats occupied positions of political influence and high social standing. By the 1870s, Muslim trade houses dominated the intermediary niche of the colonial economy. Some got their start in trade following their fathers who entered trade in the escales. Others began as the employees of métis habitants in the gum trade. Still others entered the middleman trade as the agents of French firms. Hamet Gora Diop began as an agent for Gaspard Devès, and Bacre Waly Gueye entered trade in Bakel and Podor as the agent for the French firm Rabaud.[42] By the 1870s, Muslim traders operated highly capitalized trade houses specializing in the middleman trade on the frontiers of French expansion in upper Senegal, lower Niger, and Saloum. They owned barges, river craft, and rental property in Saint Louis, dominating the peanut trade as habitants had in the heyday of the gum trade.

In addition to operating successful trade houses, Saint Louis traders occupied a strategic position in colonial affairs. On the one hand, they maintained close ties with colonial authorities who relied on Muslim traders to provide information and act as mediators with ruling elites in the interior. On the other hand, Saint Louis traders established important relationships with Sufi clerics and Futanke chiefs.[43] They supplied ammunition, tobacco, and other valued goods to chiefs and clerics. Saint Louis traders acquired both Islamic and French education. They were among the first originaires to enter institutions like the chambers of commerce and the General Council. At the turn of the century, their sons organized and mobilized the African electorate to break métis dominance in electoral politics.[44]

Others gained notoriety as interpreters for the colonial bureaucracy and as judges for the Muslim tribunal. Tamsir Hamat Ndiaye Anne and Tamsir Dudu Seck (known as Bu el Mogdad) earned reputations as scholars. In 1857, Faidherbe named Hamet Ndiaye Anne tamsir of the Muslim tribunal. Dudu Seck, having studied with Sufi clerics in Mauritania, also entered administrative service and took over responsibilities for Arabic correspondence in the political affairs bureau.[45] In 1879 Ndiaye died, and the administration chose Seck to replace him as tamsir. Seck died the following year. In a sign of the administration's dependence on these interlocutors, the political affairs office turned to the sons of both men and others within the Saint Louis trading community to fill key positions in the colonial bureaucracy. The administration continued to rely heavily on the support of Muslim residents to ease their relations with African rulers and clerics in the interior.

Muslim notables used their close ties with colonial officials to negotiate for power and privileges. The position of Saint Louis traders in the colonial economy contributed to their leverage in urban politics. After 1850, traders Bacre Waly Gueye and Pedre Alassane Mbengue served as mediators for French officials in areas where they had strategic trade interests and the French had little knowledge of the political and social environment. In the 1880s, Abdoulaye Mar sat on the municipal council and became deputy mayor and one of the first African members of the chamber of commerce. Hamet Gora Diop used his Saint Louis home on the south side of the island to hold meetings for métis and originaire candidates. He also organized town residents to lobby the administration to reinstate the Muslim tribunal after the judiciary's reorganization in 1905.[46] Although denied access to politics in proportion to their numbers, Muslim town residents constituted an influential force in the political life of the towns.

The métis held positions of influence as lawyers, physicians, businessmen, and soldiers, but participation in electoral politics afforded them a certain degree of autonomy from the colonial state. Métis traders increasingly faced competition from Muslim Saint Louis traders for control over the middleman sector of the colonial economy. While some became agents of French firms, others maintained highly capitalized independent trade firms that rivaled Bordeaux merchants. Operating their own trade houses, acting as agents for French firms or as employees of other métis merchants, or becoming entrepreneurs strengthened métis ties to the colonial economy. In the 1860s and 1870s, the métis capitalized on new areas of commercial expansion in Sin and Saloum and as far south as Mellacourie and Boké and relied on long-established client networks, kin ties, and commercial interests on the north bank of the Senegal and with African rulers in Cayor, Walo, and Fouta Toro. Métis family firms, albeit fewer than in the heyday of the gum trade, continued to play key roles in the colonial economy

Well-born individuals of Saint Louis had looked to the military as avenues of socioeconomic mobility since the late eighteenth century. Métis sons of European military officers followed a path of higher education to the military academy St. Cyr and returned to Senegal to fill positions in lower-level administration or in the military.[47] In 1854 Faidherbe formed the Tirailleurs Sénégalais to establish a regiment of trained and reputable soldiers recruited from recently subjugated territories in the interior. Previously, the military used indentured servants and runaway soldiers who arrived in Saint Louis to make up the rank and file of the colonial army.[48] Métis men, however, trained in the French naval academy and returned to the colony to become part of the officer corps. Despite becoming notable figures in the Saint Louis community, the tirailleurs rarely advanced beyond the rank of lieutenant because of colonialism's racial ideologies.

In the era of conquest, military service became a less attractive option for the métis. Those who entered the military and achieved high rank contributed to the political machinery of the administration. General Alfred Amédée Dodds supervised the most violent and repressive colonial wars from Senegal to the Indian Ocean colonies and Indonesia.[49] The son of a métis director of the postal office and signare Marie Charlotte Billaud,

Dodds grew up in Saint Louis. In 1862, he graduated from St. Cyr and achieved the rank of lieutenant five years later. In Senegal, Dodds orchestrated campaigns in the Senegal River valley, led garrisons to defeat Lat Dior Diop of Cayor, and participated in the final campaigns to suppress resistance in Fouta Toro. He supervised the suppression of revolts in Réunion and orchestrated the defeat of King Benhazin of Abomey (Benin). Named commandant supérieur de la marine, General Dodds served in the president's war cabinet from 1903 to 1907.

Outside of business and commerce, the professions, and the colonial bureaucracy, the métis focused their attention on electoral politics. Commune politics provided an avenue to articulate their interests and negotiate with colonial authorities but also to interfere in colonial affairs. The electoral institutions afforded the métis the ability to develop a degree of autonomy from Bordeaux commerce and the colonial administration. The ambiguous laws and statutes over the legal status of commune residents and voting laws, combined with the cultural politics of colonialism, worked to give métis men advantages over Africans of the communes in the political arena. While women faced categorical exclusion from the democratic institutions, regardless of race or religion, métis women exercised power in informal ways because they conformed to the ideal notion of republican womanhood.

Citizenship in the colonies remained an ambiguous idea fraught with difficulties. For French authorities, citizenship implied conformity to Eurocentric cultural values. Polygamy, lack of literacy in written and spoken French, customs deemed superstitious or primitive, and non-European dress and dwellings seemed incompatible with being a citizen of the republic. Outside of the enclave of citizens in the communes, only a handful of African individuals ever achieved recognition as French citizens in the entire history of French rule in Africa.[50]

On 5 November 1830, the monarchy issued a decree to clarify voting rights in Senegal. The decree specified that all free adult men born and living in Senegal could enjoy the same rights as those granted to French citizens by the civil code. The Second Republic elaborated on the political rights of Senegal's inhabitants by including a provision in the decree granting Senegal legislative representation, which specified that residents of the colony did not have to show proof of naturalization but only five years residency in order to vote. From that point, tradition in the towns held that all individuals born in the communes had the right to vote in local elections regardless of their customary status. French observers, officials, and members of the judiciary, however, considered the subject of African voting rights open to debate and interpretation. In the 1890s and early 1900s, the issue emerged again as originaires demanded recognition of their legal status as citizens. As more originaire traders, interpreters, and colonial employees lived and worked in the interior and interacted with Africans subject to protectorate rule, colonial officials sought to limit originaire claims to citizenship.[51]

In late nineteenth-century Senegal, most registered voters in commune elections were Africans, but they did not vote in proportion to their numbers. Those who voted often did so with instructions from one of the dominant coalitions. The census taken prior to the 1871 deputy elections recorded 3,427 registered voters for Saint Louis, yet only 1,587 actually voted.[52] Moreover, the law required candidates to prove literacy in French in order to run for electoral office. Muslim traders consistently appeared on the list of registered voters because commerce enhanced participation in politics and because they counted among the French-educated population of the town.

The habitants had long established a tradition of democratic governance in Saint Louis. Mayors, advisory councils, short-lived assemblies, and other republican practices became a part of urban life in the capital. The emergence of the Third Republic stimulated new democratic traditions in France that had a direct impact on how France understood and carried out colonial rule in West Africa. In Senegal, the existence of an enclave of republican laws and democratic institutions in the coastal towns stood in stark contrast to the pursuit of colonial conquest and the arbitrary and authoritarian practices employed to enforce French power. The urban community was located at the intersection of these two competing notions. They blurred the boundaries between town, countryside, and metropolis.

The establishment of electoral institutions by the Third Republic worked to the advantage of the métis, who were among the three groups competing for power. Their knowledge of French law, their connections to the monopoly capital trade houses, and their familiarity with French republicanism allowed them entry into electoral politics in the late nineteenth century. As a result, the métis used the institutions as a basis for maintaining their influence in colonial affairs during the period of conquest. The field of electoral politics, therefore, provided a new avenue for social and economic mobility that enabled the métis to assert power in ways that colonial authorities did not anticipate.

6

Electoral Politics and the Métis (1870–90)

The decade of the 1870s offered new opportunities for the métis to assert power and influence within the colonial system. Although they had lost their monopoly over the middleman sector of the colonial economy, the economic, cultural, and social networks that métis families had developed allowed them entry into the political arena. In the 1870s, when the Third Republic expanded electoral institutions in Senegal, the métis capitalized on these reforms by winning seats in the local assemblies. Because of their education, ties to metropolitan commerce and the administration, and their familiarity with the local situation, the métis were well positioned to take advantage of the expansion of democratic institutions, and French officials relied on their cooperation.

Histories of modern politics in Senegal tend to cast the late nineteenth century as an intermediary phase between a politics of French hegemony and the emergence of African nationalism, in which "electoral clans" dominated commune politics and candidates relied on patron-clientage to mobilize African voters in support of their candidates.[1] Racial identity had little to do with political alliances. The métis supported political parties that identified with Bordeaux commerce, the clergy, and Gaspard Devès's coalition of "Senegalese interests." Prominent African town residents organized the African electorate to support candidates with whom they had established ties, regardless of race. Saint Louis held particular importance as the capital of the colony, the headquarters of the General Council, and the commune with the largest population. Politics in Senegal's capital differed little from city politics in metropolitan France. Commune politics involved strategic alliances, questionable tactics, and even "buying" votes.[2]

Democratic institutions in the colonies served as an extension of the French idea of assimilation. While they existed as a means of providing representation for certain interests and constituencies in the political process, politics also functioned as a mechanism for imposing colonial control. In Senegal, the electoral institutions served a dual purpose of introducing western political systems and facilitating colonial control.

A closer examination of métis activities in electoral politics during the late nineteenth century reveals a complex and at times uneasy relationship between the republican institutions and colonial officials. The expansion of electoral politics in the towns at the same time that France engaged in violent campaigns for control over strategic territories of the interior presented a dilemma for French officials. The administration relied on cooperation from individuals in the urban community to achieve their imperialist aims, and French officials viewed the local assemblies as a key mechanism for cultivating relations of cooperation. The métis, however, took the practice of republican citizenship seriously. The establishment of electoral institutions in the colony expanded the field of power for the urban community, but it also raised concerns among colonial officials who increasingly viewed the interference of the assemblymen of the first arrondissement problematic for imposing colonial control.

Forming Coalitions: The First Generation

In the late nineteenth century, Louis Descemet and Gaspard Devès emerged as major figures who established successful political coalitions. Between 1884 and 1902, both men advanced lists of candidates that dominated assembly elections and played key roles in electoral campaigns for Senegal's representative to the Chamber of Deputies. A wealthy businessman and merchant, Devès held office but also put forth candidates for elections and shaped local debate. Born in 1827, Devès was the son of Bordeaux merchant Bruno Devès and a Fulbe woman who was also known as Sylvie Bruno. Bruno Devès arrived in Senegal in the 1820s. He joined his brother Justin, and they established an export firm and became prominent wholesale merchants in the gum trade. In 1851, the company merged with Gustav Chaumet to form J. Devès, Lacoste, and Company. The new concern specialized in peanut exports and maritime equipment, and opened one of the first peanut processing factories in Bordeaux. There is little evidence to suggest a close relationship between Gaspard and the Bordeaux company.[3]

In keeping with Saint Louis custom, Bruno Devès sent his Senegalese son to Bordeaux for education. Gaspard completed his studies and returned to Senegal, probably in the midst of the gum crisis. In 1851, Devès married Catherine Foy, the daughter of métis habitants Guillaume Foy and Henriette Cecile Descemet. A year later, following the birth of their daughter, Elisabeth, Catherine died, leaving Elisabeth to inherit her fortune. In 1872, when Guillaume Foy died, Elisabeth inherited his wealth. As his daughter's legal guardian, Gaspard managed her estate, combining his resources with hers to build a fortune that totaled two million francs in assets, interest, and revenue from property upon his death in 1901.[4]

Devès entered commerce following the decline of the gum trade. He began as a junior partner to métis habitant John Sleight. In 1851, when Sleight left Senegal to replace Durand Valantin in the Paris legislature, he granted Devès his contract to supply the administration with grain.[5] Over the next two decades, Devès expanded his business interests to include investments in property and steamship transportation. He became a major importer of guinées and invested in a textile manufacturing company in Pondicherry, India, that specialized in them. In addition, Devès established his own factory for peanut exports along the Mellacourie River and maintained strategic trade interests along the upper Senegal.[6] Going beyond middleman exports to control a significant aspect of the import market allowed Devès to build a commercial enterprise that rivaled the Bordeaux merchants, who enjoyed a monopoly over the export sector of the colonial economy. He commanded a network of employees and creditors in the fishing village of Guet Ndar and owned a brick factory on a nearby island. Devès entered into an agreement with the Trarza emir to buy the island of Arguin in Mauritania and acted as creditor to Lat Dior, the damel of Cayor.[7]

Although Devès joined an established métis family in his marriage to Catherine Foy, his second was a mariage à la mode du pays. He entered into this union with Madeleine Tamba, a Sarakole woman of Guet Ndar. The marriage resulted in nine children, six of whom lived to adulthood.[8] Three sons and two daughters became active in politics and the family business. In 1889, they formalized their union with the civil registry shortly before their son married Charlotte Crespin, the daughter of their main political ally. Gaspard Devès's marriage to Madeleine Tamba made the Saint Louis neighborhood of Guet Ndar one of his main bases of support in commune elections.

Devès's business interests and capital investments allowed him to develop an extensive network of client ties in Saint Louis and with ruling elites in strategic regions of the interior. Creating a merchant firm that competed with the Bordeaux corporations also allowed Devès significant influence in colonial affairs as well as a high degree of autonomy from metropolitan commercial interests. In 1875, Governor Brière de l'Isle named Devès mayor of Saint Louis. As the Third Republic expanded Senegal's political rights, Devès founded a coalition that defined itself as an advocate for "Senegalese" interests. His political allies included lawyers Jean Jacques Crespin of Saint Louis and Léopold Angrand of Gorée. Devès also developed partnerships with key figures in metropolitan politics. He cultivated close ties to Alexandre Issac, a man of color and senator from Guadeloupe who argued for racial equality in French politics. Issac was also a member of the Ligue des Droits de l'Homme, the human rights organization that pressured lawmakers to address the problem of slavery in France's overseas territories and monitored human rights abuses in the colonies. Devès's relationship with Issac extended his network to metropolitan lawmakers who had authority over administrative officials in Senegal.[9]

Louis Descemet organized the second major coalition that competed for power in commune politics during the 1870s and 1880s. The Descemets trace their lineage to a French soldier, Pierre Louis Descemet (1771–1825), who arrived in Senegal in the 1790s, and Signare Suzanne Dobbs, the daughter of Mame Coumba and John Dobbs, a British soldier who arrived in the mid-eighteenth century. Their son, Pierre (1804–69), married Louise Elisa Marie Morel Boirard (1809–47) of Saint Louis, and they were the parents of Louis and Roger Descemet, who were among the first scholarship recipients in France. Louis completed his studies at the Lycée de l'Orient and returned to Senegal to begin a career in the administration. He served as secretary to Governor Faidherbe until 1862. Roger attended St. Cyr and died leading Faidherbe's forces in the battle of Médine. In 1865, Louis Descemet married Adelaide Duchesne, the daughter of a habitant gum trader.

The Descemets distinguished themselves in the colonial bureaucracy and the military, developing relations with administrative officials. Descemet's network also extended to Bordeaux commerce through his relatives' connections to the commercial firm, Buhan and Teisseire. After leaving the administration, Louis Descemet formed a modest trade interest with Omer Teisseire. They held a contract to supply cattle for French settlers in

Dakar. Descemet was related to most of the métis families. In the 1880s, Germain d'Erneville, Leon d'Erneville, Theodore Carpot, and Charles Molinet joined his coalition. In addition, Descemet supplied credit to Foutanke chiefs in Fouta Toro.[10]

In the late nineteenth century, the Devès family positioned themselves as leaders of an oppositional group in commune politics. Gaspard Devès's knowledge of French politics, his skill in business, and his connection to powerful leaders of commerce and government in metropolitan France solidified his position. His assertive personality, his extensive client network, and his close ties to African rulers and residents of Guet Ndar generated support for his candidates. Descemet relied on support from the most influential habitant families, Bordeaux commerce, French officials, and the clergy to bolster his group's position in the electoral assemblies. Far from monolithic, the Devès and Descemet groups differed in important ways, yet both viewed the electoral institutions as a way to assert influence. While colonial officials relied on métis cooperation to consolidate French power in the countryside, the actions of the assemblymen raised suspicion. By the end of the 1880s, officials expressed concern over the role of the councilors in colonial affairs and began to question the logic of democratic institutions in the colony.

Commune Politics and the Saint Louis Community (1871–79)

From 1871 until 1884, Bordeaux interests dominated commune elections. Elections in Saint Louis remained the most important to the colony, since Rufisque and Dakar were only emerging as important commercial centers and French commerce concentrated on gaining ground in Sin, Saloum, and the Southern Rivers rather than on controlling politics in the communes.[11] Auguste de Bourmeister, a French lawyer who married into a métis family in Saint Louis, emerged as a central candidate backed by Bordeaux commerce. Alfred Gasconi, a métis candidate, also developed an important following and enjoyed the support of the clergy and the administration. Gaspard Devès formed another coalition in this period that distinguished itself as being independent of the merchant lobby, the administration, and the clergy.

As lawyers and businessmen were knowledgeable about French politics and their livelihood depended on the strength of the colonial economy, a group of métis men gained influence in the political life of the colony by winning election to the municipal council or being appointed to serve on the governor's private council. The candidates for the 1871 legislative election

included Alexandre Caminade, a pharmacist from Rochefort; Frederic Car-
rere, a member of the judiciary; Clement de Ville-Suzanne of Bordeaux; Albert Teisseire, born in Saint Louis of Bordeaux parents; J. J. Crespin; and
Jean-Baptiste Laffon de Fongauffier, a naval officer. Louis Descemet, Leon
d'Erneveille, and John Sleight backed Albert Teisseire. Gaspard Devès
formed a group called the Comité Sénégalais to advance the candidacy of
Clement de Ville Suzanne, their "Bordeaux relative" who had spent five years
living in Saint Louis as a trader. The Comité Sénégalais argued that their
candidate was truly independent of the metropolitan corporations and thus
completely devoted to liberal principles and the progress of their country.
Laffon de Fongauffier won the election with 1,186 votes. De Ville-Suzanne
came in second with 312 votes, and Teisseire trailed with 158 votes.[12]

Although the 1871 decree granted Senegal representation in the National
Assembly, legislators expressed reluctance to grant the colony additional republican institutions. As the Third Republic became stronger, the Saint Louis
community pressured the government to extend political rights to the colony.
The merchant lobby and the métis argued for more electoral institutions. In
1869, Bordeaux merchants and métis habitants sent a petition to the naval
ministry requesting that the government reestablish Senegal's General
Council. Two years later, the habitants of Saint Louis used their new representative to lobby legislators in Paris. They petitioned the legislature to grant
Senegal a municipal council and a general council.[13] Laffon de Fongauffier,
moreover, campaigned on establishing commune government, a civilian administration, and a general council for Senegal. Their efforts resulted in the
municipal decree of 1872 that granted Saint Louis and Gorée commune status
and called for municipal elections held at the end of the year.

The question of a general council remained unresolved for Senegal. In
the 1840s, when Paris instituted the short-lived assembly, lawmakers were
still reluctant to afford Senegal such a revered institution. They considered
their West African territory a commercial outpost, not one of the Grandes
Colonies. After the Third Republic reintroduced a general council in the
French Antilles and Réunion, the Saint Louis community petitioned Paris
to reestablish a similar assembly in Senegal.

On 2 May 1878, Brière de l'Isle proposed suppressing the municipal
councils of Saint Louis and Gorée. His private council deliberated on
whether the powers attributed to the two municipal councils should be
subsumed under the newly created General Council for the colony. Some

maintained that there was no need for two elected assemblies, while others argued that the functions of the municipal council should be attributed to the General Council. The issue, according to Gaspard Devès, had to do with whether political rights for Senegal would be expanded or limited under the Third Republic. Devès argued that those who "do not want Senegal as a colony, who only want to permit it to be a commercial enterprise to exploit, hinder the play of our institutions." Devès predicted that the commission named by the minister to study the necessity of the General Council would rule in Senegal's favor. He concluded that the ministry would "know how to discern between these intentions and we will soon see that Senegal is not in Bordeaux but among us."[14]

The distinction between metropolitan capital interested solely in the extraction of Senegal's resources for the metropolitan industry and those who sought to protect "Senegalese interests" shaped the struggle for power. Establishing a general council in Senegal followed republican ideals and corresponded with the idea of assimilation because it afforded Senegal's town residents the same political rights as French citizens living in Algeria and the Antilles. In the municipal elections of 1875, Devès's candidates won a majority of seats on the town council. Brière de l'Isle named Gaspard Devès mayor, even though there was strong opposition to his candidacy from the Bordeaux firms. Devès's opponents criticized his municipal council for being ineffective and costly. Devès, however, succeeded in carving out his position as a "defender of indigenous society" and an advocate of assimilation in contrast to the merchant lobby that sought control of the town council.[15]

On 4 February 1879, Paris decreed the creation of Senegal's General Council. The naval minister explained the decision as part of the logical progression of French policy that extended republican institutions to residents of the colony who have "shown real aptitude in the management of local affairs."[16] In the first General Council election in September 1879, representatives of the French trading houses gained fourteen of the eighteen available seats, including three previously held by Gasconi's candidates. Louis Descemet became the assembly's president. Devès resigned as mayor after the merchant lobby criticized his work. The administration then appointed Charles Molinet as his replacement.[17]

The expansion of republican politics increased the numbers of registered voters, and electoral campaigns became important annual events. The competition between candidates also gained momentum. In the 1879 legislative election, J. J. Crespin ran against Marechal, a European civil servant, and Alfred Gasconi. Gasconi had a strong base of support among the clergy, the métis who opposed Devès, African voters, and the tacit support of the administration. He won the legislative election in the second round, defeating the other two by 1,158 votes. In September 1881, Crespin, Marechal, and Eugene Mounier, the editor of a Parisian journal, emerged as candidates for the legislative position. Gasconi and Crespin competed in the second round. Gasconi won the election in part because he had succeeded in getting a running water system for town residents.[18]

From 1881 to 1884, the merchant lobby had control of the General Council and the deputyship and asserted significant influence on the municipal council in the capital. In December 1881, Auguste de Bourmeister and his candidates won the majority of seats in the municipal elections. The merchant lobby succeeded in their attack against Gaspard Devès by targeting his management of the Saint Louis municipality and his affiliation to Brière de l'Isle. Between 1876 and 1886, a sequence of events illustrated the nature of the struggle for power in commune elections. The merchant lobby sought to influence colonial policy in support of their aims over Devès, who represented the commercial interests of the Saint Louis community. These events solidified Devès's reputation as an opponent of metropolitan commerce and also raised colonial officials' suspicions of the interference of the Saint Louis community in colonial affairs. Interference by local assemblymen complicated the process of achieving conquest and imposing colonial control over African territories in the interior.

Colonial Affairs and the Métis (1876–86)

In 1876, Colonel Louis Alexandre Brière de l'Isle arrived in Senegal, becoming governor during a period of "pacification," as France had put a halt to further military expansion. A strong governor with totalitarian tendencies, Brière de l'Isle disapproved of civilians being able to influence how the military conducted conquest and designed colonial policy. Relations between the governor and the Saint Louis community deteriorated during his time in Senegal, as he earned a reputation for being hostile to the exercise of their political rights as well as unconcerned with French commercial interests. Ironically, Gaspard Devès became Brière de l'Isle's closest ally.

One of the events that fueled tensions between the governor and Bordeaux commerce concerned a new customs regime that was introduced to

regulate the import of guinées in Senegal. Allocation of the colony's revenues from import duties involved a complex negotiation between administrators in Saint Louis, the Bordeaux Chamber of Commerce, Paris legislators, and members of the General Council. Since Saint Louis could not rely
on consistent funding from Paris to finance infrastructure, military expeditions, and commercial expansion, negotiations over customs played a central role in generating revenue.

Guinées remained a profitable import for Bordeaux commerce long
after Senegal's gum trade declined. Moors who specialized in the overland
transport of produce from peanut-producing regions in Cayor continued
to trade their goods for supplies of the blue cloth because it remained in
high demand among local consumers. On 19 July 1877, Paris lawmakers
introduced protectionist legislation that changed the customs regime in
Senegal.[19] This new decree reduced the tariff for textiles imported to the
colony from Pondicherry, the French colonial outpost in India that specialized in the manufacture of guinées. Under the new customs law, cotton
originating from factories in Liverpool, Rouen, and Havre were subject to
higher duties than guinées from Pondicherry.[20] Since the majority of the
French companies in Senegal obtained guinées from England or textile
manufacturers in northern France, this put them at a disadvantage. As a
representative of the textile company that produced guinées in Pondicherry,
Gaspard Devès had a monopoly over imports from French India.[21] The
Bordeaux commercial houses complained to the Chamber of Commerce
in Bordeaux that the regulation gave Devès an unfair advantage.

Métis employees and allies of the French firms attacked Brière de l'Isle
for proposing the new law as a means of increasing revenues to support his
goals for military expeditions to the upper Senegal and lower Niger. At the
1879 opening of the first session of the General Council, the assemblymen
debated the matter. Gasconi, Senegal's representative in Paris, brought the
issue before the Chamber of Deputies and the colonial ministry. In addition, the Bordeaux Chamber of Commerce weighed in on the debate by
placing their support with the "Bordeaux merchants of Senegal," in a report
they sent to the government asking lawmakers to repeal the law.[22]

On 17 October 1880, the minister of colonies reduced the customs duties on all textile imports in Senegal due to pressure by the Bordeaux merchant lobby. This issue proved to be an economic victory for the French
companies, and it strengthened their position in the political life of

Senegal's capital. The guinée debate fueled complaints against Gaspard Devès's administration of the municipality. Brière de l'Isle, who described Devès in a letter to his son as the "only notable in Senegal for whom I kept a fond memory," was pressured into forcing the mayor's resignation and dissolving the Saint Louis municipal council.[23] The issue added to the criticism of the administration by members of Senegal's local assemblies. Brière de l'Isle's removal and the appointment of René Servatius, Senegal's first civilian governor, one year later was due in large part to the negative publicity campaign orchestrated by Senegal's representatives and their insistence on replacing the military regime in the colony with civilian government. Servatius, perhaps having understood Brière de l'Isle's trouble with the Saint Louis community, paid much greater attention to the demands of elected officials during his tenure as governor.

The construction of the Dakar–Saint Louis railroad had implications for the people of the Wolof states where France annexed territory to build the railroad, but it also affected the relationship between the Saint Louis community and the colonial administration. In 1878, officials proposed building a railroad to connect Dakar, the new port of the peanut basin, with Saint Louis. French merchants viewed the railroad as a way to impose peanut culture and to expand their capitalist objectives beyond the coastal enclaves and into the country's rural areas. The colonial ministry supported the railroad, in part, because it satisfied the growing propaganda for colonial projects among proponents of French overseas expansion who were firmly in control of the government at home. Construction of the railroad required support from the damel of Cayor. During the 1860s, officials in Saint Louis had interfered with succession disputes in Cayor but had not succeeded in gaining firm military control over the kingdom, nor could they count on its ruler's voluntary compliance.[24] Lat Dior, the damel, walked a fine line between cooperating with Saint Louis and resisting colonial officials' efforts to encroach upon the kingdom's territory.

In 1879, Governor Brière de l'Isle proposed a treaty to annex part of Cayor's territory in order to build their railroad through the region. Lat Dior, whom France recognized as sovereign, agreed to the treaty because France guaranteed the damel military protection against internal uprisings. In addition, Lat Dior sought French support against Samba Laobe, his nephew and chief rival for the title of damel, who opposed the railroad over concerns that it would end the tradition of long-distance caravan transport. Historically, the Trarza who controlled the caravan trade maintained close trade relations with Cayor. In May 1881, Lat Dior reversed his decision to comply with the French request by announcing his opposition to the railroad and forbidding his subjects to engage in commerce with the colony. Lat Dior's anti-French stance led Governor Servatius to launch a series of military expeditions in Cayor, eventually isolating and weakening Lat Dior. On 16 January 1883, the governor announced Saint Louis's recognition of Samba Laobe as damel with the condition that France could construct a fort at Louga and annex key territory along the railway route to begin construction.[25]

Faced with violent reprisals by colonial officials, Samba Laobe and Lat Dior turned to members of the Saint Louis community for support in their opposition to the railway. In an April 1883 letter to the minister of colonies, Governor Servatius claimed that certain people were hostile to the railroad project. He singled out Gaspard Devès, Justin Devès, and J. J. Crespin of the General Council as well as the interpreter Samba Fall among the fiercest opponents to the railway construction.[26] Lat Dior and Samba Laobe were indebted to Gaspard Devès, leading the governor to speculate that Devès was motivated by a desire to maintain members of the Cayor aristocracy as his clients. Officials accused Crespin of simply seeking to stir up bitter feelings against the administration. French authorities feared that construction of the railroad had become a rallying point for Saint Louis traders, Muslim and Wolof-speaking residents of the capital who supported Lat Dior, and members of the local assemblies who considered the transportation system detrimental to the well-established history of diplomatic and trade relations between the people of Saint Louis, the Trarza caravan leaders, and Cayor.[27]

The construction of the Dakar–Saint Louis railroad revealed key differences over how French colonialism should progress. For the administration and metropolitan commercial firms, the railroad symbolized the triumph of French technology and the penetration of French capital into the countryside. For traders and others in the Saint Louis community invested in trade with Cayor, the railroad and violent military expeditions were destabilizing forces that threatened to disrupt established relationships with African rulers that they depended on for their livelihood. Gaspard Devés objected to the railway project, in part, to preserve his relationship with one of his most important creditors in the Cayor aristocracy. Regardless of motive, opposing the railroad solidified the Devés coalition's reputation for being openly antagonistic to French policy.

In addition, colonial authorities became increasingly suspicious of Gaspard Devès's dealings with the Trarza, which had the potential to disrupt French efforts to gain control of the north bank of the Senegal and the southwestern region the Sahara. Gaspard Devès claimed to own the Atlantic island of Arguin, having acquired it in a deal with the Trarza emir. In February 1882, Devès contested the administration's decision to grant a Marseille company a concession to exploit the natural resources of Arguin.[28] He registered his grievance with officials in Saint Louis and the colonial ministry in Paris, claiming that he owned the island and planned to establish his own fishing and salt collection company there. Devès provided a bill of sale, dated 2 June 1880, that was signed by Ely, the Trarza emir, and registered in Saint Louis. In March 1882, the governor informed Devès that the ministry found that Arguin belonged to France and declared his contract with the Trarza emir null and void.

Tensions between the administration and Gaspard Devès appeared to have intensified in the mid-1880s. Regardless, French administrators continued to rely on trusted relationships with Muslim traders and the métis of Saint Louis to ease economic and political relations with ruling elites, traders, and clerics who recently experienced violent campaigns in the middle Senegal. Yet this uneasy cooperation raised concerns about the potential for these diplomatic missions to have unintended consequences for the cohesive imposition of French power. On the one hand, Saint Louis needed trusted allies who had knowledge of local issues to mediate imperial expansion. On the other hand, the assemblymen viewed the General Council as their arena and sought to exercise their autonomy from colonial officials by asserting their influence in colonial affairs. The commandant of Podor raised concerns about the activities of the assemblymen in the upper Senegal during their visit to the region.

In August 1886, a delegation from the General Council took a steamship voyage along the upper Senegal to strengthen trade relations between the administration in Saint Louis and rulers of the region. The French officer in Podor described the mission as "neither official nor commercial." Officials in Saint Louis conceived of the mission as a way to create and maintain political and economic relations between the assemblymen and several "grands chefs indigènes" after the losses that French commerce and Saint Louis traders sustained during the most recent French campaign in the region.[29] Louis Descemet, president of the General Council, headed the delegation. He also served as a commercial agent for the Bordeaux firm A. Teisseire. Raymond Martin, a representative of Buhan and Teisseire, Leon d'Erneville, an agent for the French firm Rabaud, J. J. Crespin, and Bacre Waly Gueye, the proprietor of an influential commercial network that operated from Podor, participated in the mission. The delegation represented the notable inhabitants of Saint Louis. The assemblymen traveled to the upper Senegal as liaisons for Saint Louis in their diplomatic relations with people of the region, but they also had strategic interests of their own in strengthening commercial ties there.

During their two-month voyage along the Senegal, the commandant responsible for accompanying the councilors reported to the political affairs bureau about various meetings the visitors had with chiefs and notables of the territory. The commandant called attention to the close ties that already existed between Descemet and Lam Toro Sidikh, a former ruler from Fouta Toro, whom the French had deposed two years earlier. Sidikh, the report claimed, owed Descemet for a number of purchases, and according to the commandant, the two were joined by a certain "*lieu de parenté.*" The officer noted his "great surprise" in finding Lam Toro Sidikh meeting with the General Council president on two occasions to solicit his assistance for being reinstated by the governor as the region's legitimate chief.[30]

Other chiefs and traders from the region used the occasion to present their complaints to the Saint Louis delegation. A group of traders in the upper Senegal voiced their concerns about the unfair commercial practices of the Brakna on the river's right. The chief of Bosse sent his own representative to request that the governor enlarge his kingdom. The Saint Louis delegation used their visit to Bakel to question local residents and traders about conditions in the country. According to the commandant, the assemblymen "promised their protection" to the individuals who claimed to be innocent of charges leveled by the commandant, and the Saint Louis delegation promised traders of Bakel restitution for the goods they lost as a result of French military campaigns.[31] The rulers and traders that the delegation met with considered the assemblymen to be representatives of French authority who had the power to address their problems. From the administration's point of view, the travels of the Saint Louis delegation suggested an overreach of their influence with African authorities in the interior. This event, combined with rising suspicions of other métis interference in colonial affairs, signaled to French administrators the potential problem of relying on the métis as go-betweens with Africans in the interior.

More than a strict trade mission, the Saint Louis delegation used the mission to assert themselves as representatives of French authority. They acted as mediators between the colony and African rulers in the protectorate, but they also used the authority of their position to assert their own interests in ways that positioned them above the commandants on the ground. For officials in Saint Louis, this event signaled the potential for elected representatives from the communes to disrupt the imposition of a cohesive structure of French rule in the interior and suggested that the métis, in particular, could use their position to supersede the governor's authority and that of the colony's highest officials.

These events—beginning with the dispute over import duties on guinées and evolving into the unforeseen consequences of the General Council delegation to Podor and Bakel—confirmed that the assemblymen could create problems for the maintenance and consolidation of French control over strategic regions of Senegal's interior. Gaspard Devès and his ally, J. J. Crespin, ran afoul of the administration by publically contesting French authority. Yet the report on the mission to Podor suggested to French authorities that even allies like Louis Descemet could exercise a high degree of autonomy from French officialdom.

A report in the newly constituted independent press regarding Cayor damel Samba Laobe's death at the hands of the French military confirmed Devès's reputation as anti-French. Governor Genouille authorized a military campaign against Samba Laobe to make him comply with the 1883 treaty he signed with the French and to prevent him from reestablishing Cayor's sovereignty. On 6 October 1886, a battle ensued at Tivaouane, the primary commercial depot in Cayor, in which the French captain of the regiment and Samba Laobe were killed. The administration's report of the incident in the *Moniteur du Senegal* called the incident "a glorious day for France," in which Lieutenant Chauvey "punished the damel for his insolent provocation." Four days later, the *Réveil du Senegal* published an article entitled, "The Execution of Samba Laobe." The *Reveil* author accused Governor Genouille of deliberately planning a mission to kill the damel.[32] An opinion article in the sister paper, *Le Petit Sénégalais,* launched stronger complaints against the French for inciting violence in Cayor, disrupting trade in the "breadbasket of the colony," and depopulating the region so that people could not farm. The article coincided with an electoral season that witnessed an intensification of the struggle between the two competing interest groups in Saint Louis. The independent press report of the campaign in Cayor demonstrated the willingness of Devès and his allies to openly oppose and publicize the administration's practices in the interior.

Commune Politics (1885–90)

By the mid-1880s, Senegal's political landscape had changed significantly. The "scramble" for territory resulted in French campaigns along the Niger. The administration in Saint Louis concentrated on consolidating territories in the peanut basin and the Senegal River valley as well as suppressing resistance by African rulers and clerics in the interior. From Brière de l'Isle's departure in 1881 until Genouille's appointment in April 1886, a series of weaker and somewhat less effective governors held the office in Saint Louis.[33] Most served one year or less in the colony, thus necessitating reliance on the Saint Louis community, and the métis in particular, to facilitate their aims. Elections to the republican institutions in the communes gained momentum. Saint Louis remained the nexus of political power for the urban community, and elections in the capital increasingly centered on the struggle between Gaspard Devès and Louis Descemet. Both men led influential coalitions and advanced lists of candidates for election to the local assemblies.

In the 1880s, Gaspard Devès openly criticized the administration and took actions that interfered with official orders. Devès entered the debate over secularism that played an important role in metropolitan political debates. Devès and his allies supported anticlericalism, thus straining their relationship with clergy in the colonial capital. As associates or members of the Freemasons and founders of an independent press, Devès and J. J. Crespin identified with secularists and radical-leaning republicans in metropolitan France. In addition, Devès built a coalition of advocates for "Senegalese" interests that distinguished itself from the interests of metropolitan commerce. The strategies that Devès employed situated him as someone who acted independently and outside of the administration's approval.

The *Reveil du Senegal* appeared in August 1885 just in time for the beginning of the campaign season. The newspaper criticized the administration and the monopoly commercial firms. The journals also gave their own accounts of the General Council meetings and kept close tabs on the nature of the colonial administration's dealings with African rulers in the interior.[34] In doing so, the independent press broke the administration's monopoly over print media in Senegal. Devès also strengthened his group's standing by building his coalition of supporters in the municipal council while also bolstering support for his interests by gaining seats on the General Council from the second arrondissement (Gorée, Dakar, Rufisque). In 1885, Justin Devès returned to Senegal from France and won election to the General Council. Three years later, Hyacinthe moved to Rufisque and won election to the assembly from the second arrondissement. Leopold Angrand of Gorée, who had strong ties to the Lebou of Dakar and Rufisque, was elected to the General Council during same year and joined Gaspard Devès's coalition. The 22 June 1889 marriage between Hyacinthe Devès and Charlotte Crespin cemented the coalition between Devès and J. J. Crespin, two of the most influential members of the General Council.[35]

In the fall 1889 elections, the Devès coalition accomplished a major electoral victory when their candidate, Amiral Aristide Vallon, won the legislative election. Crespin did not enter the campaign, despite having run for the position in every campaign, and instead deferred to Vallon. A naval officer from Brest, Vallon participated in French military campaigns in Senegal from 1856 to 1869. In 1882, he served briefly as governor. Alfred Gasconi sought his third term in the Chamber of Deputies, having represented Senegal in Paris since 1879. Gasconi had the backing of the métis and Bordeaux commerce.

In the fall 1889 elections, Vallon won some support from merchant interests but also gained strong backing from the African electorate. The administration must have considered Vallon to be their ally because of his career in the navy and the time he spent in Senegal. It is possible that the administration did not fully comprehend his connection to Gaspard Devès. The administration's support together with support from Devès, a major patron among African voters in the capital and the second arrondissement, certainly bolstered support for Vallon among the African electorate. In the first round of elections, Vallon came in with only 84 more votes than Gasconi. In the second round, Vallon won the election by only 289 votes.[36]

During the campaign, voters accused Gasconi and his supporters of using fraudulent tactics to gain votes. Complaints of corruption were also lodged against the current mayor, Bourmeister, and certain members of the Saint Louis Municipal Council who were allied with Gasconi.[37] Their tactics gave the Devès coalition reason to attack the legitimacy of the mayor and town council. The day after the election, Vallon demanded that the governor dissolve the Saint Louis Municipal Council and called for new elections. On 13 April 1890, the list of candidates proposed by Gaspard Devès won the majority of seats on the Saint Louis Municipal Council. Moreover, J. J. Crespin became mayor. Devès and his allies emerged as the dominant group in commune politics with control of the legislative office, the town council in the capital, and the majority of seats in the General Council. By the beginning of the new decade, they were well positioned to exercise their authority and test the extent of their power in the colony.

The expansion of democratic institutions in the communes under the Third Republic led to the growth of civil society in Senegal's colonial capital. As town residents closely affiliated with French power, the métis population took advantage of the reforms that liberalized politics in the colony by monopolizing positions of power in the local assemblies. The struggle that emerged during this period involved competition between metropolitan merchant firms interested in capitalist expansion and members of the Saint Louis community who articulated an agenda distinct from the mainstream—Bordeaux commerce, the clergy, or the administration. The political struggle that took place in the capital brought forth new ideas about what constituted "Senegalese" interests in ways that had not occurred before.

The métis competed for power within the political arena, but they all understood electoral politics as the primary field to advance their interests as an urban elite. Gaspard Devès and Louis Descemet used their affiliation with French officials and metropolitan capital as well as their understanding of local politics to assert their influence in the interior. Their network of kin and client relations and their intimate familiarity with the politics of Senegal's countryside gave them an advantage over colonial officials that proved useful to the administration in achieving conquest, but these same relations could also serve to undermine metropolitan authority. The tensions inherent in the relationship between the Saint Louis community and colonial officials reached its apex by the turn of the twentieth century. For the métis, the local assemblies served as the arena for articulating their views about French republicanism and engaging in contests for power over the nature of democratic politics and colonial rule in Senegal.

7

Urban Politics and the Limits of Republicanism (1890–1920)

And there it is gentlemen, the accusations that help those who
would succeed in introducing in a country the prejudice of color! . . .
You know that in no other country do elections take place with as
much calm and courtesy between candidates and voters; that far from
making choices based on origin, each list [in Senegal] includes black,
white and mulatto candidates. The reasoning of Mr. Sonolet is, therefore, in all
points contradictory to the truth and it is enough to destroy the arguments of
he who opposes the Declaration of the Rights of Man and Citizen, to remind
him that in this country we have always firmly followed the sublime principles
of the Revolution summarized by these words inscribed in the frontispiece of
all the public monuments, "liberty, equality and above all fraternity."

—*Georges Crespin, General Council session, February 1912*

M. Louis Sonolet, like many twentieth-century observers, considered the
existence of democratic institutions in Senegal to be an anomaly. In his
view, republican institutions such as the General Council amounted to a
premature and dangerous gesture that placed the weighty responsibility of
governance in African hands.[1] On the eve of World War I, French objectives
in West Africa no longer concerned managing two coastal settlements and
a handful of river trade posts. Instead, French rule involved maintaining
authority over a territory of approximately 4.7 million miles and a vast
population of different linguistic, cultural, and political identities.[2] Assimilation no longer seemed a logical or rational system for colonial administration. Officials in Dakar and Saint Louis looked to consolidate their

power, despite the precarious nature of French rule, and to present the colonial state as a unified, hegemonic force in the region. The notion that colonial subjects could become cultural Frenchmen or that metropolitan political systems could be replicated in the colonies gave way to an insistence that the differences be respected. Association and its emphasis on *mise en valeur* (rational economic development) replaced assimilation as the dominant ideology of colonial policy in West Africa.

The theories and practices of colonial administration in French West Africa are well understood, yet the role that commune politics played in shaping official ideas about colonial rule and how it should operate in the colony are less well known. The establishment of a governor general for French West Africa and the bureaucratic system of this federal administration generated a new cadre of metropolitan civil servants and bureaucratic officials who shaped colonial policy in Dakar rather than in Paris.[3] The governor and governor general underestimated the aggressiveness of the Saint Louis community and its ability to interfere in colonial affairs. In the 1890s and early 1900s, the struggle for power intensified between the colonial administration and the métis who demonstrated their willingness to complicate the consolidation of French power. They used the local assemblies to challenge colonial policies that sought to deny Senegal political rights, and they used the republican institutions in the town to act as watchdogs over abuses of power by the colonial regime.

The period between 1890 and 1920 witnessed an intensification of the struggle between the métis and the colonial administration. Increased scrutiny by colonial officials, the rise of new settler interests in Dakar and Rufisque, and political challenges from originaires forced the métis to adopt new strategies to maintain their influence in the political arena. In general, the métis opted to bolster their support among the originaire electorate by responding to issues that concerned African town residents and by relying on their kin and client ties with ruling elites in the interior, Muslim clerics, and Lebu and Wolof voters of the communes. In the 1890s and early 1900s, the strategies of negotiation and contestation that the métis elite employed proved a thorn in the side of French officials seeking to consolidate control and achieve metropolitan industry's goals for the extraction of raw materials. At the same time, originaire challenges threatened to end métis control of the electoral institutions. This struggle for power reordered politics among urban elites in Senegal's colonial towns and presented new challenges for members of the métis elite who sought to reconcile the practice of republican citizenship with the reality of colonial rule.

Building Coalitions: The Second Generation

A new generation of métis rose to prominence. These young men attended schools in Saint Louis with the children of Muslim traders, grumets, and African rulers. They obtained degrees from the most prestigious law schools and medical schools in France. They witnessed the rise of the Third Republic and participated in the dominant debates of the era. They were also aware of the transformations taking place in Senegal. They witnessed the impact of conquest and the effect of the colonial economy on Saint Louis traders, market sellers in the towns, and farmers in the countryside. Métis experienced the changing dynamics of race relations in Senegal and the larger French Empire. Whereas class served as a primary marker of difference in the urban community of the nineteenth century, racial categories became more pronounced in the colonial society of the twentieth century. Colonial categories mattered in a new way for this generation.

By the end of the 1890s, the Devès and Carpot brothers took over as the leaders of political coalitions in the local assemblies. Gaspard Devès established his reputation as a defender of Senegalese interests and thus attracted individuals in commune politics whose ideologies aligned with his. His sons Justin, Hyacinthe, and François defined themselves in similar ways as members of the General Council and Municipal Council. The Devès family and their allies distinguished themselves by being willing to oppose the colonial administration and go against the metropolitan commercial lobby.[4]

Justin (b. 1858), Hyacinthe (b. 1859), and François (b. 1861) Devès began their education at the school run by the Ploërmel Brothers, then attended Lycée Michel Montaigne in Bordeaux. All three completed their law studies at the University of Bordeaux and returned to Senegal, having obtained the *licence en droit*. Justin married Marguerite Laplène, the daughter of his French business associate. Marguerite's father, Albert Laplène, began a business venture in Saint Louis and married up and into the Saint Louis elite. He married Adèle Dumont, the daughter of habitant Blaise Dumont, a former mayor of Saint Louis. Justin and Marguerite's only daughter, Elisabeth, was born in 1894 (fig. 5). In June 1889, Hyacinthe married Charlotte Crespin, strengthening the relationship between Gaspard Devès and his main ally, J. J. Crespin. Two sisters, Catherine and Constance, never married and did not play a public role in business or politics. They managed the family business following the death of their brothers and continued to contest the administration's denial of the family's claim to the island of Arguin. They also became godmothers to children of African Catholics in Saint Louis.[5]

In the late 1890s, Gaspard Devès retired to Bordeaux and left his sons to run the family's affairs in Senegal. Justin Devès worked for the family firm and pursued his own entrepreneurial interests, which included a questionable scheme—to recruit laborers from Senegal for construction of the railroad in Belgian Congo—devised by Devès and his father-in-law, Albert Laplène. Justin won election to the General Council in the mid-1880s. Hyacinthe managed the family's business affairs in the peanut basin in Cayor and Baol. In 1888, he won election to the General Council from Rufisque, strengthening his family's coalition with voters from the second arrondissement. François acted as the family's representative in Mauritania and joined the assembly in the 1890s. Hyacinthe earned a reputation for being a masterful and passionate orator in the General Council, where he remained a member until his death in 1910. Justin served as mayor of Saint Louis and ran the family's coalition in commune politics until his death in 1916. François managed the family's affairs and remained on the General Council until his death in 1919.[6]

In the 1890s, the Devès family experienced a series of personal, financial, and political crises. They came under more intense scrutiny from the administration for their anti-French activities in the protectorate. In 1894, the administration launched an investigation of Justin and François's business practices. In 1895, Justin and Gaspard Devès declared bankruptcy. This dealt a significant blow to Gaspard, once the administrator of the Bank of Senegal. In addition, a personal dispute between Gaspard Devès and J. J. Crespin caused a rupture in their political alliance.[7]

After Gaspard Devès retired in Bordeaux, his sons became the recognized leaders of the family business. Their primary commercial interests were in Mauritania, an area still under nominal French control. François, Justin, and their Saint Louis associates (fig. 8) maintained their relations with the Trarza and the Peul of Fouta Toro. Since the 1860s, the Devès network of commercial agents operated in the Senegal River posts and in the peanut basin.[8] In the early 1900s, the Devès served as intermediaries for French prospectors seeking concessions for gold mining in French Sudan and worked with European import firms to obtain supplies of guinées. Justin Devès sought to exploit the salt mines of the island of Arguin and the fish stocks off the coast, despite the administration's denial that the Trarza emir had sold the land to the Devès.[9]

The extensive investments of the Devès and their intricate network of kin, clients, employees, and business associates afforded it greater independence in political affairs than other families in the Saint Louis community. The Devès advocated for originaire rights. Lawyer and advocate of workers' rights Louis Huchard of Gorée joined the Devès coalition in the General Council. Hyacinthe Devès, Huchard, and Devès ally Leopold Angrand formed a coalition in the second arrondissement that countered French settlers and commercial interests and gained the support of Wolof and Lebu voters in Dakar and Rufisque. Hyacinthe championed reforms to guarantee originaires equal access in the General Council and defended originaires, African workers, and farmers at the French court in Dakar.[10]

Justin Devès led the family's coalition in Saint Louis. He relied on support from Guet Ndar, where his family had long established kin and client ties, to mobilize support for his electoral campaigns. Devès also mentored Galandou Diouf, an emergent originaire leader. Born in Saint Louis, Diouf attended Catholic school and worked as a clerk for the administration before establishing a trade house in the peanut basin. In the 1909 General Council elections, Devès included Galandou Diouf on his list of candidates. Diouf became the first African elected to the assembly since Bacre Waly Gueye and the first to represent the second arrondissement. Political relationships proved difficult to maintain, however. Prior to the 1913 General Council elections, Diouf wrote a letter to the editor of *Le Petit Sénégalais* that accused Devès of undermining his reelection to the assembly. Devès sued Diouf for libel, causing a rift in the political alliance.[11]

The Carpots are commonly cast as rivals to the Devès brothers in commune politics. At times the two groups opposed each other, but occasionally their interests were aligned. The Carpots' authority partly stemmed from their ability to trace their ancestry to an eighteenth-century Frenchman and Signare Suzanne Dobbs. The Carpot family's ties with the administration, their knowledge of French law, and their business interests provided a pathway for developing an important coalition in commune politics during the late 1890s and early 1900s. Theodore (1855–1921), Charles (1857–1905), and François Carpot (1865–1936) also attended the Ploërmel school. All three received scholarships to attend Lycée Michel Montaigne in Bordeaux. Theodore, a commercial representative and entrepreneur, entered commune politics in the 1880s. Charles attended medical school in France and later became the first Senegalese doctor at the Civil Hospital in Saint Louis. François received a *doctorat d'état* from the prestigious Paris law school. He worked in the prefecture of Corrèze in France for a few years before returning to Senegal to open a law practice. In the mid-1890s, he joined his brother Theodore on the General Council.[12]

Their father, Pierre Carpot, worked for the administration, and their relative Durand Valantin became Senegal's first representative to the National Assembly in 1848. Charles Carpot married Louis Descemet's daughter, Henriette.[13] Theodore married Georginie Pecarrère, whose family also traced its lineage to the eighteenth century and the métis of Gorée. François Carpot married Marguerite Teisseire, a descendant of the Bordeaux commercial house. Their marriages reaffirmed the Carpots' connection to key constituencies in the Saint Louis community, including Bordeaux commerce, the métis elite, the clergy, and the administration.

Portraying the Carpots as collaborators with the administration is too simplistic. The Carpots remained on good terms with the administration, but the officials in Dakar and Saint Louis were also suspicious of François Carpot's ability to mobilize the originaire electorate. The Carpots adjusted to the emergence of a new group of western-educated originaires by seeking to align their interests more closely with originaire concerns. François Carpot relied on Louis Descemet's network in the Senegal River valley and kin ties with the family of Malik Sy, an influential Tijani cleric, to guarantee support for his candidacy among Muslim voters in Saint Louis and Wolof and Lebu voters in Dakar and Rufisque.[14] He campaigned in Wolof and promised to address originaire concerns regarding their legal and political rights.

In the 1890s, politics in Saint Louis changed as métis assemblymen from the first arrondissement faced greater scrutiny. Competition from French shopkeepers and merchants of the second arrondissement and challenges from originaire candidates threatened to break the influence that the métis gained in the republican institutions in the 1880s. The local assemblies provided an arena for the métis to negotiate with French officials and challenge the legitimacy of certain policies and practices. Still the métis walked a fine line between cooperating with colonial authorities and remaining committed to republican ideals. The Devès, in particular, proved adept at using electoral politics to advance their interests and obstruct the hegemonic practices of the administration. In the 1890s, the métis had to navigate the structural ambiguities created by the growth of civil society in Saint Louis at the same time that colonial officials sought to consolidate power and authority over Senegal's countryside.

Colonial Rule and the Métis Community (1890–1902)

The final phase of French campaigns to suppress resistance among ruling elites in the Senegal River valley and the peanut basin affected urban life in Senegal's colonial capital. Officials in Saint Louis concentrated on consolidating French control over the protectorate and organizing a more effective bureaucracy. In the previous decade, the métis demonstrated their ability to complicate the establishment of French authority in the interior by using the electoral institutions to their advantage. In the 1890s, the series of governors and political affairs directors who arrived in Senegal viewed the assemblymen with suspicion and electoral politics as problematic for the realization of their objectives.

Despite the existence of democratic institutions, the administration possessed tools to exert control over commune politics. The governor, who supervised the electoral process, could interfere in elections by rescheduling the vote or invalidating the list of registered voters. He could also suspend the representatives.[15] In the 1880 Saint Louis municipal elections, the governor used this power, and then nullified the 1889 election and appointed his own representative. In the 1890s, the administration brought in independent inspectors from the colonial ministry in Paris to investigate electoral institutions for suspected mismanagement or corruption. Governors Henri de Lamothe and Jean Baptiste Chaudié used the office of inspector to launch official investigations of individuals or institutions that gained too much power or interfered with French objectives. Ironically, new reforms eased restrictions on government control of electoral institutions in metropolitan municipalities and departments while the administration intensified oversight of electoral politics in colonial Senegal.[16]

Candidates for public office could respond to the administration's actions by taking their grievances to the Conseil d'État in Paris.[17] For example, the métis could mobilize support among lobbyists or government officials in the metropolis to protest a decision or publicize antidemocratic practices. The independent press also served as a valuable tool. The Devès coalition often used all available options to protest French actions and thus became subject to surveillance by the administration.

In 1889, Governor Léon Clément-Thomas announced the removal of certain areas in Walo and Cayor from the direct administration of the first arrondissement. This declaration, called disannexation, placed these locations under protectorate authority, moving them beyond the jurisdiction of the General Council. Disannexation affected the territories surrounding Saint Louis that the assemblymen considered part of their sphere of influence. The new policy succeeded in reducing the General Council's budgeting authority in these areas of the interior and indicated a change in French attitudes toward the Saint Louis community.[18]

At the end of Clément-Thomas's term, an event involving the Devès family and the rulers of Futa Toro created even greater alarm among administrators about the influence of the Devès and the potential problems that individuals in the Saint Louis community could cause in the protectorate. In September 1890, the director of political affairs sent Abel Jeandet to Podor just as the French were completing what they termed "pacification" in Futa Toro. Shortly after his arrival, a newly demoted soldier murdered Jeandet. A hasty investigation by the administration found Lam Toro Sidikh, the former ruler of Toro, and two others guilty of conspiring with the assassin.[19] Members of the Saint Louis trading community, including Bacre Waly Gueye, Gaspard Devès, and Louis Descemet, had established relations in Podor and commercial interests in the region. Gaspard Devès and his supporters became involved in the incident following the public execution of the three alleged culprits at Podor. The French administrative district operated as an important base for the Devès operations in the upper Senegal, where they had an extensive client network. A summary execution that took place on French territory raised concerns among critics of the administration about human rights violations. That provided a rallying point for the Devès to regain support among the originaire electorate. The scale of Gaspard Devès's business and his extensive network in France afforded him the ability to challenge the execution. Doing so undoubtedly bolstered his reputation among his clients in Futa Toro.[20]

Devès and his allies criticized Clément-Thomas and the political affairs director for their handling of the investigation and the execution of the alleged perpetrators on French soil. They persuaded the interim governor and the head of the judiciary to launch an inquiry into the actions of the officials in Podor. Devès then rallied the support of Alexandre Issac, their ally in the senate, and Vallon, their newly elected representative in the

Chamber of Deputies. Both men publicized the event in France and put pressure on the ministry of colonies to respond to their demand for an inquiry.[21]

While the ministry eventually dismissed the issue, Gaspard Devès's involvement created a scandal for the administration. Senegal's judiciary included magistrates who served in the Antilles and expressed concern over human rights issues. In addition, the involvement of a senator from Guadeloupe concerned with human rights disrupted the administration's attempts to justify the execution. To show his resolve in dealing with those who opposed the administration, the new governor, Henri de Lamothe (1891–95), immediately acted against judicial officials who sided with the Devès family by transferring them out of Senegal and assigning them to other posts.[22]

De Lamothe arrived in Senegal in the interim between the assassination and Clément-Thomas's departure. The Jeandet assassination solidified de Lamothe's opinion that Senegal's electoral institutions had too much influence over the business of colonization and that it was imprudent to extend political rights to African subjects. Writing in the year following his departure from the colony, de Lamothe rationalized his decision to reduce the General Council's authority by arguing that creating further separation between the communes and the protectorate would contribute to progress in the interior and provide a way to avoid the "irritating debates and angry indiscretions" of the councilors.[23] The Jeandet incident raised the governor's awareness of the threat posed by the Devès family and made him more adamant about suppressing the power of a coalition he considered adversarial to French interests.

During his administration, de Lamothe concentrated on continuing Clément-Thomas's policies by separating town from country even further, limiting the authority of the electoral institutions, and reducing the influence of métis leaders in commune politics. He relied on Faidherbe's governing approach, which drew a line between citizens of the towns and subjects of the protectorate. Furthermore, de Lamothe maintained that the "former states of native Muslim and tiedos" under French control should be governed by their own customs and not by French law.[24] In the 1890s, the administration's attitude toward the Saint Louis community turned from one of cooperation to greater hostility and outright confrontation. As a result, the Saint Louis community found themselves on the defense and their influence in political affairs significantly diminished.

One of the governor's first steps in the wake of the Jeandet assassination involved eliminating the dominance of the Devès family. Devès and his allies gained control of the local assemblies, and their candidate won election to the Chamber of Deputies. On 14 February 1891, de Lamothe issued an administrative order calling for the municipal council to be dissolved and for J. J. Crespin to be removed from the mayor's office. The governor appointed Jules Couchard, a petit colon and an old friend of Clément-Thomas, to replace Crespin. Couchard and his allies won the majority of seats on the municipal council in the June 1891 election despite protests from the African electorate.[25] Crespin protested the results at the Conseil d'État in Paris claiming irregularities in the voting process. Although the administrative council sided with Crespin and nullified the election, Couchard won the next election, undoubtedly with the administration's help.

The second major decision that affected the métis elite concerned de Lamothe's decree limiting the budgetary authority of the General Council. A conflict with council members over approval of funds to reopen the School for the Sons of Chiefs and Interpreters convinced the governor to further Clément-Thomas's earlier efforts to strengthen the administration's ability to operate freely in matters relating to the protectorate. On 13 December 1892, de Lamothe announced the creation of a separate budget for the protectorate that came under the direct authority of the governor.[26] This measure restricted the General Council to approving only expenses involving those areas under direct rule, with no consultative role in crafting the budget for the colony.[27] By eliminating the input of the General Council from decisions regarding a major portion of the colonial budget, this decree dealt a striking blow to the councilors, who considered budgetary authority their most important responsibility.

In addition to these efforts, de Lamothe intensified the administration's scrutiny of the Devès family and its business interests in Senegal. In March 1894, colonial inspectors implicated Justin Devès in an official investigation of alleged abuses of African workers in the Belgian Congo labor recruitment scheme. In August of the same year, that administration sued François Devès for fraud involving customs duties on a shipment of goods. Senator Alexandre Issac, a family friend, represented François and succeeded in winning his acquittal on all charges. In a letter to Gaspard Devès, Issac wrote that upon hearing the verdict, the Saint Louis courtroom erupted in loud applause.[28]

De Lamothe's successor, Jean-Baptiste Chaudié (1895–1902), continued the administration's assault on the Devès family by scrutinizing the practices of the Bank of Senegal. After learning of generous loans made to Gaspard and Justin Devès, Governor Chaudié called for an inspector from the colonial ministry in Paris to investigate the bank's operations. The inspector found habitant Charles Molinet, the bank's director, guilty of mismanaging funds and abusing power.[29] According to the investigation's report, Molinet authorized credit valued at 322,000 francs to Gaspard and Justin knowing that Gaspard had recently declared bankruptcy, thereby compromising the bank's liquidity.[30] In addition, the inspector found that Molinet and his treasurer, Jean Duchesne, borrowed money from the bank under family members' signatures to avoid repayment. Molinet accepted bank notes underwritten by his wife and his brother-in-law to construct homes in Saint Louis. He later replaced their signatures with that of his daughter, whom the inspector described as "a widow without resources." In light of the inspector's report, the governor forced Molinet to resign and leave Senegal in disgrace.[31] Chaudié appointed a bureaucrat from the ministry in Paris to replace Molinet and required all civil servants and employees in his administration who took loans from the bank to repay their debts immediately. In 1901, the colonial ministry closed the bank.

The Bank of Senegal was important to the métis because it provided access to capital. Most of its clients were métis men and women, Muslim traders, and a few members of the French merchant community. In the 1880s and 1890s, the bank afforded the métis the ability to buy property and finance their business ventures when they had little access to capital in France. Louis Descemet and Omer Teisseire, for example, borrowed money from the bank for their trade house. Frederic Michas and Charles Carpot depended on the bank to finance their electrical lighting company.[32] The bank helped the métis to finance the construction of a building to house the General Council. Although the investigation was aimed at the Devès family, the bank's collapse and the scandal affected the métis. The bank helped to sustain the financial viability of the métis elite despite the losses they suffered during the economic crisis of the 1850s. The closing of the bank dealt a severe blow to their economic standing in the colony.

Commune politics reflected the tensions affecting the Saint Louis community. Couchard's victory in the municipal council elections in the capital raised concerns about the strength of the Devès coalition and the role of

Bordeaux commerce in commune politics. Although not tied to the metropolitan corporations, Couchard enjoyed the backing of the administration. His candidates gained a majority in the General Council. In the 1893 legislative election, Gaspard Devès decided to support his former rival, Gasconi, instead of their longtime ally, J. J. Crespin, thereby facilitating Couchard's election as deputy.[33] Couchard became the first French man from Dakar to succeed in commune politics without long-standing ties to the Saint Louis community. His close relationship to the governor indicated a greater involvement by the administration in commune politics than had occurred before. To the métis, these developments surely appeared as an encroachment on the independence of their institutions.

In 1894, Jean Jacques Crespin won the Saint Louis Municipal Council elections but died less than a year later. Couchard and his supporters held the majority of seats on the General Council, where French settlers and agents of metropolitan commerce of the second arrondissement became rivals of the métis. Since the 1870s, race had little to do with the formation of political coalitions. In the mid-1890s, race and class consciousness began to inform political coalitions in new ways. Theodore and François Carpot joined the Devès coalition on the General Council. Louis Huchard and Leopold Angrand joined the Devès-Carpot alliance, thus strengthening the group's support among originaire voters from the second arrondissement. Finally, Louis Descemet joined the new coalition, breaking from his affiliation with the administration and metropolitan merchants. On 3 May 1896, the Devès-Carpot-Descemet coalition defeated Couchard in the municipal council elections. The Devès-Carpot coalition won the majority of seats on the town council, and Louis Descemet became mayor of Saint Louis.[34]

The revival of an independent press, spearheaded by the métis in Saint Louis and their allies in Gorée, Dakar, and Rufisque, revived the debate over the role of the urban community in colonial affairs. Appearing in 1896, *L'Afrique Occidentale* criticized the administration and spoke out against the unjust practices of monopoly commerce.[35] Louis Huchard became the major contributor to the paper. He was a lawyer and assemblyman who fought for the rights of African farmers and traders in the peanut basin, and his editorials reflected a growing concern with the expansion of cash crop agriculture and the exploitation of farmers. The newspaper criticized the protectorate administration created by Clément-Thomas and de Lamothe and spoke out against Couchard and the commercial interests he represented.[36]

In addition to these issues, *L'Afrique Occidentale* emphasized the exploitation of workers by French commercial firms and cast its critique of metropolitan capitalists in radical terms. The editors argued that "the colonies are farms of which the populations are without a doubt cattle" and called for the paper's readers to oppose "the transformation of our soil into a farm and its people into cattle."[37] The authors editorialized on racism against *gens du couleur* throughout the empire. One editorial speculated that racial prejudice motivated a decision to remove General Alfred Dodds from command in Indochina.[38] The editorials in the journal reflect doubt among its editors of France's commitment to the idea of assimilation and the universal principles that France espoused in its nineteenth-century imperial projects. As occurred for people of color in other regions of the French Empire, upward mobility for the métis of Senegal seemed less stable at the turn of the century than it had a generation earlier.

In fall 1897, André Lebon, the minister of colonies, visited Senegal. His visit to Saint Louis encouraged youth of the capital to demonstrate. In October 1897, Lebon arrived in Saint Louis for the inauguration of the Faidherbe Bridge. The impressive steel bridge, a symbol of French technological achievement, linked the island to the mainland. A journalist from *Le Temps*, the Parisian daily covering Lebon's visit, remained in the town and reported on the General Council elections taking place on 7 November 1897. The reporter wrote that, on the eve of the elections, a crowd of "blacks led by some *jeunes gens du pays* [métis]" ran through the town manifesting their anger at the regime and shouting, *"A l'eau les Blancs! A bas les Français! Nous sommes les maitres! A nous le Sénégal!»*[39]

The protest marked a turning point in Senegal's political history, in which the saying «Senegal for the Senegalese» became an anticolonial slogan in a public demonstration by the town's youth. The demonstration may have encouraged Africans in the communes to form the Jeunes Sénégalais, the organization that supported originaire candidates. The event signaled a transition from urban politics controlled by the Saint Louis elite who came of age in the era of conquest to politics by a new generation of western-educated youth. In choosing to sack the house of Bacre Waly Gueye, the oldest assemblyman, the Saint Louis youth expressed their disappointment with the status quo.[40] The demonstration must have also served as a wake-up call for the métis, who had to adopt a new strategy in order to maintain their influence in the electoral arena.

Theodore and François Carpot responded to the changing political momentum by bringing together the main interest groups in the communes and appealing directly to the growing concerns of originaires. Their good standing with the administration, the Church, and metropolitan merchants assured them of support from the traditional representatives of French authority. François Carpot's background in law made him a particularly attractive candidate for the deputy position. In 1898, he ran for the office but lost by a small margin to Hector d'Agoult, the candidate of the metropolitan commercial lobby. In 1902, Carpot ran again with the support of both Louis Descemet's and Gaspard Devès's networks. This time he based his campaign on appealing to the interests of Muslim traders and grumets in the Saint Louis community as well as Lebou voters in Rufisque and Dakar. Carpot gave speeches in Wolof. He called himself an *enfant du pays* and promised to defend the rights of local people and fight for Senegal's place in the federation. Louis Descemet's connection to Tijani cleric Malik Sy, who had support among Muslim traders in Saint Louis and the Lebu of Dakar, Rufisque, and Gorée, strengthened Carpot's appeal among the originaire electorate.[41] On 27 April 1902, François Carpot became Senegal's representative in Paris. The campaign produced the highest voter turnout of any legislative election. In the fall elections, Theodore Carpot's list gained the majority of seats on the General Council, and he became the president of the assembly.

In the 1890s, the métis faced new assaults from the administration. The Devès family experienced greater scrutiny by administrative officials but proved adept at being able to use their networks and the electoral institutions to their advantage. Knowledge of French legal and political systems gave métis candidates the advantage of being able to protest administrative interference, but colonial officials managed to constrict métis power by limiting the authority of the electoral institutions. The emergence of western-educated African town residents shifted the balance of power in commune elections at the end of the century. François and Theodore Carpot as well as Justin, Hyacinthe, and François Devès and others among the métis elite had to confront new pressures from officials in Dakar, French interests in the second arrondissement, and the originaire electorate.

The Struggle over Electoral Politics (1902–20)

The opening of the twentieth century witnessed Saint Louis's decline as the economic, administrative, and cultural center of French rule in West Africa.

Modern facilities at Rufisque and Dakar replaced the Saint Louis port. Traders shifted their operations to the peanut basin, but also faced the contraction of the middleman trade as French commercial houses relied on their employees and Lebanese and Syrian immigrants to facilitate the sale of retail goods and the purchase of exports from farmers in the interior. Saint Louis remained the capital of Senegal, but the transfer of the federation's capital to Dakar removed Saint Louis even further from the center of power. In addition, the governor general's office enacted a series of reforms that diminished the role that electoral institutions played in making decisions regarding political, economic, and social matters for commune residents and the colony.

In 1895, the ministry of colonies established a federal system of administration for French West Africa, grouping Senegal, Soudan, Guinea, and Ivory Coast under the administration of a governor general. In 1902, the colonial ministry appointed Ernest Roume governor general. Two years later, the ministry moved its office from Saint Louis to Dakar. The move satisfied metropolitan merchants who held warehouses in Dakar and Rufisque. It also encouraged the growth of petit colons—a small class of metropolitan shopkeepers, company agents, and professionals.[42] Most French settlers who came to Dakar worked for the government general.

An experienced administrator and engineer by training, Roume considered the implementation of *mise en valeur,* or rational economic development, as his first priority. He set about implementing measures to centralize the colonial bureaucracy. He enforced secularization of educational and health services in response to metropolitan legislation that sought to eliminate the Church's role in public services. Roume ordered religious instructors from the Brothers of Ploërmel and the Sisters of Saint Joseph de Cluny to close their schools and leave the colony. He then created a new system of secular schools for the entire federation, eliminating the monopoly that métis families held on access to French schooling in Senegal and higher education in France.[43]

The Saint Louis community confronted Roume's assault on the political rights of urban residents. On 18 October 1904, the colonial ministry approved Roume's proposal to create a general budget for French West Africa that would come from the revenues of the five colonies in the federation. The budget law gave the governor general absolute authority to collect Senegal's customs duties expressly for the federal administration. This gave him the financial resources needed to run the new territory. For the métis, this measure meant the final erosion of their primary responsibility: authority over key parts of the colonial budget and the allocation of Senegal's customs duties. Roume's restructuring of the budget effectively achieved Clément-Thomas's and de Lamothe's objective to eliminate the General Council's influence in matters pertaining to the colony's financial management.[44]

In addition to budgetary reforms, French officials initiated new proposals that called for replacing the General Council with a much less powerful body. Governor Camille Guy (1902–1906) complained that assemblymen from Saint Louis sought to undermine representatives of French commercial interests from the second arrondissement. In his 1903 report to the governor general just before the General Council's annual session opened, Guy referred to the "antagonistic" relationships among the "mulatto" councilors from Saint Louis who "resolutely and surely sacrificed the interests of Dakar and Rufisque, of Sine Saloum and Casamance, for the interests of their voters and even their personal preoccupations."[45]

According to Guy, the Saint Louis councilors tampered with plans to develop peanut culture as the only export commodity from Senegal. Based in large part on the suggestions of leading metropolitan commercial firms headquartered in Dakar and Rufisque, Guy proposed suppressing the General Council and replacing it with a "simple consultative commission." He proposed creating a deliberative assembly made up of seven members chosen by universal suffrage with the remaining twenty appointed by the governor of Senegal. Roume's successors continued to argue for this plan despite the colonial minister's reluctance to eliminate such a venerable institution as the General Council. Nevertheless, Saint Louis and Dakar maintained that the General Council served a minority population of privileged town residents, whereas a less powerful, hybrid assembly would better represent "indigenous" interests and facilitate the objectives of French merchants and the administration.[46]

The most important issue that shaped the struggle between commune residents and French officials concerned the administration's attempts to deny originaires full legal and political rights. Officials in Saint Louis and Dakar concluded that France acted prematurely in extending voting rights to originaires. Guy turned to the colonial courts to challenge the legality of the 1830 decree, which granted all adult male town residents the right to vote in local elections.[47] The administration's attack on originaire rights threatened the status of African inhabitants of Saint Louis and Gorée, who had a long history of attachment to France as well as Wolof and Lebu of Dakar and Rufisque. In addition, denying originaire claims to citizenship threatened commune residents who worked as traders, clerks, interpreters, and employees of the colonial administration in the districts and trade centers of the interior.

The governor general complicated matters by seeking to restrict voting rights in the colony to Europeans and assimilated Africans in the towns. Roume maintained that allowing African town residents to hold political rights only resulted in "a mass of indigènes not knowing how to read or write French, often natives of Sierra Leone and the Gambia [British territories], becoming voters in Senegal."[48] Ten years earlier, Henri de Lamothe had suggested that French legislators should make a tabula rasa of rights that were acquired by indigènes in the colonies and place conditions on those in the towns who had already obtained voting privileges. By the first decade of the twentieth century, the idea that the residents of the colonies (regardless of race) should be afforded access to the same political institutions as citizens of the republic seemed untenable to officials in Dakar and Saint Louis. Instead, colonial authorities sought to reduce the number of voters in the communes to a narrow group of metropolitan Frenchmen and individuals who conformed to French cultural ideals.

In October 1904, the colonial ministry approved Roume's budget proposal. The budget decree eliminated the General Council's ability to make decisions regarding Senegal's customs duties and gave sole discretion over Senegal's revenues to the governor general. The November 1904 session turned into a contentious debate between the governor and the General Council over the budget decree. The assembly initially refused to vote on the budget proposed by the administration even though the governor general asserted that the budget would be passed in his private council regardless of their decision. Theodore Carpot, president of the assembly, expressed the council's objections to the governor and threatened to bring the issue before the Conseil d'Etat.[49] François Carpot used his leverage as Senegal's representative in Paris to voice his opposition to the minister of colonies. Hyacinthe and François Devès and Jules Couchard, their former opponent, joined in the protest against the new budget decree.[50] Although the issue provoked passionate debate within the assembly, the councilors reached a compromise in order to maintain good relations with French officials. The meeting ended, according to Guy, "without incident for the administration."[51]

In the General Council session of the following year, the Devès family and their allies focused on the administration's use of force to suppress African resistance in the interior. Violent attacks against African rulers and clerics disrupted commerce and created conflict with clients and agents with whom they had long-standing business and personal ties. Justin and François Devès expressed concern over the effect that French military actions had on their business in Mauritania.[52]

In the May 1905 General Council session, Hyacinthe Devès introduced a motion to denounce the government for its policies of pacification in Mauritania. The motion followed a debate between the assemblymen and the lieutenant governor of Senegal over a vote to express sympathy to the widow of Lieutenant Xavier Coppolani. Considered the architect of conquest in Mauritania, Coppolani suffered a fatal gunshot wound when he led a march into the northern territory of Adrar to suppress the last bastion of resistance by Shaykh Ma al-Aynayn and his supporters. Reminiscent of the controversy over the administration's characterization of Samba Laobe's death in Cayor twenty years earlier, Georges Crespin argued that Coppolani's death must be characterized as a casualty of war rather than an assassination as the administration termed it.[53]

Hyacinthe Devès supported Crespin's assessment. He went further in his criticism of the administration's use of force, saying, "Our duty is to show that a death so resounding as that of M. Coppolani is the sad fruit of a politics which has already accumulated many ruins." He continued:

> Sentimentalism is not our business. We are here to control; to watch that the acts of the Administration do not compromise the vital interests of the colony. When the death of a high civil servant is the consequence of a politics that has created depression of business in Saint Louis, brought the closing of shops in Guet Ndar, and suppressed the livelihood of numerous men, one is obliged to ask of oneself if the value of an event such as that should not concern the General Council and if on this occasion the representatives of the colony have not the duty to make their advice heard. [*Exclamations from many benches.*]

Hyacinthe Devès questioned the reasons why the councilors should express grief over the loss of Coppolani, saying, "M. Coppolani is not one of our dead. . . . What do you [officials] reserve for the poor Tokolors of Fouta, for indigenous gum harvesters who are dead over there and for whom no one says a word?" Devès noted that France claims "peaceful penetration" in Senegal and Morocco, yet in his estimation, colonial conquest in Senegal resulted in "the same significant and troubling results of battles and explosions" that occurred during the French wars with Prussia.[54] Devès and Crespin considered Coppolani's incursions into Mauritania as a continuation of policies that relied solely on military force to accomplish French objectives—policies that, in their view, did not improve African and French relations but rather had a detrimental effect on the lives of traders and producers in the countryside as well as middlemen, shopkeepers, and everyday inhabitants of Senegal's colonial capital.

In response to the changing political climate, the Devès family relied again on their reputation as a group willing to oppose the administration and defend Senegalese interests to defeat their rivals in commune elections. Hyacinthe and their Gorée lawyer, Louis Huchard, argued cases involving African defendants in customary courts. Justin Devès joined Saint Louis trader Hamet Gueye, who held a meeting at his house to organize the African electorate to protest the administration's attack on their political rights. In July 1906, Justin Devès presented the governor with a petition of two thousand voters that denounced Roume's attack on originaire voting rights and his plans to eliminate the General Council. The petitioners declared that the creation of a Colonial Council ignored the voting privileges of *indigènes citoyens français* and would eventually lead to the abolition of their legal rights.[55] Guy responded to this act by submitting a similar petition to Roume in support of the new assembly. Roume claimed to have support of "the principal representatives of the colony," including Theodore Carpot, Jules Couchard, Louis Descemet, and Leopold Angrand. Hyacinthe Devès, Georges Crespin, and Louis Huchard declared their "hostility" to the project, while Louis Guillabert remained neutral.[56]

The administration's attack on the political rights of originaires marked a reversal from France's recognition of Saint Louis and Gorée residents' loyalty since the eighteenth century. It also marked a departure from the idea of assimilation in the nineteenth century that gave African town residents special status in French law. Muslim traders and notables as well as grumets had long established a consciousness of citizenship. In the early 1900s, Saint Louis notables began organizing to assert their legal rights. Saint Louis traders Hamet Gueye and Papa Mar Diop organized African voters and held meetings with François Carpot and Justin Devès to pressure métis assemblymen to address the attack on originaire rights. Some métis supported the education of young originaire men in French schools and supported their careers in trade or the colonial bureaucracy.

In 1910, a group of young men formed a voluntary association called the Aurora of Saint Louis. It included western-educated town residents who worked as clerks, teachers, and interpreters. The Aurora brought together students who developed interest in music, plays, philosophy, and sports, but they also discussed the problem of British rule in South Africa, the political careers of blacks in the French Antilles, and the work of black American Booker T. Washington. In 1912, the men of the Aurora formed the Jeunes Sénégalais (Young Senegalese), an organization founded to discuss politics and develop strategy for breaking the métis monopoly in the local assemblies and asserting originaire rights. The Jeunes Sénégalais argued for better pay for originaire civil servants and complained about poor schools, the lack of jobs for commune residents, and limited access to higher education.[57]

The Jeunes Sénégalais also followed the careers of Galandou Diouf and Mody Mbaye, who emerged as influential figures in commune politics. Born in Saint Louis, both men attended the secondary school run by the Brothers of Ploërmel. Galandou Diouf worked in the postal service before establishing himself in trade and agriculture in the region outside of Rufisque. An employee of the administration in Baol, Mbaye became the subject of numerous confrontations with French officials over his role as an official letter writer for Africans in the district. Diouf followed the political careers of Justin Devès and François Carpot. He became Carpot's representative among Lebou voters in Rufisque and with Africans in neighboring regions of the interior. Louis Huchard served as Mody Mbaye's lawyer in his disputes with the administration. Mbaye formed a network among rural inhabitants of Baol that collected information exposing abuses of power by commandants. He wrote letters of complaint to the administration on behalf of his clients in the protectorate.[58]

By 1906, the métis confronted the reality of the administration's attempt to reduce the authority of the General Council and restrict the political influence of the Saint Louis community. While sympathetic to the métis, the administration began to fear the radicalization of originaires from Saint Louis and their influence over rural farmers in the peanut basin. Métis responses to the colonial attack on the political rights of town residents reveal their ambiguity over maintaining a monopoly over political power and responding to the exclusion of originaires. The métis had personal and economic interests in perpetuating the colonial system, but they also had a vigorous critique of how French rule should operate. Many had personal and familial ties to African residents of the town, but they also had close relations with agents of metropolitan commerce and French officials.

In order to maintain political power, métis assemblymen included more African town residents in their electoral campaigns. In the 1904 campaign for the Saint Louis Municipal Council, Louis Descemet recruited originaire Pierre Chimère for his list of candidates. Justin Devès appealed directly to his supporters in the fishing villages of Guet Ndar. On 4 July, Justin Devès's list of eight black, six métis, and six European candidates won the Saint Louis municipal elections. Devès defeated the mayor, Louis Descemet, by mobilizing voters in the fishing villages and supporting more originaire candidates than Descemet. Devès lost the May 1908 municipal council elections, but protested the decision at the Conseil d'État in Paris. The Conseil d'État nullified the election results, finding fault with the decision by Senegal's judiciary that unfairly struck the majority of Africans from the list of registered voters. The Devès list won when new elections were held on 4 July 1909.[59]

Justin Devès's electoral victory generated new surveillance from the administration. Officials in Saint Louis accused Devès of publically defying their authority and considered him a threat to the colonial system in his role as mayor. The political affairs office monitored Devès's activities because they feared he would use his position to influence African rulers in the protectorate to resist French authority. The inspector characterized Devès as a dictatorial administrator who used the mayor's office to his advantage by implementing his own policies. In one case, Governor Peuvergne claimed that Devès sought to desegregate a school by arguing that financial constraints required closing the Saint Louis school reserved for children of Europeans and *assimilés*. The governor accused Devès of seeking to implement "his personal doctrine in matters of democratic equality by forcing young white girls to attend school with *indigènes*."[60] Adding insult to injury, Devès refused to accompany the governor to the opening meeting of the General Council in May 1910. According to Peuvergne, this act constituted an expression of Justin Devès's "desire to completely break relations with the government of the colony."[61]

Saint Louis dealt with the threat Devès appeared to present to the colonial order by questioning his management of the town's affairs. Peuvergne called in an inspector from the governor general's office in Dakar to investigate Devès's management of the municipality. The inspector found that Devès had created unnecessary jobs with inordinate salaries for friends and relatives. The report also accused the mayor of mismanaging funds for the roads and public works department in the commune. Peuvergne corroborated the inspector's findings with reports from his officers in the *cercles* of Dagana, Louga, Thies, and Podor that suggested that Devès offered gifts to local rulers for whom he promised to reinstate slavery and had even claimed he possessed powers superior to that of the governor and governor general.[62] This led Peuvergne to conclude that "Devès always makes himself known by an attitude of haughtiness and gross hostility against the administration." The governor concluded that Justin Devès "considers himself invested with a new force permitting him to enter most energetically in conflict with the local administration." On 15 July 1910, the governor announced Devès's suspension as mayor and ordered the dissolution of the municipal council. Devès protested his dismissal and the council's dissolution at the Conseil d'État, but lost the case.[63]

While allegations against Devès may have been partially true or not at all, the incident revealed the degree to which the administration felt threatened by the assemblymen in Saint Louis and the power they held over clients in the interior. Devès and his allies continued to act in opposition to the administration. In 1910, Hyacinthe Devès died, leaving a void in the General Council and in the Devès coalition of the second arrondissement. In the 1910 General Council elections, Devès included Galandou Diouf on his list of candidates from the second arrondissement. Diouf won the election, becoming the first originaire elected from Rufisque.[64] A year later, Justin Devès won reelection as mayor of Saint Louis by popular vote. In 1913, he defeated Theodore Carpot, becoming president of the General Council, but the same election witnessed a rupture in his relationship with Galandou Diouf. French mobilization for the war effort distracted officials in Saint Louis and Dakar from their plans to restrict originaire voting rights and eliminate the General Council.

In 1914, Blaise Diagne returned to Senegal from Paris to level a challenge against the métis in the legislative election. He presented the greatest challenge to both Carpot and the Devès candidate, Henri Heimburger. Born in Gorée to a Catholic family with ties to the Portuguese senhoras of Joal on the petit côte, Diagne attended Catholic primary schools and the secular lycée in Saint Louis before making a name for himself as a customs officer in Réunion and French Guiana (South America).[65] Diagne had a close relationship with the Saint Louis elite. He referred to his mentor, Adolphe Crespin, as Oncle Adolphe. Diagne's experience in France and his career as a customs officer bolstered his viability as a candidate. The Young Senegalese supported Diagne's candidacy, considering him the first Wolof-speaking originaire who could successfully challenge métis dominance in commune politics. On 9 May 1914, after the second round of elections, Blaise Diagne won election to the French National Assembly.[66]

His victory proved a signal achievement for the originaires who broke the métis monopoly of electoral politics. Since 1906, Muslim and black Catholics of Saint Louis had gained representation on the local assemblies, but Diagne's victory broke the color barrier in French national policies, giving African town residents a representative in Paris. Most notably, Diagne's position in the Chamber of Deputies occurred at a key moment in French history. France turned to Senegal's representative in Paris to assist in mobilizing reluctant troops from French West Africa to serve as infantrymen. Blaise Diagne's most infamous act as Senegal's deputy involved gaining consensus in the National Assembly for passing legislation to confirm the legal status of originaires as French citizens rather than as subjects of protectorate rule. In return, Diagne recruited African soldiers to support the French war effort.[67]

Diagne's victory reordered urban politics in Senegal, concentrating power in the electoral institutions among African town residents. Closing Senegal's General Council, however, had a profound effect on disrupting the power of commune residents in colonial affairs. When World War I came to a close, Dakar focused attention on eliminating the General Council and creating a new consultative assembly. Governor General Martial Merlin served as political affairs director under Henri de Lamothe and was aware of the influence that traders and assemblymen from Saint Louis held over chiefs, clerics, and farmers in the interior. In one of his first acts as governor general, Merlin presented the colonial ministry with Roume and Guy's proposal for the creation of a new assembly in Senegal modeled after the Colonial Council of French Indochina. On 4 December 1920, the ministry decreed the creation of the Colonial Council, and the governor general announced plans to dissolve Senegal's General Council.[68]

The new assembly was composed of forty-four members representing the towns and the protectorate. Voters in the Four Communes elected eighteen representatives to the body. The *chefs du canton* and *chefs du province* of the interior chose representatives to fill the remaining twenty-six seats. The reorganization included representation from the rural regions, but it also worked to the advantage of colonial officials, who could pressure appointed chiefs to follow the administration's orders in key decisions before the assembly.[69] The first meeting of the Colonial Council reflected the makeup of the new assembly (fig. 9).

While the Colonial Council seemed like a republican institution, it was not quite the same. The Colonial Council held none of the budgetary authority that the General Council coveted, and while commune residents continued to advise the administration in their capacity as assemblymen, the institution no longer served as the main political field for the Saint Louis community. A hybrid institution, the assembly reflected Dakar's idea of a republican empire that created a sharp distinction between town and country. For Dakar, electoral politics could only be entrusted to a small group of Africans who achieved a certain level of "civilization" while the majority of Senegalese should be governed through "traditional" structures appropriate for their level of development. Originaires of Senegal's communes achieved formal recognition as French citizens and limited political representation, but colonial officials deemed the republican institutions that afforded town residents budgetary authority and influence in policy untenable in the twentieth century.

After 1920, the métis population lost their dominant role in urban politics. Some individuals left Senegal for France. François Carpot, for example, spent the rest of his life in Paris. Some integrated into metropolitan society, leaving little trace of their Senegalese past. Others remained in Senegal and continued to participate in politics. In June 1916, Justin Devès died, leaving his brother François to serve as the last of his family's representatives in the local assemblies. He died in 1919. One of his last acts was to accept money from his Belgian business partner to host a reception honoring Senegalese soldiers returning home from the Great War.[70] Louis Guillabert succeeded Justin Devès as president of the General Council. His officers on the council included vice president Pierre Chimère and secretaries Jhon Ka and Ambroise Mendy.[71]

Much is made of the rivalry between political factions and the internal disputes that gave way to Blaise Diagne's victory over François Carpot, and yet social and cultural ties among the urban elite mitigated these conflicts.

Louis Guillabert joined Diagne's coalition in commune politics. In 1916, Diagne wrote a letter to Guillabert following the passage of the Diagne laws in the Paris legislature that confirmed French citizenship for commune residents. In the letter, Diagne called upon Guillabert to encourage "blacks, mulattos, and Europeans" to work together to achieve their common objectives after the war.[72] Guillabert occupied an important role symbolically and politically. He provided continuity for the new generation of originaires in commune politics and also served as a reminder of the historic role that métis families played in shaping Senegal's democratic institutions.

On 11 October 1921, Guillabert, as president of the newly constituted Colonial Council, gave a speech honoring the visit of Minister of Colonies Albert Sarraut. He referred to the long tradition of republicanism in Senegal and called on the administration to make more efforts to extend democratic rights and privileges to all inhabitants of the colony.

> In this forum as before, mister minister, you will find men entirely devoted to the mother country having profound attachments in the colony. Some are of pure race of this country while others are their brothers in race, sons of the first Frenchmen who planted the venerable flag here.... Several Europeans of democratic sentiments have come to join these men who think that freedom can even spread to West Africa and who generously defend without other motives and sometimes against their personal interests, the democracy of this country.... How can one apply a policy of association and uplift if at each step that he takes the *indigène* finds himself lowered four ranks under the pretext that he is Senegalese?[73]

By 1920, the economic, social, and political landscape in Senegal had changed significantly. The métis were products of a nineteenth-century vision of French interaction in Senegal. In the French Empire of the early twentieth century, the métis of Senegal served as a reminder of the universal ideals espoused by the Third Republic and its unintended consequences for the development of French colonial rule in West Africa.

Conclusion

The métis strongly claimed the same rights for Senegal as for the French people from the metropolis in the intellectual, moral, and political fields. In the General Council of Senegal, the métis families—Descemet, Guillabert, Carpot, Devès, and others—expressed themselves according to the framework of that time, i.e., a French one in favor of assimilation. This claim was not appreciated by the colonial administration.

—*Christian Valantin, vice president, Senegal National Assembly*

Justin Devès died on 22 June 1916. Two months later, a delegation representing all of the town's neighborhoods (Nord, Sud, Guet Ndar, Ndar-Toute, and Sor) presented a proposal to Saint Louis's municipal council that called for establishing a monument to honor him. They called it "an act of recognition that we devote to the memory of our deceased mayor." Devès's deputy mayor, Pierre Chimère, concluded that no matter what one thought of Devès, "he was a mayor who did a lot of good for the indigènes." The municipal assembly agreed that the front of the monument should read, "The indigène acknowledges." The council voted unanimously to erect a statue and create a public square for Devès. The only other public squares in the town included one at the governor's palace in honor of Faidherbe and another facing the train station that honored the doctors who died caring for the ill during the yellow fever epidemic of 1878. The council meeting adjourned with the new mayor agreeing to present the idea to the administration and to begin collecting donations.[1]

Today, no public square or monument dedicated to Justin Devès exists in Saint Louis. A street sign in Guet Ndar bears his name as a reminder of the coastal fishing village's long-standing support for the Devès family and evoking the connection between the mayor and his mother's family home. It is unclear why the memorial never materialized. Perhaps the town council failed to get financial backing, or French authorities, preoccupied with the war effort, simply ignored the request. By 1916, the administration had succeeded in discrediting the Devès family. Questionable business practices and scandals over Justin Devès's administration of municipal government further eroded the family's position among the wealthy and powerful in the urban community. These factors may explain the erasure of the Devès family from popular narratives of modern nationalism in Senegal. Michel-Rolf Trouillot writes that concrete evidence of a historical moment provides a "materiality of the socio-historical process" that sets the stage for the production of knowledge about the past. The absence of a monument or marker may account for silences regarding the role of the Devès in narratives of Senegalese nationalism.

The history of the métis in Senegal has either been told in terms of the golden age of the gum trade or as a footnote in the emergence of modern nationalism. As a result, historians fail to understand the role of Senegal's métis population in the broad sweep of political, economic, social, and cultural transformations that shaped nineteenth-century Senegal. My aim in writing this book is to provide a perspective on the formation of métis identity and society that takes into account the long durée. The métis emerged as a self-conscious group in the late eighteenth century, but the social and cultural transformations that occurred in the first half of the nineteenth century solidified their distinctive identity. The ability to trace one's ancestry to a signare and a European merchant or soldier who arrived in the colony in the late eighteenth or early nineteenth century distinguished the métis of Saint Louis and Gorée from people of mixed race who were the products of twentieth-century French West Africa.

In writing this book, I deliberately placed Saint Louis at the center of the analysis. As the nexus of métis social and cultural life, a study of Saint Louis offers a new framework for understanding nineteenth-century urban life in West Africa. Histories of the Atlantic World often consider West Africa's Atlantic towns as locations for departure for African people who entered New World societies. Colonial studies often view these locations as the center of European power without regard for the societies that lived in close proximity. The permanent inhabitants of Senegal's coastal towns interacted with and responded to the geopolitical and cultural changes affecting the Atlantic World and the expansion of the French Empire. Senegal's coastal residents made transatlantic crossings that brought them to Bordeaux, Haiti, Réunion, and Martinique and then back to Senegal. Similarly, Europeans and people of color came to Senegal at various times in the nineteenth century, bringing new ideas and establishing transatlantic networks. In the eighteenth century, the métis, grumets, and signares embodied the characteristics of cosmopolitan inhabitants of the Atlantic World. They had the linguistic dexterity, knowledge of mercantile commerce, and a worldly outlook that helped them navigate geopolitical and cultural change. At the same time, they were intimately familiar with the religion, language, and practices of the people of the Senegal River valley.[2]

As the "country wives" of European men and the mothers of métis children, signares provided continuity between African and European society. In the eighteenth century, they played key roles in establishing dual identity for town residents. Signares of Saint Louis adopted Catholicism but observed Islamic holidays and followed Wolof traditions of the town, yet in the nineteenth century, these women became the objects of cultural hegemony. Colonial domination did not simply involve gaining control over the production of raw materials for export to capitalist markets or suppressing resistance through overwhelming military force. It also required imposing a new cultural order. French authorities attempted to "regularize" interracial mixing in the colony by eliminating signares' "superstitious" practices, enforcing Catholic orthodoxy, and imposing French civil law. In the minds of French officials, women, family, and private life were central to reproducing colonial society. Faced with a region long influenced by Islam, French officials focused their civilizing mission on signares and their métis children. Race and class worked to create a culturally assimilated elite in the colony. At the same time, these categories shored up bourgeois identity in metropolitan society.[3]

What studies of colonialism's culture often fail to take into account is how individuals who lived and worked in colonial cities interpreted the changing world. The métis were products of the expansion of French imperialism, but they were also intimately tied to the social, economic, and political changes occurring in Senegal. Islam played a key role in the development of urban life. The expansion of Umar Tal's Tijani movement in the middle and upper Senegal had important implications for the Saint Louis population. Colonial officials cultivated relations of cooperation with Muslim clerics and notables who served as interpreters for the colonial bureaucracy. The growth of Muslim traders in the Saint Louis community also transformed the social and economic landscape of the towns. Whereas in the eighteenth century French authorities relied on the métis and grumets to be cross-cultural brokers, in the nineteenth century, colonial officials needed the cooperation of Muslim town residents.

Economic historians have shown that coastal middlemen proved more resilient than previously assumed to the restructuring of the colonial economy in the nineteenth century. Métis habitants suffered significant financial losses in the wake of the gum crisis. Contemporary observers and historians examining the role of métis merchants predicted the disappearance of the métis habitants as viable intermediaries in Senegal's colonial economy after 1850. Recent research has revised the notion that coastal intermediaries could not adapt to the transition from the slave trade to "legitimate" trade, showing that Muslim Saint Louis traders developed thriving businesses in the escales and in the peanut basin.

These works neglect the resiliency of métis habitants who established operations on the frontiers of the colonial economy. They also capitalized on their networks in the Senegal River valley, relied on their relationship with Bordeaux commercial houses, and profited from acting as creditors to African rulers in the interior. The ability to generate capital through the Bank of Senegal and control urban real estate furthered their position. The extent of Gaspard Devès's success as a merchant and businessman, for example, afforded him a high degree of autonomy from the metropolitan commercial firms and the colonial administration. Research on urban land tenure and the transfer of wealth in the Saint Louis community after the abolition of slavery has already yielded important insights into growth of entrepreneurs in Saint Louis after 1850. Further research on métis business ventures will contribute to a broader understanding of the economic power of the Saint Louis community and the interdependent relationship between métis merchants and Muslim traders.[4]

In examining the role of the métis in nineteenth-century Senegal, I have deliberately emphasized transformations in identity and society. Ethnographers writing about Senegal in the early twentieth century reduced Senegal under colonial rule to binary categories such as colonizer and colonized, European and African, citizen or indigène. Sociologists writing in the twentieth century described the métis as part of a homogenous category of the colonizer. My examination of the transformation in métis identity from the late eighteenth century to the early twentieth century shows that these dichotomies are too simplistic and do little to explain how inhabitants of the colonial towns defined themselves. It also allows for an understanding of mixed racial identity that goes beyond a focus on the nameless, timeless signare described by European travel writers.

The métis adopted visible markers of identity that strengthened their position as French-educated, Catholic, property-owning bourgeoisie. Marrying within the group affirmed exclusivity. In conforming to the teachings of the Church and following the appropriate habits of republican womanhood, métis women strengthened their families' reputation as pious, morally upstanding members of society. Dress styles, consumption habits, and domestic choices conveyed an image of the métis that placed them on equal footing with French authorities, captains of industry, and the educated classes in metropolitan society. Pursuing French education also provided a pathway for maintaining socioeconomic status. Attending French schools, monopolizing scholarships for higher education in France, and entering the liberal professions allowed the métis to benefit from what historian David Roediger refers to as the psychological advantage of proximity to whiteness.[5] Access to French institutions of higher learning, for example, allowed métis to transition from being the dominant commercial elite to the dominant French-educated elite in the colony. In particular, it shored up their claim to participation in republican politics and bolstered the notion that they were best suited to lead modernization in the colony.

While close proximity to French officialdom conferred certain advantages for the métis of Senegal, it also proved problematic for establishing colonial authority. Urban life in nineteenth-century Senegal illustrates the structural ambiguities produced by a colonial system that professed republican principles in the coastal enclaves while subjecting African people in the interior to the authoritarian and arbitrary practices of the protectorate regime. The existence of republican institutions in Senegal highlighted these contradictions.[6] The métis took advantage of their knowledge of Senegal, their role in the colonial economy, and their intimate familiarity with republican law to establish themselves as power brokers. Senegal's General Council became the nexus of métis power and also the central institution for contesting French authority. Far from monolithic in their outlook, the métis used the assembly to debate republican politics and to insert their interests into the decision-making apparatus of the colonial regime. Colonial authorities underestimated the aggressiveness of the Saint Louis assemblymen and their ability to interfere in the affairs of the protectorate.

Collaboration does not adequately account for the range of responses by individuals within the Saint Louis community to colonial rule. The métis served as commandants, employees of the colonial bureaucracy, and decorated soldiers who distinguished themselves in wars of conquest. They also guarded their autonomy from the colonial administration, upheld the political and legal rights of Senegalese, and challenged what they considered to be abuses of colonial power. In establishing Senegal's first independent press and forming an oppositional coalition in commune politics, some métis gave the colonial administration fits. Being métis in colonial society, as Francoise Vergès suggests, could cause disruption, transgression, and even subversion of the colonial order.[7]

This study pays particular attention to the origins of democratic institutions in Africa. The literature on modern politics in colonial Africa tends to emphasize the weakness of the colonial state. Yet little attention is paid to how politics actually operated in the late nineteenth century. In Senegal, African and métis town residents organized as civil society. Democratic traditions had existed since the late eighteenth century, but the expansion of republican institutions under the Third Republic stimulated the growth of civil society. The consolidation of French rule in the early twentieth century and the subsequent closing of the General Council dealt a blow to the originaires, but it also restricted the influence of the urban elite on colonial policy.

Finally, research on urban politics in nineteenth-century Senegal intervenes in scholarship on the emergence of modern nationalism in West Africa. Historians typically consider Blaise Diagne's election to the National Assembly on the eve of World War I as the watershed moment in the emergence of national consciousness. While the first political histories of Senegal corresponded to the need for a cohesive national narrative, it is now time to reexamine the development of national consciousness in the late nineteenth century. Gaspard Devès articulated the idea of Senegalese interests as a counterpoint to the interests of metropolitan corporations. The schools run by the religious orders acted as microcosms of Senegalese society, bringing together young people of towns of varying social and economic backgrounds with former slaves, soldiers, and children of the ruling elite in the interior. Town residents used the cry "Senegal for the Senegalese!" when confronted with an administrative attack on their political rights. The métis of Senegal operated, as Christian Valantin suggests, in an assimilationist framework. They sought equal rights within the French system—not independence from it. In arguing for political rights, the métis contributed to the emergence of a consciousness about Senegal and being Senegalese that redefined urban politics at the end of the nineteenth century.

APPENDIX: FAMILY HISTORIES*

Alin—Jean Jacques Alain (1777–1849), called l'Antillais or l'aîné (the elder), arrived in Senegal with his parents, Louis (1744–1821) and Rose Dessources (1759–1839), in 1799. The Alains were part of a company of one hundred free blacks sent to develop loyalty to France in the aftermath of the French Revolution. Jean Jacques Alain married Signare Marie Paul Benis (1793–1860) and served as part of the town's guard under Blanchot at the beginning of Napoleon's empire. A distinguished habitant and gum trader, Alain was mayor of Saint Louis from 1829 to 1848. Two of their daughters, Charlotte Alain and Louison Alin, married Crespin brothers, Joseph "Dio" and Germain. The Alains are an example of the integration of free people of color from the French Antilles into Saint Louis society during the revolutionary era.

Angrand—One of the principal métis families of Gorée, the Angrands trace their lineage to the mid-eighteenth century. Pierre Angrand (1819–1901), a commercial agent, married Helene de Saint Jean (1826–59), of a notable Gorée family. His son, Leopold Angrand, participated in trade in

---

* The families described are based on a selected list that is relevant to this work. I composed these biographical sketches from a variety of sources. The principal secondary references are Johnson, *The Emergence of Black Politics*; Idowu, "Café au Lait: Sénégal's Mulatto Community"; Zuccarelli, *La vie politique Sénégalaise*; Natalie Reyss, "Saint Louis du Sénégal"; and Sylvain Sankale, "A la mode du pays . . . chroniques Saint Louisianes." Notarized documents and private family archives assisted me in compiling this information. Guillaume Guillabert, "Arbre généaogique des familles Descemet-Guillabert"; Yves Teisseire, "La famille d'Erneville"; Georges Crespin, "Liste de descendance de Benjamin Crespin"; notarized documents, Saint Louis, Senegal, 1881, and Gorée, Senegal, 1880, 1Z107, ANS; http://www.senegalmetis.com/S%C3%A9n%C3%A9galm%C3%A9tis/Genealogie.html. Personal communication with Xavier Ricou, Christian Valantin, Sylvain Sankale, Ibrahima Diallo, Madeleine Devès Senghor, and Moustapha Crespin provided further clarification.

Saloum and the Gambia. A lawyer politically linked to the Devès family, Leopold won election to the General Council from the second arrondissement and won election as deputy mayor of Gorée in 1890. Leopold married Mathilde Faye of Bathurst and Madeleine Diouf. Two of his sons, Armand (1892–1964) and Joseph (1893–1935), participated in the Jeunes Sénégalais. Armand Angrand was mayor of Dakar from 1934 to 1939.

Carpot—Michel Carpot d'Estrourelles (1763–1803) arrived in Senegal to serve as Governor Blanchot's secretary in the 1790s. He married Signare Suzanne Dobbs in his first union, the daughter of Mame Coumba and a British soldier who arrived in Senegal in the mid-eighteenth century. Charles Carpot (1799–1880), a property owner and trader, married Sophie Renaud-Valantin (1832–86). Four sons, Theodore (1855–1921), Charles (1857–1905), François (1863–1936), and Ernest (1867–1956), studied in France. Theodore became a commercial agent, won a seat on the General Council, and served as president of the assembly from 1902 until 1914. He also operated the first electrical lighting company in Saint Louis. Charles, a physician, became director of the Civil Hospital in Saint Louis and was noted for his work during the yellow fever epidemic of 1878. François Carpot graduated from the University of Paris law school and practiced in France before returning to Senegal in the 1880s. The Carpots emerged as one of the main political coalitions in commune politics in the 1900s. In 1902, François Carpot won the legislative election, becoming the first métis to represent Senegal in Paris since his ancestor, Durand Valantin, held the office during the Second Republic.

Crespin—Benjamin Crespin (1769–1811), a merchant from La Rochelle, arrived in Senegal in the late eighteenth century. He entered a mariage a la mode du pays with Signare Caty Wilcock (1765–1831), a property owner who traced her lineage to British occupation of the mid-eighteenth century. Their sons, Germain (1803–70) and Joseph "Dio" (1806–58), developed trade houses in the gum trade era. Both married daughters of Jean Jacques Alain. Germain married Louison Alain and then entered a mariage à la mode du pays with Kayeta Macoumba Leye (1819–94), his children's nurse, following his wife's death. Joseph and Charlotte Alain had twelve children. Of them, Jean Jacques Alain (1837–95), also known as J. J. Crespin, specialized in law and had a distinguished career in commune politics. Another son, Adolphe (1854–1933), worked for the ministry of colonies in Paris and mentored Blaise Diagne. J. J. Crespin married Hanna Isaacs of Sierra Leone, the daughter of British explorer Nathaniel Isaacs, whom he met while trading in the Southern Rivers region. Their daughter, Charlotte (1864–1956), married Hyacinthe Devès, son of J. J.'s ally, Gaspard. Their son Georges (1869–1918), also pursued law and entered commune politics. Another son, Germain (1876–1957), began as a trader, studied law, and later became deputy mayor of Cotonou (Benin).

Descemet—the Descemets trace their lineage to the late eighteenth century. Pierre Louis Descemet (1771–1828) was a soldier who arrived in Senegal in the 1790s or early 1800s. He married Signare Suzanne Dobbs (1769–1845) after the death of her first spouse, Michel Carpot, in 1803. Their daughter, Henriette, married Guillaume Foy, a habitant and successful gum trade merchant whose daughter wed Gaspard Devès. Roger (1833–57) and Louis (1839–1921) are the best known of this family. Both were among the first scholarship recipients. Roger attended St. Cyr military academy in France, then returned to Senegal. A military officer under Governor Faidherbe, he died in the battle against Al-Hajj Umar Tal's forces at Médine. Louis studied at the Lycée de l'Orient, returned to Senegal, and worked as secretary to Faidherbe. In the 1860s, he left the administration and formed a trade house with Omer Teisseire. Descemet's ties to the habitant elite, the administration, and Bordeaux commerce facilitated his rise in commune politics. He served as president of the General Council from 1879 to 1890. Descemet was president of the Saint Louis Chamber of Commerce from 1881 to 1889 and mayor of Saint Louis from 1895 to 1911. His kin and client networks extended to Fouta Toro, where he served as creditor to rulers in the region and traded in cattle.

Devès (the Bordeaux branch)—The Devès family of Senegal originated in the nineteenth century. Justin (1789–1865) and Bruno Devès were born in Bordeaux. In 1807, Justin left France after their family suffered bankruptcy en route to Philadelphia. In 1810, he arrived at Gorée aboard a slaver; Bruno followed later. They represented a new generation of private wholesale merchants who entered the export trade in gum, hides, ivory, and probably slaves from the Senegal River. In 1850, the company founded by Justin Devès merged with Lacoste to capitalize on peanut exports. In 1865, the firm merged with Gustav Chaumet. Devès and Chaumet specialized in peanut and textile imports, military supplies, and river and ocean sailing vessels. They built a factory to manufacture peanut oil in Bordeaux.

Devès (the Senegalese branch)—Bruno Devès entered a mariage à la mode du pays with a Fulbe woman named Coumbel Ardo Ka, also called

Silvie Bruno. Their union produced a son, Gaspard. Bruno sent Gaspard to France for schooling. He returned to Senegal and entered business, having received John Sleight's contract to supply grain to the colonial administration. Gaspard Devès married Catherine Foy (1832–51). He built a commercial enterprise that rivaled the Bordeaux firms. His networks extended from the Trarza on the north bank of the Senegal to trade centers in the peanut basin. He maintained a network of agents in Podor and as far south as Melacorie on the border with Sierra Leone. His business interests included a brick factory in Saint Louis, an investment in a textile factory in Pondicherry (India), fisheries on the island of Arguin, and gold mines in eastern Senegal. Gaspard Devès served as creditor to ruling elites in the interior and as employer to Saint Louis residents. Mayor of Saint Louis from 1876 to 1880, member of the General Council, and administrator for the Bank of Senegal, Devès formed one of the most important coalitions in commune politics. Following the death of his first wife, Gaspard Devès entered a second union with Madeleine Tamba. Likely of Sarakolle origin, she came from the coastal fishing village of Guet Ndar. Three sons completed secondary education in France and law school in Bordeaux. François (1854–1919), Justin (1858–1916), and Hyacinthe (1859–1910) won election to the General Council. Hyacinthe represented Rufisque, shoring up the family's support in the second arrondissement. A fourth son, Guillaume, studied medicine in France. The Devès represent the height of métis wealth and power in the late nineteenth century, and they were skilled at using the republican institutions to their advantage.

Dodds—Englishman John Dodds (1790–1874) arrived in Senegal during the Napoleonic Wars. In 1816, he married Sophie Feuiltaine (1797–1866), the métis daughter of Antoine Feuiltaine and Marie Bamby-Amady. Their son, Henry Dodds (1818–82), worked for the administration as director of the post office. He and Charlotte Billaud (1823–90) had ten children. One son, Alfred Amédée Dodds (1842–1922), became a decorated military officer who joined Faidherbe's forces in the battle of Médine against Al-Hajj Umar Tal, led campaigns in Cayor and the middle Senegal, and led the battle to unseat Behazin, the king of Dahomey, in 1892. Virginie Dodds (1862–1951) married Léonce Le Bègue de Germiny (1850–1922), a president of the General Council and mayor of Gorée. Edouard Dodds (1856–1939) served as secretary for the mayor of Saint Louis. His son, Prosper Dodds (1915–73), became the first Senegalese appointed bishop of the Saint Louis diocese.

D'Erneville—Charles Jean Baptiste d'Erneville arrived in Senegal in the revolutionary period. Born in New Orleans, Louisiana, he followed his father to France and became a soldier after serving several years in a debtors' prison. Arriving in Senegal when the French returned in 1785, d'Erneville wed Signare Catherine Miller. When d'Erneville left Saint Louis for an assignment on Gorée, he established a new household with Hélène Pateloux. The d'Ernevilles were related by marriage to most of the nineteenth-century métis families, including the Valantins, Sleights, Armstrongs, Pattersons, Alsaces, O'Haras, Turpins, Duchesnes, Descemets, Crespins, and Andres. In the nineteenth century, Bordeaux merchants Auguste Teisseire, Raymond Martin, and Henri Jay married d'Erneville women. Hippolyte d'Erneville (1834–87) established a trade house in Boké on the Southern Rivers where he married Moussou Camara. Their son, Victor Hipployte "Hipo," continued in trade and married Marie Pierre Turpin, the daughter of Fine Turpin, a prominent métis merchant located in Saloum. In the 1890s, Leon and Germain "Gino" d'Erneville joined Louis Descemet on the General Council. Germain became president of Alliance Française in Saint Louis and served as president of the General Council.

Foy—Guillaume Foy (1803–69) was a successful property owner and trader. Born in 1803 to Charles Foy and Marie Allemaney N'Diaye, Foy came of age at the end of the Napoleonic Wars and the height of the gum trade. A noted habitant, Guillaume Foy married Henriette Descemet (1809–53). In 1851, their only child, Catherine Foy (1832–51), wed Gaspard Devès. Catherine died giving birth to their daughter, Elizabeth. Guillaume Foy participated in the governor's advisory council and was mayor of Saint Louis from 1850 to 1854. Guillaume Foy's granddaughter, Elizabeth, inherited the wealth he gained during the heyday of the gum trade.

Guillabert—Antoine Guillabert (1748–1849) of Marseille arrived in Senegal as the king's employee when the monarchy regained control of Senegal after the Napoleonic Wars. Guillabert settled in Senegal, entered commerce, and married Signare Felicité Bouba. He formed a second union with Hélène O'Hara and a third union with Marie Victoire Krialla Diouf. His sons were employees of the administration. Augustin Henri "Louis" Guillabert (1866–1932) completed primary education in Saint Louis and studied law in Toulouse. He was named supernumerary in Bordeaux and Paris before returning to Saint Louis. He married Suzanne Descemet and worked as an employee of the administration and a public notary. Louis Guillabert entered electoral politics in the early twentieth century, becoming a member of the General Council. He served as this assembly's last president (1916–18) and the first president of the Colonial Council (1921–23).

Huchard—Louis Huchard (1857–1922) became an important figure in commune politics, representing Gorée in the 1900s. Huchard's father worked as a trader and agent for a French trade firm in Rufisque and married a Dakar businesswoman, Marie Lapolice. The Huchards were firmly established in the second arrondissement. Nicholas Huchard (1850–93) was a public works employee in Dakar. Ursule Huchard (1855–89) married François Potin, a métis wholesale agent located in Bissau (Portuguese Guinea). Louis Huchard (1857–1922) became a lawyer, founded *L'Afrique Occidentale*, and gained a reputation for defending the rights of Senegalese with grievances against the administration. In the late 1890s, Huchard won election to the General Council. He joined the Devès coalition, which shored up the Devès family's support among Lebou voters in Dakar, Gorée, and Rufisque.

Teisseire—Auguste Teisseire (1813–94) was one of the Bordeaux traders who established an interest in Senegal in the early nineteenth century. He followed other Bordeaux traders who married into the Saint Louis community. In 1836, Auguste married métis habitant Marie Anne d'Erneville (1817–58). He began as an exporter of birds, feathers, and trade goods, then became a wholesaler. In 1870, his son Albert (1843–82) formed the company Buhan and Teisseire with his father-in-law. Albert entered electoral politics as a candidate for the legislative position and as a member of the General Council. His brother Omer (1840–86) and Louis Descemet established a trade interest that supplied cattle for Dakar and Saint Louis. Omer Teisseire's daughter Marguerite (1869–1943) married François Carpot. The Teisseires are an example of the integration of metropolitan merchants with métis society. They also illustrate the close relationship between Bordeaux commerce and the electoral institutions.

Valantin—Barthelemy Durand, a merchant from Marseille, arrived in Senegal in the late 1780s when France regained control of Saint Louis. He entered a mariage à la mode du pays with Signare Rosalie Aussenac. The union produced thirteen children. Three sons rose to the rank of négociant (wholesale merchant) in the gum trade. Etienne Valantin (1804–59) operated from Gorée. François (1793–1838), John (1802–23), and Barthelemy "Durand" (1806–64) Valantin established a trade house in Saint Louis. Durand Valantin studied in Marseille and became an important political figure in the colony during the 1830s and 1840s. The governor appointed him mayor of Saint Louis, and he served on the governor's advisory council. In 1840, Durand Valantin won election to the newly constituted General Council and served as Senegal's first representative to Paris from 1848 to 1851. He also served as public notary for the town. The Valantins were related by marriage to some of the earliest métis families of Saint Louis and Gorée, such as the Lloyds, Duboises, de Saint Jeans, and Feuiltaines as well as the Carpots, Descemets, d'Ernevilles, and Crespins, who trace their ancestry to the late eighteenth or early nineteenth century.

NOTES

INTRODUCTION

1. Guillabert was elected mayor of Louga and Saint Louis. Henri Louis Valantin was ambassador to London, and Pierre Devès was appointed ambassador to the Vatican. Members of the Crespin family served in Senegal's judiciary. Alfred d'Erneville became a decorated officer in the armed forces. The bulletin of the Catholic Church in Saint Louis reported on the achievements of members of their congregation and also reproduced key milestones for the community from the Church newsletter that circulated in the late nineteenth and early twentieth centuries. "Pages d'Histoire" and "Actualité," *Unir: L'Echo de Saint Louis* 10 (June 1969), 5–7.

2. O'Brien made these observations in her sociological study of European society in Senegal based on fieldwork conducted in the 1960s. Rita Cruise O'Brien, *White Society in Black Africa: The French of Senegal* (Evanston, IL: Northwestern University Press, 1972).

3. Abdoulaye Sadji, *Nini: Mulâtresse du Sénégal* (1957; reprint, Paris: Présence Africaine, 1988). Historian H. Oludare Idowu confirms that tensions existed between the Senegalese and the métis over the latter's role in politics. In 1963 and 1965, he interviewed descendants of the métis and Senegalese in the towns who reported the use of racial expressions to condemn the métis during contentious political campaigns such as the elections of 1914. My interviews revealed less animosity perhaps because almost fifty years had passed since independence, giving rise to new political and economic realities where the métis no longer exercised political power. H. O. Idowu, "Café au Lait: Senegal's Mulatto Community in the Nineteenth Century," *Journal of the Historical Society of Nigeria* 6 (December 1972): 271. For the concept of métissage in Senegalese literature, see Daouda Loum, "Métis et métissages: L'Eclairage littéraire en miroir," *French Colonial History* 9 (2008): 79–102.

4. Spitzer compares the psychology of a Krio family of Freetown, a mulatto family of Brazil, and a Jewish family in Austria to illustrate the social and moral dilemmas for such groups in the late nineteenth and early twentieth centuries. Leo Spitzer, *Lives in Between: The Experience of Marginality in a Century of Emancipation* (New York: Hill and Wang, 1999).

5. Ferdinand Brigaud, interview with author, 4 December 2000, Saint Louis.

6. Brooks's seminal contribution focuses on the role of signares as entrepreneurs rather than only as the sexual companions of European men. George E. Brooks, *EurAfricans in Western Africa* (Athens: Ohio University Press, 2003). For a treatment of the material world created by signares and their descendants in this era, see Peter Mark,

"Portuguese" Style and Luso-African Identity: Precolonial Senegambia, Sixteenth–Nineteenth Centuries (Bloomington: Indiana University Press, 2002).

7. Ira Berlin coined this term to capture the stage in the formation of African American identity represented by the "charter generations." This definition emphasizes culture over birth. Others have expanded on this concept for ports of Spanish-speaking America and the Bight of Biafra in West Africa. Yet research on precolonial Africa shows that mixing was also a conscious strategy of rulers and merchants who placed a premium on dependents with "wealth in knowledge" or the linguistic and cultural dexterity to move between groups. Ira Berlin, "From Creole to African: Atlantic Creoles and the Origins of African American Society in Mainland North America," *William and Mary Quarterly* 53 (April 1996), 253–55; Randy Sparks, *The Two Princes of Calabar: An Eighteenth-Century Atlantic Odyssey* (Cambridge: Harvard University Press, 2004); and Jane G. Landers, *Atlantic Creoles in the Age of Revolutions* (Cambridge: Harvard University Press, 2010). On mixing in Africa, see Jean-Loup Amselle, *Mestizo Logics: Anthropology of Identity in Africa and Elsewhere*, trans. Claudia Royal (Stanford: Stanford University Press, 1998), and Jane I. Guyer and Samuel M. Eno Belinga, "Wealth in People as Wealth in Knowledge: Accumulation and Composition in Equatorial Africa," *Journal of African History* 36 (1995): 91–120.

8. "Etablissements Devès et Chaumet, Bordeaux, à Centre de Recherches et de Documentation du Sénégal, Saint Louis," 3 April 1981. This information comes from a letter sent from the headquarters of Devès and Chaumet in response to a request for information pertaining to the exhibit "La Société Créole à Saint Louis." I am grateful to Fadel Dia for making it available to me.

9. Several dissertations examine the golden era of the métis: Michael David Marcson, "European-African Interaction in the Pre-Colonial Period: Saint Louis, Senegal, 1758–1854" (Princeton University, 1976); Natalie Reyss, "Saint Louis du Sénégal à l'époque précoloniale: l'émergence d'une société métisse originale, 1658–1854" (Université Paris I, 1983); Sylvain Sankale, "A la mode du pays . . . Chroniques Saint Louisiennes d'Antoine François Feuiltaine, Saint Louis, Sénégal, 1788–1835" (l'Université de Montpellier II, 1998); and Amanda Sackur, "The Development of Creole Society and Culture in Saint Louis and Gorée, 1719–1817" (University of London, 1999). For a comparison with mixed-race groups of British and American descent in Senegambia during the same period, see Bruce L. Mouser, "History of Trade and Politics in the Guinea Rivers, 1790–1865" (PhD diss., Indiana University, 1971).

10. Abdoulaye Ly, *La compagnie du Senegal* (Dakar: Présence Africaine, 1958); Philip Curtin, *Economic Change in Precolonial Africa: Senegambia in the Era of the Slave Trade* (Madison: University of Wisconsin Press, 1975). For more recent treatments of the relationship between the Atlantic economies and Senegalese society, see Boubacar Barry, *Senegambia and the Atlantic Slave Trade*, trans. Ayi Kwei Armah (Cambridge: Cambridge University Press, 1998), and James F. Searing, *West African Slavery and Atlantic Commerce: The Senegal River Valley, 1700–1860* (Cambridge: Cambridge University Press, 1993).

11. The most strident advocate of this view is Roger Pasquier, who argued for the subjugation of African middleman to merchant capital much earlier than Samir Amin, who considered the rise and fall of the Senegalese bourgeoisie in terms of a longer trajectory beginning in the nineteenth century and collapsing with the consolidation of colonial rule and the domination of monopoly corporations in the colonial economy by 1920. Samir Amin, "La politique coloniale française à l'égard de la bourgeoisie commerçante Sénégalaises, 1820–1960," in *The Development of Indigenous Trade and Markets in West Africa*, ed. Claude

Meillassoux (Oxford: Oxford University Press, 1971); and Roger Pasquier, "Le Sénégal au milieu du XIXe siècle: la crise économique et sociale" (PhD diss., Paris IV, 1987).

12. Laurence Marfaing, *L'évolution du commerce au Sénégal, 1820–1930* (Paris: Harmattan, 1991) and contributions to Boubacar Barry and Leonhard Harding, eds., *Commerce et commerçants en Afrique de l'Ouest: Le Sénégal* (Paris: Harmattan, 1992).

13. L. H. Gann and Peter Dunigan, *Colonialism in Africa, 1870–1900* (London: Cambridge University Press, 1969); Ronald Robinson, "Non-European Foundations of European Imperialism: Sketch for a Theory of Collaboration," in *Studies in the Theory of Imperialism,* ed. Roger Owen and Bob Sutcliffe (London: Longman, 1972).

14. Berman and Lonsdale refer specifically to metropolitan merchant capital, local African producers, and white settler interests. While British rule in Kenya supported a large white settler population, I find that the expectations of this group are similar to the demands that the métis population placed on the state to respond to their legal rights for political representation. Bruce Berman and John M. Lonsdale, *Unhappy Valley: Conflict in Kenya and Africa* (Athens: Ohio University Press, 1992), 77–95.

15. Jean and John Comaroff, *Of Revelation and Revolution,* vol. 1, *Christianity, Colonialism, and Consciousness in South Africa* (Chicago: University of Chicago Press, 1991) and vol. 2, *The Dialectics of Modernity on a South African Frontier* (Chicago: University of Chicago Press, 1997), and David Robinson, *Paths of Accommodation: Muslim Societies and French Colonial Authorities in Sénégal and Mauritania, 1880–1920* (Athens: Ohio University Press, 2000). For a general treatment of intermediaries in colonial Africa, see Benjamin N. Lawrence, Emily Lynn Osborn, and Richard L. Roberts, eds., *Intermediaries, Interpreters, and Clerks: African Employees in the Making of Colonial Africa* (Madison: University of Wisconsin Press, 2006).

16. Examples include Michael Crowder, *Senegal: A Study in French Assimilation Policy* (London: Methuen, 1967); A. S. Kanya-Forstner, *The Conquest of the Western Sudan* (London: Cambridge University Press, 1969); William B. Cohen, *Rulers of Empire: The French Colonial Service in Africa* (Stanford: Stanford University Press, 1971); Jean Suret-Canale, *French Colonialism in Tropical Africa, 1900–1945,* trans. Till Gottheiner (New York: Pica Press, 1971); and Jacques Marseille, *Empire colonial et capitalisme français: histoire d'un divorce* (Paris: Albin Michel, 1984).

17. Seminal in this regard are Anne McClintock, *Imperial Leather: Race, Gender, and Sexuality in the Colonial Contest* (New York: Routledge, 1995); Julia Clancy-Smith and Frances Gouda, eds., *Domesticating the Empire: Race, Gender, and Family Life in French and Dutch Colonialism* (Charlottesville: University Press of Virginia, 1998); and Ann Laura Stoler, *Carnal Knowledge and Imperial Power: Race and the Intimate in Colonial Rule* (Berkeley: University of California Press, 2002).

18. Frederick Cooper argues that scholarship on colonialism in Africa has focused on taking a "pro-colonial" or "anti-colonial" stand at the expense of examining Africans as historical actors within specific systems of power. Alice Conklin has pointed out that French imperial studies has neglected the cultural ways that colonial operated. As a result, urban elites have largely been seen as the unwitting dupes of hegemonic colonial power. Frederick Cooper, *Colonialism in Question* (Berkeley: University of California Press, 2005), 3–32; Alice Conklin, *A Mission to Civilize: The Republican Idea of Empire in France and West Africa, 1895–1930* (Stanford: Stanford University Press, 1997). Another work that focuses on the connection between modern French history and colonial history is Gary Wilder, *The French Imperial Nation-State* (Chicago: University of Chicago Press, 2005).

19. On urban elites in British West Africa, see Jacob Ajayi, *Christian Missions in Nigeria, 1841–1891: The Making of a New Elite* (London: Longman, 1965); Abner Cohen, *Custom and Politics in Urban Africa* (Berkeley: University of California Press, 1969); Barbara E. Harrell-Bond, Allen M. Howard, and David E. Skinner, *Community Leadership and the Transformation of Freetown, 1801–1976* (The Hague: Mouton, 1978); Leo Spitzer, *The Creoles of Sierra Leone* (Madison: University of Wisconsin Press, 1974); and Kristin Mann, *Marrying Well: Marriage, Status, and Social Change among the Educated Elite in Colonial Lagos* (Cambridge: Cambridge University Press, 1985).

20. For a treatment of the relationship of religion and citizenship for Senegal's urban elite, see Mamadou Diouf, "Assimilation coloniale et identitaires religieuses de la civilité des originaires des Quatre Communes (Sénégal)," *Canadian Journal of African Studies* 34, no. 2 (2000): 565–87, and Catherine Coquery-Vidrovitch, "Nationalité et citoyenneté en Afrique occidentale français: originaires et citoyens dans le Sénégal colonial," *Journal of African History* 42 (2001): 285–305. See also G. Wesley Johnson, "The Senegalese Urban Elite, 1900–1945," in *Africa and the West: Intellectual Responses to European Rule*, ed. Philip D. Curtin (Madison: University of Wisconsin Press, 1972).

21. The seminal account of Blaise Diagne's rise to political power is G. Wesley Johnson, *The Emergence of Black Politics in Senegal: The Struggle for Power in the Four Communes* (Stanford: Hoover Institution, 1971). Another work that takes the same approach is François Zuccarelli, *La vie politique Sénégalaise: 1798–1940* (Paris: CHEAM, 1987).

22. One example of the first wave of Africanist scholarship on nationalism is James Coleman, *Nigeria: Background to Nationalism* (Berkeley: University of California Press, 1958). For a nuanced interpretation of class, urban elites, and politics, see Shula Marks, *The Ambiguities of Dependence in South Africa: Class, Nationalism, and the State in Twentieth-Century Natal* (Baltimore: Johns Hopkins University Press, 1986).

23. Mamdani makes this argument to explain the weakness of the colonial state and its legacy on civil society in Africa today. Mahmood Mamdani, *Citizen and Subject: Contemporary Africa and the Legacy of Late Colonialism* (Princeton: Princeton University Press, 1996), 9–18.

24. For an analysis of *Creole* as a term of social classification and its particular meaning in the context of race in Louisiana, see Virginia R. Dominguez, *White by Definition: Social Classification in Creole Louisiana* (New Brunswick, NJ: Rutgers University Press, 1986). On miscegenation and the notion of hybridity in colonial discourse, see Robert J. C. Young, *Colonial Desire: Hybridity in Theory, Culture, and Race* (London: Routledge, 1995).

25. Idowu remarked on the confusion over Gasconi's identity when he asked this question of his informants in the 1960s. According to Zucarelli, Gasconi grew up in Marseille and fought in the volunteer army that defended the Papal States against Prussian invaders in 1871. In Senegal, he referred to himself as a lawyer from Marseille, and he died in France with "français" recorded on his death notice. The arbitrary nature of racial categories for people of color in nineteenth-century France meant that individuals like Gasconi may have been categorized as *français,* whereas a métis from Guadeloupe would be labeled as *gens du couleur.* Idowu, "Café au Lait," 272; Zuccarelli, *La vie politique,* 52.

26. Scholarship has shown that race is a social construct and that biological definitions are no longer tenable. Fields's contribution to the ideology of race in American history pushed scholarship on the construction of race in the formation of European empire. Barbara J. Fields, "Ideology and Race in American History," in *Region, Race, and*

Reconstruction: Essays in Honor of C. Vann Woodward, ed. J. Morgan Kousser and James M. McPherson (New York: Oxford University, 1982).

27. For colonial studies and postcolonial studies scholarship that goes beyond mixed race identity as mimicry to examine how métissage produces anxieties that can potentially thwart colonial power, see Françoise Vergès, *Monsters and Revolutionaries: Colonial Family Romance and Métissage* (Durham: Duke University Press, 1999), and Françoise Lionnet, *Autobiographical Voices: Race, Gender, and Self-Portraiture* (Ithaca: Cornell University Press, 1999). Recent studies of racial identity in African societies tend to focus on formal or late colonialism in Africa. See Giulia Barrera, "Patrilinearity, Race, and Identity: The Upbringing of Italo-Eritreans during Italian Colonialism," *Quaderni Storici* 37 (April 2002): 21–53; Christopher Joon-Hai Lee, "The 'Native' Undefined: Colonial Categories, Anglo-African Status, and the Politics of Kinship in British Central Africa, 1929–38," *Journal of African History* 46, no. 3 (2005): 457–58; Carina E. Ray, "Policing Sexual Boundaries: The Politics of Race in Colonial Ghana" (PhD thesis, Cornell University, 2007), and Rachel Jean-Baptiste, "Miss Eurafrica: Men, Women, Sex, and Métis Identity in Late Colonial French West Africa, 1945–1960," *Journal of the History of Sexuality* 20, no. 3 (2011): 568–93. For a treatment of racial thinking in Africa under colonial rule, see Jonathan Glassman, *War of Words, War of Stones: Racial Thought and Violence in Colonial Zanzibar* (Bloomington: Indiana University Press, 2011).

28. Hulstaert (1900–1990), an ethnographer and linguist in the Belgian Congo, expressed common anxieties about métis in Africa forming a "separate caste" that would fit neither African nor European society. G. Hulstaert, "Le Problème des Mulâtres," *Africa* 15, no. 3 (1945): 129–44; G. Hulstaert, "Le Problème des Mulâtres (suite)," *Africa* 16, no. 1 (1946): 39–44.

29. For an analysis of interracial sexuality in French West Africa and the problem of métis identity for the colonial administration, see Owen White, *Children of the French Empire: Miscegenation and Colonial Society in French West Africa, 1895–1960* (Oxford: Oxford University Press, 1999). For other treatments of the legal and cultural construction of mixed race identity in French empire, see Emmanuelle Saada, *Les enfants de la colonie* (Paris: Editions la Découverte, 2007) and Sylvie Kandé, ed., *Discours sur le Métissage, Identités Métisses* (Paris: Harmattan, 1999).

30. In 1850, a journal published by this association, *L'Eurafricain,* appeared in French West Africa. The origins and circulation of the publication are unclear, but the founder associates it with a group called the Union Nationale des Métis. The newspaper argued for the application of French civil law regarding the right of individuals born in the colony to research their paternity. It appeared during a surge of applications among Africans in the colonies for French nationality. *L'Eurafricain: Bulletin d'Information et de liaison de l'union des EurAfricains de l'A.O.F. et du Togo* no. 7 (Dakar).

31. For a definition of *domnu ndar* and an overview of the specific cultural traditions that characterized Saint Louis du Senegal, see Abdoul Hadir Aïdara, *Saint Louis du Sénégal: d'hier à aujourd'hui* (Brinon-sur-Sauldre, France: Editions Grandvaux, 2004), 21–43, and Fatou Niang Siga, *Reflets de modes et traditions Saint-Louisiennes* (Dakar: Khoudia, 1990). The term *enfants de la terre* may have originated with the Portuguese *filos de terra,* the offspring of Luso-Africans in Cape Verde and Bissagos.

32. Alfred Stepan, *Rethinking Military Politics: Brazil and the Southern Cone* (Princeton: Princeton University Press, 1988); Jean François Bayart, *The State in Africa: The Politics of the Belly* (New York: Longman, 1993); Mahmood Mamdani, *Citizen and Subject;*

and John L. and Jean Comaroff, eds. *Civil Society and the Political Imagination in Africa* (Chicago: University of Chicago Press, 1999).

33. Leonardo Villalon, *Islamic Society and State Power in Senegal* (Cambridge: Cambridge University Press, 1995); Donal B. Crusie O'Brien, Momar Coumba Diop, and Mamadou Diouf, *La construction de l'état au Sénégal* (Paris: Karthala, 2002).

34. It may be more accurate to talk about civil society in the communes as "colonial civil society," since the development of civil society could only occur in a limited form within the context of colonialism. The policy of assimilation created structural ambiguities in French West Africa by granting citizenship rights and democratic government to a very limited population in Senegal's colonial towns.

35. Stepan, *Rethinking Military Politics*, chap. 1.

36. Bourdieu's analysis of family and educational strategies among the French upper classes contains important parallels with the métis case. For a discussion of the role of schools in the production and reproduction of the educated elite in France, see Pierre Bourdieu, *The State Nobility: Elite Schools and the Field of Power,* trans. Lauretta C. Clough (Stanford: Stanford University Press, 1989).

37. Pierre Bourdieu, *Outline of a Theory of Practice,* trans. Richard Nice (Cambridge: Cambridge University Press, 1977; reprinted 1995), 58–61, 171–83.

38. Popular depictions of this era of Senegal's history are rendered through romanticized representations of signares with little attempt to recover the names of these African women and to analyze the role that women played in establishing métis households and bolstering their reputations. The merits of oral history for getting at Africa's colonial past have been widely debated. Jan Vansina dismisses "reminiscences" for their lack of historicity. Others argue that African oral histories, regardless of their flaws, lend an invaluable perspective on archival histories. I agree with the latter. On this debate, see Jan Vansina, *Oral Tradition as History* (Madison: University of Wisconsin Press, 1985), and Louise White, Sephan F. Miescher, and David William Cohen, eds., *African Words, African Voices; Critical Practices in Oral History* (Bloomington: Indiana University Press, 2001).

39. On "tin trunk literacy" as a methodology for uncovering African self-representations, see Karin Barber, ed., *Africa's Hidden Histories: Everyday Literacy and the Making of the Self* (Bloomington: Indiana University Press, 2006), 1–24. For a compelling example of the recovering of métis history and the use of new technologies to interpret family documents and make them available to the public, see Xavier Ricou, "Sénégalmétis," at http://senegalmetis.com/Senegalmetis/Accueil.html.

40. The *Moniteur* was the country's first newspaper. It was founded by Governor Faidherbe to circulate military, administrative, commercial, and scientific information about the colony. The first publication appeared on 16 March 1856. The journal ran until 29 December 1887. In 1888, it was replaced by the *Journal Officiel du Sénégal et Dépendances.*

41. For a recent example of this argument, see Mamdani, *Citizen and Subject.*

42. A classic example of this approach is Johnson's *Emergence of Black Politics.* For a critique of this approach, see James Searing, "Accommodation and Resistance: Chiefs, Muslim Leaders, and Politicians in Colonial Senegal, 1890–1934" (PhD diss., Princeton University, 1985), 364–65.

1. SIGNARES, HABITANTS, AND GRUMETS IN THE MAKING OF SAINT LOUIS

1. A noble family of Normady, the d'Erneville name can be traced to the tenth century. Charles Jean-Baptiste's father, Pierre Henri, was a naval captain. He married Dame

Pelagie Fleuriau of New Orleans, Louisiana. Pierre Henri returned to France after falling on hard times and finally lost the family's fortune in the New Orleans fire of 1786. The family's financial troubles led to Charles Jean-Baptiste's imprisonment in France. His appointment to Senegal appears to have been an opportunity for advancement after being released from debtors' prison. Teisseire, "La famille d'Erneville," genealogy (courtesy Sylavin Sankale, Dakar), 244–47, 260–63; Xavier Ricou, "Sénégalmétis," http://www.senegalmetis.com/Senegalmetis/Genealogie.html; and G. Crespin, interview with author, Paris (8 June 2011).

2. The Alain family arrived in Saint Louis from Martinique in 1799. Louis Alain (1744–1821) and his wife, Rose Dessources (1759–1839), were born in Martinique and died in Saint Louis. The Alains arrived in Senegal as part of a company of one hundred free blacks from Martinique, Guadeloupe, and Saint Domingue who were sent to Senegal to develop loyalty to the Republic in the aftermath of the French Revolution. Their eldest son, Jean-Jacques Alain (1777–1849), was born in Lamentin, Martinique. He married Signare Marie Paule Bénis of Saint Louis. Jean-Jacques Alain was mayor of Saint Louis from 1828 to 1848. For more on the small group of West Indians who settled in Senegal during the era of the Haitian Revolution, see Marcson, "European-African Interaction in the Pre-Colonial Period," chap. 2, and Natalie Reyss, "Saint Louis du Sénégal," 103.

3. Literary interpretations range from works that evoke colonial nostalgia such as Pierre Loti's 1873 novel, *Le Roman d'un spahi,* and director Bernard Giraudau's 1996 film, *Les Caprices d'un Fleuve,* based on the journal of the infamous Chevalier de Boufflers. Tita Mandelou departs from the idealized portrait of African and European romance by placing signare agency at the center of her historical novel, *Signare Anna* (Dakar: NEAS, 1991). Jean Pierre Biondi's work *Saint Louis du Sénégal: mémoires d'un métissage* (Paris: Edition Denoël, 1987) takes a nostalgic view. For interpretations by historians that emphasize agency, see George Brooks, "The *Signares* of Saint Louis and Gorée," in *Women in Africa,* ed. Nancy Hafkin and Edna G. Bay (Stanford: Stanford University Press, 1976), and James Searing, *West African Slavery and Atlantic Commerce.*

4. Other scholars have made this observation with regard to Saint Louis and Gorée, but few have placed women at the center of analysis of the expansion of global capitalism to Senegal's interior and the development of a class of coastal traders. The classic interpretation of the importance of Afro-European trade diasporas in Senegal's economic history is Philip Curtin, *Economic Change in Precolonial Africa.* For a feminist critique, see Anne McClintock, *Imperial Leather,* 4–9, and Ann Laura Stoler, *Carnal Knowledge and Imperial Power,* 1–13.

5. David Robinson, "France as a Muslim Power in West Africa," *Africa Today* 46, no. 3 (1999): 105–27, and Christopher Harrison, *France and Islam in West Africa* (Cambridge: Cambridge University Press, 1988). For a discussion of travelogues and captivity narratives by western observers about the Sahara and the stereotypes they perpetuated about the frontier between white Moors of the Sahara and black Africans of the Senegal's southern bank, see Ghislaine Lydon, *On Trans-Saharan Trails* (Cambridge: Cambridge University Press, 2009), 36–43.

6. During the thirteenth century, these kingdoms were united under a single centralized Jolof empire that included the Serer kingdoms of Sin and Saloum and the Tekrur kingdom of the upper Senegal. Disintegration of the empire occurred in the mid-sixteenth century, causing the separation of the Wolof, Serer, and Fouta Toro (Tekrur) kingdoms. Jolof remained in existence but as a much weaker and isolated polity that never regained

supremacy. For an overview of the populations and states of the region between the Senegal and Gambia rivers, see Boubacar Barry, *Senegambia and the Atlantic Slave Trade*, 10–17.

7. The first definitive mention of the fort by the French appears in 1660. The fort was named after the first ship to arrive there, the *St. Louys*. Although France traded in West Africa prior to 1659, Saint Louis was the first French *comptoir* (literally bank branch or trade station) in West Africa. Cayor established relations with European commerce dating to the era of the Portuguese in the sixteenth century because of the kingdom's close proximity to the petite côte, a region of the coast suitable for ship-to-shore trade. Cayor, according to historian Mamadou Diouf, remained a secondary zone of commercial interest for Europeans until the slave trade accelerated in the early eighteenth century. See Boubacar Barry, *Le royaume du Waalo* (Paris: Karthala, 1972), 90–91, and Mamadou Diouf, *Le Kajoor au XIXe siècle* (Paris: Karthala, 1990), 76–79, 106–107.

8. Historian Ravane Boy claims that the old village of N'da is located near present-day Leybar on the mainland adjacent to Saint Louis. Camille Camara writes that the first record of the mayor calling the town Saint Louis, not Ndar, occurred in 1862. On the origins of Ndar, see Barry, *Le royaume du Waalo*, 42, 89; Regine Bonnardel, *Saint Louis du Sénégal: Mort ou Naissance?* 21–22; Ferdinand Brigaud and Jean Vast, *Saint Louis du Sénégal ville aux mille visages* (Dakar: Editions Clairafrique, 1987), 17; and Camille Camara, *Saint Louis du Sénégal* (Dakar: IFAN, 1968), 34.

9. On company government, see Abdoulaye Ly, *La compagnie du Sénégal*, and Philip Curtin, *Economic Change*.

10. Bruë's memoir disappeared sometime in the eighteenth century but was copied in Père Labat's account, *Nouvelle Relation de l'Afrique Occidentale*. Bruë's report is reproduced in a reprinting of Labat's account, which was included in a compilation of European travelers' accounts found in the rare book collection of the Library of Congress. See *Histoire Générale des Voyages*, vol. 3, ed. Antoine François Prévost (Holland: Pierre de Hondt, 1747), 317–18.

11. The comprehensive work on Gajaaga is Abdoulaye Bathily, *Portes de l'or: le royaume de Galam, Sénégal de l'ère musulmane au temps des négriers, viiie–xviiie siècle* (Paris: L'Harmattan, 1989). See also François Manchuelle, *Willing Migrants: Soninke Labor Diasporas, 1848–1960* (Athens: Ohio University Press, 1997). Saint Louis residents refer to the Soninke of Gajaaga as Sarakolle.

12. British and French rivalry over trade in North America is well documented. Seventeenth- and eighteenth-century rivalries also involved British and French footholds in West Africa. Britain seized Saint Louis for a short time from January to July 1693, but the period from 30 April 1758 to 11 February 1779, when Britain took control of Saint Louis and Gorée, marks the first period of sustained British occupation. The Treaty of Paris of 1763, which ended the Seven Years' War, resulted in the loss of all French possessions in Senegal. In April 1776, Senegambia was declared a British Crown colony.

13. For an account of the British invasion and occupation of Senegal in 1758, see Reverend John Lindsay, *A Voyage to the Coast of Africa in 1758* (London, 1867). Lindsay was chaplain of the Crown ship that took Gorée. On British attitudes toward Senegalese, see documents in Hargreaves, *France and West Africa: An Anthology of Historical Documents* (London: Macmillan, 1969), 76.

14. O'Hara was an Irish Protestant. The original petition of grievances presented by the habitants of Senegal against Colonel O'Hara can be found in the Public Records

Office, London C.O. 267/12. The petition was written in English, but as Hargreaves notes, no African in Senegal spoke English in 1758. For a reprint of the petition, see Hargreaves, *France and West Africa*, "The Rights of Senegalese," 76–83.

15. Boufflers (1738–1815) is a well-known figure in the history of French administration in Senegal. An aristocrat who was related to the king of Poland, Boufflers distinguished himself as a novelist, poet, and military officer. During his short governorship in Senegal (1785–87) he corresponded regularly with his French lover and future wife, Anne de Sabran. Signare Anne Pepin became Boufflers's companion while he lived in her house on Gorée. See A. Paul Bouteiller, *Le Chevalier de Boufflers et le Sénégal de son temps, 1785–1788* (Paris: Editions Lettres du Monde, 1995), and Mark Hinchman, "The Travelling Portrait: Women and Representation in Eighteenth-Century Senegal," in *Interpreting Colonialism,* ed. Byron R. Wells and Philip Stewart (Oxford: Voltaire Foundation, 2004), 35–39.

16. The best known accounts by French travelers from this period are Jean-Baptiste Léonard Durand, *A Voyage to Senegal* (London: Richard Phillips, 1806); Silvester Meinrad Xavier Golbéry, *Travels in Africa*, trans. W. Mudford, 2nd ed. (London, 1808); Geoffroy Villeneuve's *L'Afrique ou histoire, mœurs et coutumes des Africaines* (Paris, 1814); Pierre Labarthe, *Voyage au Sénégal pendant les années 1784–1785* (Paris, 1802); and M. Lamiral, *L'Afrique et le people Afriquain* (Paris, 1789), 50–53.

17. A number of recent studies have illustrated the extent to which the revolutionary discourse of the French Revolution spread to the colonies of the West Indies, Louisiana, Alabama, and South America. Laurent Dubois shows that beyond having an impact on people of the colonies, the very idea of universal rights, thought of solely as a product of Europe, was actually shaped by the struggle over slavery and citizenship in the French Caribbean. See Laurent Dubois, *A Colony of Citizens* (Chapel Hill: University of North Carolina Press, 2004). See also David Barry Gaspar and David Patrick Geggus, eds., *A Turbulent Time: The French Revolution and the Greater Caribbean* (Bloomington: Indiana University Press, 1997), and Christopher L. Miller, *The French Atlantic Triangle* (Durham, NC: Duke University Press, 2008).

18. The connection between the Haitian Revolution and Saint Louis is obscure. Marcson shows that some Haitian soldiers were deported to Senegal after having revolted under Toussaint L'Ouverture. The gens du couleur who formed part of this group of soldiers threatened Governor Lassere, who with habitant support deported the gens du couleur from Senegal. Marcson, "European-African Interaction," chap. 2.

19. Several colonies of the ancient regime sent their grievances to the Estates-General when it met in 1789 to challenge the nobility and the Church, which dominated government but paid no taxes. Delegates representing free people of color from the West Indies sent a petition calling for full rights of French citizenship. Dominique Lamiral presented the habitants document in Paris because Cornier, the mayor of Saint Louis, was denied entry to France in April 1789 due to his race. Lamiral, *L'Afrique et le peuple Afriquain.* On the origins of the document and its veracity, see William B. Cohen, *The French Encounter with Africans* (Bloomington: Indiana University Press, 1980, 2003): 100–115.

20. Lamiral, *L'Afrique et le peuple Afriquain,* 208.

21. Searing cites these statistics from a 1736 report on the role of "blacks and whites" in the service of the company. The document gives a report on the state of the workforce in all locations under company control (Gorée, Saint Louis, and Galam). See Searing, *West African Slavery,* 103, and Jean Bernard Lacroix, *Les français au Sénégal au temps de la compagnie des Indes* (Vincennes: Service Historique de la Marine, 1986).

22. Adopted from the Portuguese word *grumete, grumet* (alternatively *gourmets/gour-mettes*) referred to a cabin boy or apprentice seaman in medieval Europe. Writing in the mid-nineteenth century, David Boilat defined Senegal's grumets as baptized blacks. Boilat, *Esquisses Sénégalaises* (Paris: P. Bertrand, 1853), 39.

23. Marcson, "European-African Interaction," 16.

24. In the worst years (1741, 1742, 1746, and 1753), a quarter to a third of company employees died. For a study of the mercantile company personnel, see Lacroix, "Les français au Sénégal."

25. For a useful assessment of the Saint Louis population in the mid-eighteenth century, see James Searing's analysis of the February 1754 document, "Réponse du Conseil Supérieur au Sénégal du mémoire et observations." While population data is fragmentary, officials conducted this report in response to critics of the company who blamed the famine on the overconsumption of food by French and British slave ships and on the expanding population of Saint Louis and Gorée. Searing, *West African Slavery*, 103–104.

26. A system of slave and free wage labor existed in Saint Louis. The nature of this system as part of the mercantile practices of the town will be discussed in further detail in chapter 2.

27. Official data for population is scarce for the period when the French regained control. Accounts by French writers estimate the population numbered between 5,000 and 6,000. Although administrators did not conduct an official count of the population in this period, this estimate corresponds with official reports of an increase in the town's population due to the reliance on slave labor and free workers recruited from Galam. Durand, *A Voyage to Senegal*, 115–16; Lamiral, *L'Afrique*, 12.

28. Golbéry, *Travels in Africa*, 110.

29. Marcson, "European-African Interaction," chap. 1.

30. See petition presented by the inhabitants of Senegal, "Requested for a redress of the injustice done to them by his Excelly. Govr Ohara," 22 August 1775, reprinted in Hargreaves, *France and West Africa*, 76–83, and Golbéry, *Travels in Africa*.

31. Maps of Saint Louis from the late eighteenth century present an idealistic vision of the town with linear graphs indicating streets and rectangular blocs indicating dwellings. This is a reflection of French architectural sensibilities that associated linear drawing with rational urban planning rather than the nature of building in a sahelian town where construction relied on local materials and knowledge. Mark Hinchman, "Housing and Household on Gorée, Senegal 1758–1837," *Journal of the Society of Architectural Historians* 65 (June 2006), and Alain Sinou, *Comptoirs et villes coloniales du Sénégal* (Paris: Karthala, 1993).

32. French travelers who wrote memoirs of their travels in Senegal typically used these terms to describe Africans and métis in Saint Louis, even though classifications such as octoroon and quadroon described degrees of African and European mixture in French colonies of the greater Caribbean. Such terms do not appear to have been used by Senegalese. Durand, *A Voyage to Senegal*, 115.

33. See Prunneau de Pommegorge's description in George Brooks, "Signares of Saint Louis and Gorée." For a description of markets, produce, and special organizations of the town, see Lamiral, *L'Afrique et le peuple Afriquain*, 67–69.

34. Here I refer to trade houses of Calabar and the Bight of Biafra, Fanti associations, and the diaspora of Krio traders from Freetown, Sierra Leone, to Fernando Po. See K. O. Dike, *Trade and Politics in the Niger Delta, 1830–1885* (Oxford, 1956); Anthony G.

Hopkins, *An Economic History of West Africa* (New York: Columbia University Press, 1973); and Roger Gocking, *Facing Two Ways: Ghana's Coastal Communities under Colonial Rule* (Lanham, MD: University Press of America, 1999).

35. There was already a mayor for Gorée when the British arrived, which suggests that the practice of appointing a mayor existed during company rule. Although Lindsay notes that the mayor of Gorée was grumet, the mayors identified for Saint Louis seem to come from métis families. A 1775 petition lists métis habitant Charles Thevenot as mayor of Saint Louis. In 1789, métis mayor Charles Cornier authored a letter of grievance presented to the Estates-General in Paris on behalf of the habitants of Saint Louis. On mayors of Gorée, see Lindsay, *A Voyage to the Coast of Africa*, 76. On mayors of Saint Louis, see reprint of petition to Colonel Ohara in Hargreaves, *France and West Africa*, 40–41, and Lamiral, *L'Afrique*, 66.

36. Johnson notes that this practice may have evolved because of the lack of European personnel in the colony between 1790 and 1814. On evidence of councils, see Johnson, *The Emergence of Black Politics*, 41–42.

37. The original copy of the document presented to the Estates-General no longer exists, but it was reprinted in Dominique Lamiral's account of his time in Senegal. Lamiral presented the document to the assembly because Charles Cornier, the métis mayor of Saint Louis, was denied entry to France in April 1789. Although Lamiral likely crafted the wording of the document, it is a representation of habitant thought. Cornier was known to have a degree of western education as did the habitants who signed their names to the petition. On the background to the petition, see Cohen, *French Encounter with Africans*, 100–115.

38. Lamiral, like other European writers of the time, mistakenly assumed Senegal was a tributary of the Niger. A copy of the petition, "Trés humbles doleances et remontrances des habitants du Senegal aux citoyens Français tenant les Etats-Generaux," is reproduced in Lamiral, *L'Afrique*.

39. Lamiral's views are consistent with the history of racial thinking that developed as a result of French encounters with native peoples in North America. Belmessous argues that when French officials failed to "assimilate" native peoples by making them Catholic, then culture rather than physical traits became the basis of constructing racial difference. I think the same holds true for Senegal. Salhia Belmessous, "Assimilation and Racialism in Seventeenth- and Eighteenth-Century French Colonial Policy," *American Historical Review* (April 2005): 322–49, and Lamiral, *L'Afrique*, 208.

40. Senhoras appeared in Senegambia in the fifteenth century, when Portuguese sailors and merchants established a presence at Joal, Portudal and Rufisque, Portugal's principal ports on Senegal's Petit Côte. Luso-African society flourished in these locations. Signares of Gorée reportedly took French versions of Portuguese names, suggesting that some may have come to Gorée and Saint Louis from southern Senegambia. Golbéry, *Travels in Africa*, 20. On Luso-Africans at the court of the Damel of Cayor, see Curtin, *Economic Change*, 98–100. For more on Luso-African identity and the decline of this society, see Mark, *"Portuguese Style*; George Brooks, *EurAfricans*, 50–55; and Jean Boulègue, *Les Luso-Africains de Senegambie XVI–XIXe siècle* (Senegal: Universite de Dakar, 1972), 93–100.

41. Economic historians have written mainly about the role of Afro-Europeans in establishing networks of male traders with European men and male rulers in the Senegal River valley. Less attention has been paid to the household as the key unit of economic organization for the development of African and European commercial relations in the

precolonial era. Natalie Reyss first argued that interracial unions in Senegal's coastal towns developed because company employees and European officials were faced with overcoming problems of poor health, poor living conditions, and the need to find the most efficient means of carrying out long distance trade in a kin-based society. See Reyss's concept of "mariage comme moyen du survivre" in "Saint Louis du Sénégal a l'epoque pre-coloniale," pt. 1, chap. 3.

42. Golbéry, *Travels in Africa*, 110; Lamiral, *L'Afrique*, 50–53; Durand, *A Voyage to Sénégal*, 66–67. Comparative information about marriage on Gorée is useful in understanding how marriage operated in Saint Louis. See Geoffroy Villeneuve's description of marriage on Gorée, the observations of Prelong, the director of the hospital on Gorée from 1787 to 1789, and Pierre Labarthe's description of signares on Gorée between 1784 and 1785 for insight into the practice of mariage à la mode du pays, quoted in Brooks, "Signares of Saint Louis and Gorée," 34–48.

43. Lamiral, *L'Afrique*, 50–53; Durand, *A Voyage to Senegal*, 66–67; and Lindsay, *A Voyage to the Coast of Africa*, 76–79.

44. For a comparison with Wolof marriage traditions in the first half of the nineteenth century, see Boilat, *Esquisses sénégalaises*, 321. For an analysis of marriage in Wolof society, see Abdoulaye Bara Diop, *La famille Wolof* (Paris: Karthala, 1985).

45. Golbéry, *Travels in Africa*, 110–11; Lamiral, *L'Afrique*, 46–50.

46. Hargreaves, "Assimilation in Eighteenth-Century Senegal," *Journal of African History* 6, no. 2 (1965): 177–84; Abdoulaye Ly, *La compagnie du Sénégal*.

47. De Benoist, *Histoire de l'église catholique au Sénégal* (Paris: Karthala, 2008), 76–81.

48. On habitant fear of English religion, see Lindsay, *A Voyage to the Coast of Africa*, 75. Amanda Sackur suggested that Senegal's habitants adopted Christianity to distinguish themselves from Muslim traders who operated on the Saharan side. See Amanda Sackur, "The Development of Creole Society and Culture in Saint Louis and Gorée."

49. Lamiral, *L'Afrique*, 42. On celebration of Muslim festivals and Wolof practices, see Adanson, *Voyage au Senegal* (Publications de l'Université de Saint-Etienne, 1996), and Lindsay, *A Voyage to the Coast of Africa*, 76–77. On religion in late eighteenth-century Saint Louis, see Marcson, "European-African Interaction," 34. On the designation of a parish priest for Saint Louis in the 1780s and difficulty in maintaining a permanent clergy, see Joseph-Roger de Benoist, *Histoire de l'eglise catholique*, 80–82.

50. Fiona Mc Laughlin's study of Wolof in mid-nineteenth-century Saint Louis makes a persuasive case for the emergence of urban Wolof (rather than pure Wolof) in Saint Louis before its emergence as a popular form in mid-twentieth-century Dakar. Nineteenth-century writers spoke of the pervasiveness of Wolof in Saint Louis, and European accounts of the eighteenth century include Wolof words and phrases in their descriptions of the town. On the grammatical structure of urban Wolof, see Fiona Mc Laughlin, "On the Origins of Urban Wolof: Evidence from Louis Descemet's 1864 Phrase Book," *Language and Society* 37 (2008): 713–35, and Leigh Swigart, "Cultural Creolisation and Language Use in Post-Colonial Africa: The Case of Sénégal," *Africa* 64 (1994): 175–89.

51. Golbéry, *Travels in Africa*, 108–109.

52. While most habitant men developed proficiency in spoken French, it is difficult to discern the level of proficiency in reading and writing French among the habitant population. Literacy in reading was most likely connected to one's position in the commercial hierarchy and in politics and diplomatic/bureaucratic operations of the administration. Métis men had the highest opportunity for education from their fathers, as formal

French education was not established in the colony until the 1820s, as discussed in chapter 4 of this book.

2. MÉTIS SOCIETY AND TRANSFORMATIONS IN THE COLONIAL ECONOMY (1820–70)

1. Durand Valantin epitomizes métis ascendancy in the period. His father, Marseille merchant Barthelemy Durand (1770–1836), arrived in Senegal in the 1790s. His union to Signare Rosalie Aussenac produced fourteen children. Four brothers became licensed *négociants* (wholesalers) specializing in the gum trade and operating a firm in Gorée. Durand Valantin studied in Marseille. He returned to Senegal as notary and held key political positions as a notable habitant. He was also a member of Senegal's first Masonic Lodge, La Parfaite Union. Roger Pasquier, "Les traitants des comptoirs du Sénégal au milieu du XIXe siècle," in *Actes de Colloque Entreprises et Entrepreneurs en Afrique,* ed. Catherine Coquery Vidrovitch (Paris: Harmattan, 1983), 150–53,and Sylvain Sankale, "A la mode du pays," 440.

2. Homi Bhabha argues that post-Enlightenment English colonial discourse emphasized mimicry but in reality operated through relationships of mutual dependency. Groups such as the métis of Senegal were both part of the governing structures of colonial regimes that professed free trade, equal rights, and democratic principles while also being subjected to the hegemonic practices of these regimes. Leo Spitzer labels the psychological dependence of people in between colonizer and colonized as "a predicament of marginality." Homi Bhabha, *The Location of Culture* (London: Routledge, 1994), 122, and Leo Spitzer, *Lives in Between.*

3. Ralph Austen countered the "crisis of adaptability" argument by showing that indigenous forms of trade organization continued to operate and proved problematic for European merchant firms who could only achieve the penetration of western capital into West Africa's interior by military conquest. Recent studies of the social history of West Africa's Atlantic ports examine the long durée, showing how African middlemen and town residents adopted to the transition from slave trade to "legitimate" trade. Hopkins, *Economic History of West Africa;* Ralph Austen, *African Economic History* (Portsmouth: Heinemann, 1987); and Paul Lovejoy, "The Impact of the Atlantic Slave Trade on Africa: A Review of the Literature," *Journal of African History* 30, no. 3 (1989): 365–94. See also Robin Law, *A Social History of a West African Slavering Port, 1727–1892* (Athens: Ohio University Press, 2004), and Kristin Mann, *Slavery and the Birth of an African City: Lagos, 1760–1900* (Bloomington: Indiana University Press, 2007).

4. French firms in Senegal and British firms in Gambia and Sierra Leone began hiring Lebanese and Syrian immigrants to act as retail merchants in the peanut basin. The first Syrians appear in the baptismal registry of the Catholic Church of Saint Louis in 1897: Joseph Habiff, baptized 27 May 1897, to Habiff Jabour and Faridd Joseph, Sor diocese, Saint Louis. On the displacement of Krio intermediaries in the palm oil trade, see Martin Lynn, "Technology, Trade, and 'A Race of Native Capitalists': The Krio Diaspora of West Africa and the Steamship, 1852–95," *Journal of African History* 33 (1992): 421–40.

5. In 1802, French colonists sought to compensate for the slave revolt in Saint Domingue by turning Senegal into a planter colony for sugar cultivation, using slave labor that would otherwise be exported to the Caribbean. Similar plans had been proposed by Britain in 1794 for plantation colonies at the mouth of the Gambia and in Sierra Leone. None of these schemes ever came to fruition, as colonists underestimated soil

quality and the problem of forcing Africans to leave their lands to cultivate cash crops on French-controlled land in the Senegal River valley. On the history of plantation schemes in Senegambia and the failure of the French plantation scheme at Richard Toll, see Boubacar Barry, *Le royaume du Waalo*, 203–204, 215–36.

6. Schmaltz, his wife, and a crew of four hundred personnel, including African crew members and geographers, were part of the convoy of ships that left France to accept the transfer of power from England. The raft of the *Méduse* was wrecked on a sandbar off the coast of today's Mauritania. Schmaltz was aboard the lifeboat that cut loose the raft of the *Méduse*. Schmaltz's involvement in the shipwreck and the national attention the scandal garnered in France led to his resignation in December 1817. On 13 March 1819, Schmaltz returned to Senegal for a second term, when he began to implement his plan for the plantation colony. Explorer Gaspard Mollien was aboard the ship and wrote his account of the shipwreck in *Travels in Africa to the Sources of the Senegal and Gambia in 1818* (London, 1820).

7. H. B. Gerbidon to Minister of Marine, 25 August 1827, reprinted in Hargreaves, *France and West Africa*, 90–92.

8. These river trade markets were called escales, not markets (marchés), because they differed from the year-round markets of Saint Louis, Europe, or even market towns of Africa's interior. The escales only operated during the trading season from November to January (during the petite traite) and February to July (the grande traite).

9. I rely on data collected by James Webb on the increase of river craft. For the numbers of merchants and traders in the Senegal River trade in the 1830s, see James Webb, *Desert Frontier* (Madison: University of Wisconsin Press, 1995). For population data for Saint Louis in 1835, see "Notices statistiques sur les colonies françaises jusque 1839" and "Le tableau de population de Saint Louis et Gorée pour l'année 1835," in C. Becker, V. Martin, J. Schmitz, and M. Chastanet, *Les premiers recensements au Sénégal et l'évolution démographique* (Dakar: ORSTOM, 1983), 5.

10. Mollien, *Travels in Africa*, 4–6.

11. The British held a stake at Portendick, and the Dutch maintained a fort on the island of Arguin on the southwestern coast of today's Mauritania. In the late 1600s and early 1700s, Portendick supplied the majority of exports from Senegal. The increasing aridity of the Sahara pushed acacia groves further south, making Saint Louis and French sites along the Senegal strategic locations for the gum trade. Most sources of gum for European markets came from Arabia until the eighteenth century, when the southwest Sahara became the sole supplier of gum to Europe. Webb, *Desert Frontier*, 124.

12. Webb's analysis of the political economy of this region from the seventeenth to the mid-nineteenth centuries illustrates the interconnection between gum exports, grain trade, and import of textiles. His statistics on the rise in gum consumption in Europe and increases in the volume of gum sent from Senegal shows the importance of Senegal gum on the European market. Golbéry claimed French profits of 1,000 percent from the gum trade. See Webb, *Desert Frontier*, 100. For an eyewitness account of the expansion of the gum trade in the 1780s, see Durand, *A Voyage to Senegal*, 71, and Golbéry, *Travels in Africa*, 175–78.

13. Webb, *Desert Frontier*, 115–24.

14. On the 1827 civil war and the attempted Muslim revolution, see Barry, *Le royaume du Waalo*, 243–49. For the war's demographic impact on Saint Louis and the growth of Muslim Saint Louis petty traders, see Marc Marcson, "European-African Interaction," 154–68.

15. In the 1830s and 1840s, conflicts between Trarza, Walo, and Saint Louis intensified. Habitant families had lineage ties to ruling elites in Walo. French administrators reported on the influence that the Pellegrin family had with the Trarza. In the 1830s, the habitants helped the Trarza emir Mohammed El Habib get rid of his rival, Moctar. Trarza and Walo went on to form an alliance through the marriage between the Walo princess Ndymöböt and the emir, which threatened to make Saint Louis dependent on the Trarza. Marcson, "European-African Interaction," chap. 3.

16. Many of the records of Maurel and Prom and the other Bordeaux firms that were held at the Bordeaux Chamber of Commerce were destroyed during attacks on the city during World War II. The Gironde departmental archives contain some records of Jean Germain Clamargeran and his son-in-law Pierre Delile Jay, who formed an association for business ventures in Senegal as well as Jay's correspondence regarding commercial dealings with habitants Pecarrère, Duchesne, Louis Alsace, Lazare Audibert, and Auguste Teisseire. Fonds Delile Jay, 14 J, #70, #82, #86 ADB.

17. On the political influence of the Bordeaux merchants in nineteenth-century Senegal, see Leland Barrows, "General Faidherbe, the Maurel and Prom Company, and French Expansion in Sénégal" (PhD diss., UCLA, 1974), and Joan Droege Casey, "The Politics of French Imperialism in the Early Third Republic: The Case of Bordeaux" (PhD diss., University of Missouri, Columbia, 1973).

18. J. Devès and H. Prom rented rooms from the same Bordeaux agent, M. Potin, when they arrived in Gorée. The generation of Bordeaux merchants who came to Senegal after 1850 (Cheri Peyrissac, Vezia) began as agents in the Bordeaux headquarters of Maurel and Prom, Buhan and Teisseire, or Devès and P. Lacoste (later Devès and Chaumet). On the Bordeaux branch of the Devès, see "Etablissements Devès et Chaumet, Bourdeaux, à Centre de Recherches et de Documentation du Sénégal," 3 April 1981.

19. Yves Pehaut has written the best study of the connection between Bordeaux and Saint Louis commerce that details the biographies of the Bordeaux traders: "A l'époque de la 'traite' de l'arachide: les 'bordelais' au Sénégal," *Revue historique de Bordeaux et du Département de la Gironde* 30 (1983–84): 50–53.

20. "Etablissements Maurel et Prom à M. Directeur du Centre de Recherches et de Documentation du Sénégal," Bordeaux, 10 March 1981, and Teisseire, "La famille d'Erneville." In a journal entry of 31 May 1840, Germain Crespin writes that he sent his son, Jean Jacques, to France to study. For a reprint of the private journal of Germain Crespin, see Reyss, "Saint Louis du Sénégal," annexe 1.

21. Métis acquired slaves by purchasing them in public markets in the interior or inheriting them and as debt payments, gifts, or dowries in marriage. On slave ownership in Saint Louis, see Saliou Mbaye, "L'esclavage domestique à Saint Louis à travers les archives notariés, 1817–1848," in *Saint Louis et l'esclavage,* ed. Djibril Samb (Dakar: IFAN, 2000), 141–47.

22. Mansour Aw, "Saint Louis, chef-lieu de la Concession du Sénégal et sa place dans la traite négriere aux XVIIe et XVIIIe siècles," in *Saint Louis et l'esclavage.*

23. On slavery in Cayor, see Diouf, *Le Kajoor au XIXe siècle.* For sociological treatment of slavery in Wolof society, see Abdoulaye Bara Diop, *La société Wolof* (Paris: Karthala, 1981), and Martin Klein, "Servitude among the Wolof and Serrer of Senegambia," in *Slavery in Africa,* ed. Suzanne Miers and Igor Kopytoff (Madison: University of Wisconsin Press, 1977).

24. The administration's 1835 account of the town's population reported 4,924 free people, 634 indentured workers, and 6,118 slaves. Becker et al., *Les premiers recensements,*

and Martin A. Klein, *Slavery and Colonial Rule in French West Africa* (Cambridge: Cambridge University Press, 1998), 23.

25. Aw, "Saint Louis, chef-lieu de la Concession du Sénégal," 81 and François Zucarelli, "Le Régime des engagés à temps au Sénégal (1817–1848)," *Cahiers d'Etudes Africaines 2*, no. 7 (1962): 420–61.

26. Evidence suggests a clandestine trade in young girls continued until the end of the nineteenth century. Searing, *West African Slavery*, 122.

27. Germain Crespin married Khayta Macoumba Leye, who was his principal slave and nurse for the children born of his first marriage to Louison Alin. Reyss, "Saint Louis du Sénégal," *Journal Privé de Germain Crespin*, annexe 1, 59, and Georges Crespin, interview with author. On slave women as market traders and slave owners, see Searing, *West African Slavery*, 123.

28. For a general history of Soninke labor migration and the role of Soninke as laptots in the Senegal River trade, see Manchuelle, *Willing Migrants*, 59–63.

29. Habitant and négociant Louis Alsace owned 111 slaves. Reyss, "Saint Louis du Sénégal," 144.

30. For an account of slavery in Saint Louis in the eighteenth century, see Golbéry, *Travels in Africa*, 109; Lamiral, *L'Afrique*, 60; and Adanson, *Voyage au Sénégal*, 38. For a nineteenth-century description, see Boilat, *Esquisses Sénégalais*, 213. Boilat explains that when habitants of Saint Louis baptized slaves, it was followed by an act of freedom, whereas habitants of Gorée baptized all slaves, accounting for a larger population of grumets.

31. Pasquier studied marriage contracts for nineteen métis couples between 1838 and 1850. He found that at least half of these unions brought together goods and earnings of at least 40,000 francs, which is on a par with the Parisian middle class. For documentation on métis material wealth, see Pasquier, "Le Sénégal au milieu du XIXe siècle," table 503, and Pasquier, "Les traitants des comptoirs du Sénégal," 152.

32. "Obligation par Nicholas d'Erneville à Adélaïde Crespin," 28 April 1834, 1Z3, #16, ANS. For other examples, see Sylvain Sankale, "A la mode du pays," 465–67, and Mbaye, "L'esclavage domestique," 147–54.

33. Several studies have analyzed cycles of price fluctuations in the gum-for-guinée trade and the delicate balance of the supply of guinées by importers, the cost of merchandise to traders at the coast, the price for guinées sold in the escales, and the nature of annual gum harvests, which could fluctuate because of the unpredictability of rainfall and desert wind conditions. These factors contributed to great prosperity in times of good harvests and adequate supply to meet demand, but resulted in sharp losses in times of poor harvests or oversupply of guinées. Webb's data shows that Wolof and Tokolor demand for guinées increased in the 1820s, whereas previously these markets sought goods such as coral, amber, and other types of cloth. For the specific problems in the supply and demand of the gum trade and the specific economic conditions that caused the gum crisis of the late 1830s, see Roger Pasquier, "Le Senegal au milieu du XIXe siècle," 673–751; Webb, *Desert Frontier*, 124–31; Marcson, "European-African Interaction," 170–80.

34. From 1837 to 1840, the amount of guinées for each consecutive year amounted to 138,000, 240,000, 138,000, and 109,000. This illustrates the rampant speculation on the part of metropolitan importers who bet on the ability to liquidate massive quantities of the textiles at low costs and the rising demand in Europe for the West African commodity. Compounding this problem, négociants did not stockpile guinées from year to year because of the dangers that flooding and mildew posed and because they did not want to

keep old supplies of expensive guinées if the next year's supplies were cheaper. Webb, *Desert Frontier,* 126–27, and Pasquier, "Le Sénégal au milieu du XIXe siècle," 479–592.

35. An 1836 administrative order granted French merchants direct access to the river trade posts, breaking the métis monopoly on the gum trade in the escales. Marcson, "European-African Interaction,"175–77.

36. Ibid. Although highly capitalized wholesalers, like Maurel and Prom, did not experience losses, the wild fluctuation in prices did force some metropolitan merchants who had recently opened firms in Saint Louis to get out of the import/export trade and into the upriver markets in order to avoid losses.

37. Anne Raffenel, *Nouveau Voyage dans le Pays des Nègres suivi d'études sur la colonie du Sénégal* (Paris: Imprimerie de Napoléon Chaix, 1856), and Webb, *Desert Frontier.*

38. For more on the implications of the law, see Marcson, "European-African Interaction," 188–89.

39. "Table des créanciers du Banque du Sénégal, 1895–1901," ANS Q40; Pasquier, "Les traitants des comptoirs," 154–61; Marfaing, *L'evolution du commerce au Sénégal,* 58.

40. Liste générale des traitants, négociants et habitants notables in Reyss, "Saint Louis du Sénégal," annexe 3, 61–68.

41. The decree announcing the end of slavery was one of the first measures instituted by the Republic on 27 April 1848. It was intended for the plantation colonies of the Caribbean, but had an impact on Senegal's two coastal towns.

42. Paris founded colonial banks to handle these indemnity payments.

43. Indemnity payments had not been worked out at the time of abolition, but they were in place when the Bank of Senegal opened. Ironically, Maurel and Prom bought the largest amount of indemnity payments from Saint Louis and Gorée slave owners at a lower price than that offered by the administration because signares and habitants were in debt to the firm. "Banques coloniales," Bordeaux Chamber of Commerce, Séance, 31 January 1900. For a general history of the Bank of Senegal, see Ghislaine Lydon, "Les péripéties d'une institution financière: La Banque du Sénégal, 1844–1901," in *AOF: réalités et heritages,* ed. Charles Becker, Saliou Mbaye, and Ibrahima Thioub (Dakar: Direction Archives du Sénégal, 1997), 480–81.

44. Pasquier, "Les traitants des comptoirs," 161, and Webb, *Desert Frontier,* 130–31.

45. Fréderic Carrére and Paul Holle, *De la Sénégambie française* (Paris: Librairie de Firmin Didot Frères, 1855), 353.

46. Boilat, *Esquisses Sénégalaises,* 210–11.

47. This debate has generated new documentation on Saint Louis Muslim traders and their activities in the upper Senegal ports of Bakel, Podor, and Kayes as well as in Sine, Saloum, and the Gambia. See Mamadou Diouf, "Traitants ou négociants? Les commerçants Saint-Louisiens (2ᵉ moitié du XIXe–début XXe): Hamet Gora Diop (1846–1910): étude de cas"; Babacar Fall and Abdoul Sow, "Les traitants Saint-Louisiens dans les villes escales du Sénégal, 1850–1930"; and Mohamed Mbodji,"D'une frontière à l'autre ou l'histoire de la marginalisation des commerçants sénégambiens sur la longue durée: La Gambie de 1816 à 1879," all in *Commerce et commerçants en Afrique de l'Ouest,* ed. Boubacar Barry and Leonhard Harding (Paris: L'Harmattan, 1992).

48. Financial records of métis family businesses are fragmentary. The Devès papers offer the most comprehensive view of a family firm that regained dominance in the colonial economy between 1860 and 1890. Property transactions after 1850 are recorded in notary documents but are not systematically classified. Devès papers, 1Z5–1Z18, Actes

Notaries Saint Louis, 1881. Research on urban land tenure may yield greater insights into the relationship between power and property in the towns. See Mohamed Mbodj, "The Abolition of Slavery in Sénégal, 1820–1890," in *Breaking the Chains*, ed. Martin A. Klein (Madison: University of Wisconsin Press, 1993), 197–215.

49. The British firm Foster and Smith was the first to export peanuts from the Gambia in the 1830s. Protective tariffs prevented early adoption of peanut exports in Senegal, but in 1840 the Bordeaux Chamber of Commerce began to lobby Paris to remove the protective tariffs against peanut exports to open exports from Senegal. In 1881, Cheri Peryrissac of Peyrissac et Cie founded the only peanut oil company in Senegal, located in Sor. Yves Pehaut, "Les oléagineux dans les pays d'Afrique Occidentale associes au marche commun" (PhD diss., Université de Bordeaux III, 1973), vol. 2; George E. Brooks, "Peanuts and Colonialism," *Journal of African History* 16, no. 1 (1975): 29–54; and Pierre Guillard, "Chéri Peyrissac," *UNIR: Echo de Saint Louis* 140 (December 1994): 7–11.

50. On Ponty's speech at the chamber of commerce, see Pehaut, "Les Bordelaises au Senegal," 50. For more on Bordeaux Chamber of Commerce and peanut exports from Senegal, see Fonds de la Chambre de Commerce de Bordeaux, 21 J ADB, and "Procès-verbaux," Chambre de Commerce de Bordeaux, Bibliothèque Municipale de Bordeaux, 1894–1901.

51. My understanding of the Devès family's business interests comes from reading the family papers, especially "Créances et Reconnaissances de dettes," 1913–31, 1Z10 ANS; "Emir Ely Ould Mohamed El Habib," Actes Notaires Saint Louis, 31 October 1881. On Devès interests in Mellacourie, see John Hargreaves, *Prelude to the Partition of West Africa* (London: Macmillan, 1963), 131–36, and private communication with Ibrahima Diallo, Saint Louis, Senegal.

52. Auguste Teisseire (1813–94) arrived in Senegal from Bordeaux in 1830 and became a négociant in the gum trade. He married Marie-Anne d'Erneville. Their sons, Auguste "Omer" Leopold Teisseire (1840–86) and Albert Teisseire (1842–82), were both born in Senegal and married into Bordelaise families. Guillaume Guillabert, "Arbre généalogique des familles Descemet-Guillabert," "Note sur M. Descemet," Podor, 13 February 1886, 4E4, ANS and "Auguste Teisseire," Senegalmétis, http://www.planete-genealogie.fr/xricou/familles_métisses_030510/fiche/individu/?IndiID=20950.

53. French military expansion in the interior secured new locations for trade. Faidherbe fixed the escales on the Senegal by establishing French military posts at Podor, Bakel, Matam, and Médine. Similar expansion south secured locations along the Sine, Saloum, and Southern Rivers. The administrative decree of 22 January 1852 formally recognized the right of French trade houses to set up locations in the escales as long as they took an "indigene" intermediary to conduct trade. Muslim Saint Louis traders capitalized on these developments by agreeing to act as agents in the escales for French firms. The decree of 22 March 1880 ended the protected role of African middlemen in the trade depots. On the strategies used by Muslim Saint Louis traders between 1850 and 1880, see Fall and Sow, "Les traitants Saint-Louisiens dans les villes escales du Sénégal," in *Commerce et commerçants en Afrique de l'Ouest*,

54. Recent research has recovered the biography of Theophile "Fine" Turpin, who built a commercial empire at Ndiaffate between Kaolack and Foundiougne after 1889. He was Catholic and had thirteen wives. Administrative reports typically record conflicts at the posts. But these were locations of intense interaction between Saint Louis traders and Saint Louis bureaucrats appointed as interpreters or commandants. Further research on the role of urban elites in the interior trade posts may yield additional information. On

Fine Turpin, see Laurence Marfaing, *L'évolution du commerce au Sénégal,* 253–55, and Fall and Sow, "Les traitants Saint-Louisiens dans les villes escales du Sénégal," in *Commerce et commerçants en Afrique de l'Ouest,* " 175–76. On trade rivalries at Rio Nunez and conflict between administrators and traders, see "Incident administrateur Martin-d'Erneville, commerçant," 7G9, #4, ANS, and Dossier G. Crespin, 1879–81, 7G3, #226–29 ANS. Also Christian Valantin, interview with author.

55. These young men may have been household slaves or indentures who worked as apprentices for the trade houses of métis or Europeans who educated them and relied on them to assist in their business ventures in the interior. See Jean Aly élevé chez M. Valantin entrée 1846," "François Jupiter élevé chez M. B. Pellegrin entrée 1846," "Joseph Lelieve élevé chez M. O'hara entrée 1846," and "Edouard Bambara élevé chez M. Teisseire entrée 1848," *Registry of Students of the Primary School of the Ploërmel Brothers in Saint Louis, 1843–1892* (Catholic Church, Saint Louis diocese, Sor, Senegal).

56. When faced with confusion over how antislavery law should be applied in Senegal, Faidherbe turned to the colonial judiciary to clarify policy. They developed a distinction between "subjects," who were under the sovereignty of African rulers and customary law, and "citizens," who were the inhabitants of the towns and thus subject to French law. For an overview of French antislavery policy in Senegal, see Klein, *Slavery and Colonial Rule in French West Africa.*

57. On vagabonds in Senegal's towns, see Ibrahima Thioub, "Juvenile Marginality and Incarceration during the Colonial Period: The First Penitentiary Schools in Senegal, 1888–1927," in *A History of Prison and Confinement in Africa,* ed. Florence Bernault and Janet L. Roitman (Portsmouth, NH: Heinemann, 2003).

58. Martin Klein's research on this subject confirms the persistence of child labor in the colonial towns under the guise of wardship. Despite attempts to enact reforms in the late 1870s and 1880s, the colonial judiciary and the administration only took serious measures to end slavery once military conquest had been achieved and France consolidated its territories in West Africa. "Lt. Governor to Governor General," 4 May 1904, K23, #15, ANS.

59. Between 1861 and 1863, the civil registry contains ten entries for pileuses. See Carrère's report in Klein, *Slavery and Colonial Rule,* 29–30, 73, and "Actes de Naissance de la commune de Saint Louis," Etat Civil, 1861–63, 8M/52 ANS. On the problem of sexual abuse, see Bernard Moitt, "Slavery, Flight, and Redemption in Senegal, 1819–1905," *Slavery and Abolition* 14, no. 2 (1993): 70–86.

60. It is impossible to know how many liberated slaves were assigned to métis families. Martin Klein estimates 10 percent. The Catholic registry of baptism indicates that métis men and women served as godparents for children placed in the charge of Catholic habitants. These entries also suggest that Catholic families played key roles in taking in young girls from regions of the interior, displaced as a result of slavery or conquest. For example, "Joséphine Marie Sene," 11 ans née environ Soudan de parents inconnus. Confiée à la famille Octave Armstrong, Parish registry of baptisms, 9 April 1895. Born in 1919, my informant recalled her mother's knowledge of slaves in métis households. Her mother died in 1967 at age 78 and was likely born in 1889. Georgette Bonet, interview with author, Saint Louis (Sor) Senegal, 1 December 2000.

3. RELIGION, MARRIAGE, AND MATERIAL CULTURE

1. "Devès, Jean Lazare Hyacinthe à dlle Charlotte Louise Crespin," Civil Registry of Marriage Commune of Saint Louis, 22 June 1889, ANS.

2. The act specifies that the officer performed the wedding at the Devès home because of Madeleine Tamba's illness. This is the spelling of her name as it appears in the civil registry. The standard spelling, Madeline Tambe, appears in captions written when the collection was donated to the archives in the 1980s. The surname Tamba refers to Tambacoumba, the Sarakole region of eastern Senegal where many laptots came from. Her father appears as deceased Tamba Daba Daguisery and her mother Dame Awa Souleymane N'Diaye, also deceased. "Devès, Pierre Gaspard et Madeleine Fatma Daba Daguisery dite Madeleine Tamba," Civil Registry of Marriage Commune of Saint Louis, 9 May 1889, ANS.

3. Ann L. Stoler, "Making Empire Respectable: The Politics of Race and Sexual Morality in Twentieth-Century Colonial Cultures," *American Ethnologist* 16 (November 1989): 644. For an early conceptualization of colonialism's cultural impact on both France and Africa, see G. Wesley Johnson, "Introduction: Reciprocal Influences between French and Africans in the Age of Imperialism," in *Double Impact: France and Africa in the Age of Imperialism*, ed. G. Wesley Johnson (Westport, CT: Greenwood Press, 1985).

4. Bourdieu, *State Nobility*, 272–99.

5. Although I am specifically concerned with transformations in métis society and identity, I suspect that similar patterns can be identified among Muslim habitants. My conversations with descendants of Muslim authorities and notables of Saint Louis suggest that learned clerics, who acted as interpreters for the political affairs bureau and as judges for the Muslim tribunal, played important roles in communicating piety and respectability. The Muslim tribunal also served as a mechanism in which ideologies of marriage and familial arrangements could be articulated. Almamy Mathieu Fall, interview by author, 27 May 2000 (Saint Louis); Swadou Seck and Aby Diop, interview by David Robinson, 29 and 30 June 1997 (Saint Louis).

6. Genevieve Lecuir-Nemo, *Anne-Marie Javouhey* (Paris: Karthala, 2001), 87.

7. Ibid., 80, and Benoist, *Histoire de l'eglise catholique*, 94–96.

8. The congregation of Saint-Esprit is also known as the Spiritains or Holy Ghost Fathers. For seminal works on the history of Christianity in Senegal, see Benoist, *Histoire de l'eglise catholique*; Brigaud and Vast, *Saint Louis du Sénégal: ville aux mille visages*; D. H. Jones, "The Catholic Mission and Some Aspects of Assimilation in Senegal, 1817–1852," *Journal of African History* 21 (1980): 323–40; and Jean Delacourt, *Histoire Religieuse du Sénégal* (Dakar: Editions Clairafrique, 1976), 24–26.

9. Sinou, *Comptoirs et villes coloniales du Sénégal*, 132.

10. For a complete history of the order and a biography of the founder, see Lecuir-Nemo, *Anne-Marie Javouhey*.

11. Sister Rosalie, Mother Javouhey's sister, headed the delegation in Senegal. Their brother, Pierre, accompanied them to act as their protector on the journey and in the colony, a sign of the deep fear that European men felt for unaccompanied European women in the colonies. This was especially true in 1819 Senegal, which was rumored to be exceptionally dangerous and unhealthy given the harrowing reports in France about the shipwreck of the *Méduse* only two years earlier.

12. The nuns opened a school on Gorée in 1822 and had plans to establish a school in Dagana, where the founder obtained a concession as part of the annexation of land from Walo to build a French plantation colony in this fertile region of the middle Senegal (called the *jeri*). The objective was to build a school to train an African clergy, but the plan failed when her cousin who was supposed to run the concession died. Lecuir-Nemo, *Anne-Marie Javouhey*, 165–70.

13. Amand Mamadou Sy came from the kingdom of Bondu in the region called Galam. He may have been the first of young Africans taken from kingdoms of the interior and confined in French schools as "hostages." Jean Pierre Moussa's father, Pierre, served as cantor for the church in Saint Louis. Florence came from Fouta Toro. She was liberated aboard a slave ship seized by French authorities, and then liberated (a process called *rachat* or "to buy back") by the wife of a French official. When the couple returned to France, Sister Rosalie adopted Florence, then entrusted her to serve as an interpreter for Mother Anne-Marie Javouhey when she arrived in the colony in 1822. Ibid., 170–81.

14. On their experience as seminarians in France, see Jones, "The Catholic Mission," 333–39; Benoist, *Histoire de l'eglise catholique*, 117–22; Lecuir-Nemo, *Anne-Marie Javouhey*, 181–83; and Yvon Bouquillon and Robert Cornevin, *David Boilat: Le Précurseur* (Dakar: Les Nouvelles Editions Africaines, 1981).

15. The careers of the three clergy and the difficulties that they suffered with their superiors and the administration in Senegal are well documented in the archives of the Spiritains and Saint Joseph de Cluny as well as by the administration in Saint Louis. Benoist, *Histoire de l'église catholique,* and "M. Kobès adresse à la propagande," journal of Abbé Boilat, 1852, Annales Religieuses-Dakar, 2Z1, ANS.

16. Boilat's biography is the best known because he worked as a priest in France until his death on 19 December 1901. Born 20 April 1814 in Saint Louis, Boilat was 13 when he and the others left for France. Abdoulaye Bara Diop suspects that Boilat saw the Church as family when his mother died, leaving him an orphan. Boilat compiled information for his book during his year of travels through France. He completed writing the work in the village of Seine-et-Marne, where he was named clergy of the parish. Published in 1853, it included sketches of various "types" of groups inhabiting Senegal's countryside and the signares of the towns. Boilat is buried in the cemetery of Seine et Marne. Abdoulaye Bara Diop, introduction to Boilat's *Esquisses sénégalaises*, 5–6.

17. These complaints are not uncommon in missionary reports, in part because the rhetorical device served to generate sympathy and support for their efforts at home. Boilat, *Esquisses sénégalaises*, 218–20.

18. Benoist, *Histoire de l'église catholique,* 100–102, and Boilat, *Esquisses sénégalaises*, 221.

19. Docteur d'Anfreville de la Salle, *Notre Vieux Sénégal: Son histoire, son état actuel ce qu'il peut devenir* (Paris: Librairie Maritime Coloniale, 1909), 101. Nineteen métis marriages, one signare, and two grumet marriages are noted in the Catholic registry between 1845 and 1849. "Matricule de la Mission Catholique a Saint Louis jusqu'en 1886, Notes prises par Oumar Ba en 1966."

20. Born in the late eighteenth century, Sheikh Umar Tal broke from the Qadiriyya, the dominant Sufi order among Fulbe clerics in West Africa in the early 1800s. He made three pilgrimages to Mecca, where he was guided by a North African cleric appointed by Ahmad al-Tijani, founder of the Tijani lodge. Tal considered the Tijaniyya the most important Sufi order and incompatible with others. He gained a following in Fouta Toro, on the middle Senegal. As the jihad gained momentum, French officials viewed all Foutanke (whom they called "Tokolor") with suspicion. For an interpretation of the Umarian expansion, see David Robinson, *The Holy War of Umar Tal: The Western Sudan in the Mid-Nineteenth Century* (New York: Oxford University Press, 1985). For Robinson's placement of the Umarian movement in the context of Islamic movements in the Western Sudan before Tal and after, see Robinson, *Paths of Accommodation*. On French attitudes toward Umar, see Leland Barrows, "General Faidherbe, the Maurel and Prom

Company, and French Expansion in Sénégal" (PhD diss., UCLA, 1974), 494, and Yves-Jean Saint Martin, *Le Sénégal sous le second empire: naissance d'un empire colonial, 1850–1871* (Paris: Karthala, 1989).

21. For a contemporary account of Al-Hajj Umar's 1846–47 tour of Bakel and Podor, see Frédéric Carrère and Paul Holle, *De la Sénégambie française*, 194–96. For a critical perspective on this event and the secondhand report of Umar's visit contained in the Carrère and Holle account, see Saint-Martin, *Le Sénégal sous le second empire*, 57, and Robinson, *The Holy War of Umar Tal*, 124.

22. Robinson cautions that sometimes information filtered by the Saint Louisians was not always reliable whether it involved the transmission of information to Umar about the French or transmission of information to the French about Umar. For a reproduction of the letter Al-Hajj Umar wrote to the "children of Ndar," see Robinson, *Holy War of Umar Tal*, 162–63.

23. Sinou, *Comptoirs et ville coloniales du Sénégal*, 131–36.

24. Frédéric Carrère was appointed by the king to be a judge and lawyer for Senegal's appeals court. Genealogy records suggest that he married a métis woman first and an African woman second. Born in Saint Louis in 1807, Paul Holle died at the battle of Médine, fighting against the Umarians on 6 December 1862. He was the son of métis négociant Paul Holle and Mariam Sambou. Their account depicts the expansion of Umar Tal's movement as a threat to the Saint Louis community, which in their view meant French power and métis habitants in particular. Carrère and Holle, *De la Sénégambie française*, 14–18. For works that express a similar point of view with regard to Islam and the French, see Boilat, *Esquisses sénégalaises*, 480–84, and Anne Raffenel, *Voyage dans l'Afrique occidentale française* (Paris, 1846).

25. The similarities between the role of marriage in guaranteeing the economic and symbolic capital of families for the emerging bourgeoisie in nineteenth-century France are strikingly similar to sociologist Pierre Bourdieu's analysis of marriage as symbolic capital, which had value for families in maintaining their elite status and exercising political power. See Bourdieu, *The State Nobility*, 272–90.

26. Docteur d'Anfreville de la Salle, *Notre Vieux Sénégal*, 102–103. See also Guillaume Guillabert, "Arbre généalogique des familles Descemet-Guillabert."

27. See Tableau des noms des principales familles métisses de Saint Louis avant 1854, in Natalie Reyss, "Saint Louis du Sénégal," annexe 1, 101–102.

28. Boilat, *Esquisses sénégalaises*, 222–24.

29. Barbara Cooper shows that among the Hausa of Maradi, dowry served as the most important symbolic asset for establishing a woman's worth and that of female kin. Similarly, Kristin Mann demonstrates that elite Yoruba women in Lagos relied on indirect dowry as a means of ensuring the social standing of the groom and asserting the social standing of the bride. Barbara Cooper, *Marriage in Maradi* (Portsmouth: Heinemann, 1997), and Kristin Mann, *Marrying Well*. For comparison with marriage and inheritance strategies among French elites in the nineteenth and early twentieth centuries, see Pierre Bourdieu, *State Nobility*, 261–85.

30. Lynn Hunt argues that revolutionary thinkers sought to eliminate paternalism but not patriarchy. Napoleon solidified patriarchal laws and concepts by subsuming regional practices and understandings of marriage and family life into a national code. Jurists who authored the civil code (also known as the Napoleonic code) eliminated the liberties afforded women under revolutionary law. This formed the basis of a struggle over the course

of the nineteenth century for women's access to full citizenship rights. Lynn Hunt, *The Family Romance of the French Revolution* (Berkeley: University of California Press, 1992); Rachel G. Fuchs, "Seduction, Paternity, and the Law in Fin de Siècle France," *Journal of Modern History* 72, no. 4 (2000): 944–89; Jean Elisabeth Pedersen, "Special Customs: Paternity Suits and Citizenship in France and the Colonies, 1870–1912," in *Domesticating the Empire*, ed. Julia Clancy Smith and Frances Gouda (Charlottesville: University Press of Virginia, 1998), 43–65; and Roderick Phillips, *Putting Asunder: A History of Divorce in Western Society* (Cambridge: Cambridge University Press, 1988).

31. Stoler's analysis of Foucault's history of sexuality shows how a colonial discourse on sexuality informed theoretical analysis of the making of bourgeois notions of sexuality. Ann Laura Stoler, *Race and the Education of Desire* (Durham: Duke University Press, 1995), chap. 2.

32. The civil code is the basis for family law, property rights, and individual rights, but it also established commercial and criminal law and divided civil law into property law and family law. The civil code reintroduced slavery in the colonies after it had been briefly outlawed under the revolutionary regime. For the decree promulgating the civil code in Senegal, see the decree cited in Bonnardel, *Saint Louis,* 136.

33. Code Civil, France, book I, title II, chap. 1, art. 34–39 and book I, chap. 2 and chap. 3

34. "Actes de Naissance de la commune de Saint Louis," Etat Civil, 8M/52, ANS, 1861–63, and "Actes de Mariage de la commune de Saint Louis," Etat Civil, ANS, 1885–90.

35. During the *ancien régime*, French society permitted men as well as women to engage in extramarital sexual relations. This was particularly true among the aristocracy because marriage generally revolved around family interest and not individual happiness. By the late eighteenth and early nineteenth centuries, writers, artists, and politicians looked down on female adultery, specifically, but increasingly portrayed sexual relations outside of marriage as immoral. Natalie Zemon Davis, *Society and Culture in Early Modern France* (Stanford: Stanford University Press, 1975), and Fuchs, "Seduction, Paternity, and the Law," 949–955.

36. "Actes de naissance de commune of Saint Louis," 1861–63.

37. Faidherbe spent his vacation in his hometown of Lille, France, where he married his niece Angele. When their son reached adulthood, he joined the corps of Senegalese soldiers he had founded called the Sphai (Tirailleurs Sénégalais). The son died at the battle of Médine against the Umarians. A gravestone exists in the Christian cemetery in Sor for Faidherbe's son. For a biography of Faidherbe and his marriages to Siadibi and Angele, see Barrows, "General Faidherbe," 493–94.

38. Bourdieu describes this notion of "family resemblance" as the basis for his concept of *habitus*. Bourdieu, *The State Nobility,* 273.

39. "Acts of Marriage for the Commune of Saint Louis," Civil Registry, 1885–90, ANS.

40. D'Anfreville de Salle counted the métis population as 1,200 in 1830, barely above 1,600 in 1860, but having never reached more than 1,700 in 1909. Salle, however, used this data to emphasize the "unstable" nature of the métis population due to their infertility, a common argument of the time. Precise rate of population stagnation and decline is difficult to determine because colonial officials did not use "mulâtre" to describe the métis population but instead categorized people of the colonial towns as either "French" or "indigène." It is likely that the métis population was larger than the data presented in the 1916 census report for French West Africa, which counted the "mulatto" population in

the communes at 1,600. D'Anfreville de la Salle, *Notre Vieux Senegal,* 101–102, and Idowu, "Café au Lait," 272.

41. "Actes de naissance de la commune de Saint Louis," 1861–63, 8M/52, ANS.

42. Marianne d'Erneville married Bordeaux merchant Auguste Teisseire, Anne d'Erneville married Bordeaux merchant Henry Jay, and French merchant Raymond Martin married Hortense d'Erneville. Auguste de Bourmeister, a lawyer and mayor who settled in Saint Louis, married Anna Pécarrère. Charles de Montfort, a bureaucrat and lawyer who became mayor of Gorée and a member of the General Council (1879–96), married another daughter of the Pecarrère family. Prosper Bancal, a navy medical doctor, retired in Saint Louis and married a métis woman. See A. Teisseire, "La famille d'Erneville"; "Josephine Marie Virginie Martin," 2 July 1892, Parish Registry of Baptisms, Sor diocese, Senegal; Zuccarelli, *La vie politique sénégalaise,* 52–53; Idowu, "Café au Lait," 272.

43. "Publications and Acts of Marriage for the Commune of Saint Louis, 1885–1890," ANS, and "Notes taken by Omar Ba from Catholic Marriage Register to 1886," Saint Louis, Senegal, in author's possession.

44. Researcher Xavier Ricou alerted me to evidence that suggests Anna Isaacs was the daughter of Nathanial Isaacs (1802–72), who was a British explorer and trader who joined his uncle in the merchant marine. Historians now question the veracity of his infamous eyewitness account of the rise and destruction of Shaka Zulu during his stay in Natal, after a shipwreck resulted in a six-year stay in the country (1825–31). In 1844, Isaacs settled in Sierra Leone. In 1854, the British governor accused him of slave trading and expelled him from the colony. Civil records record Anna Isaacs as the daughter of an English lord and Madeline Diole of Bathurst. Baptism records for the children of J. J. Crespin and Anna Isaacs record their place of birth as Melakore, Sherboro River (Sierra Leone). "Nathaniel George Joseph Crespin," 16 October 1870, *Parish Registry of Baptisms,* Sor diocese, Senegal, and Georges Crespin, interview with author, Paris, France, 8 June 2001.

45. Idowu, "Café au Lait."

46. Christian Valantin, interview with author, Dakar, 16 May 2000.

47. See Marie Louise Demba, daughter of François Demba and Sophie Gaye, baptized 11 April 1868, godparents Louis Alsace and Mme Alsace, and Rene Omer Durand Camara, son of Marianne Camara, baptized 12 November 1891, godparents Omer Descemet and Mme Rene Bancal, "Parish Registry of Baptisms," Sor diocese, Saint Louis.

48. Naming practices carry important meaning in West African societies and carried similar significance in the towns. Baptisms offered an opportunity to choose namesakes and reinforce relationships of clientage and affiliation. In other cases, laptots or grumets adopted surnames to indicate their regions of origin such as Madeleine Tamba, whose family likely originated from Tambacaounda. Métis families also maintained ties with African branches of their families in Senegal's countryside across generations. Madeleine Devès Senghor, interview with author, Dakar, 18 March 2000; Ibrahima Diallo, private conversation, Saint Louis, Senegal 2006; Christian Valantin, interview with author, Dakar, 16 May 2000; and Georges Crespin, interview with author, Paris, 8 June 2001. On Descemet family connection to Demba War Sall, see Omar Ba, *La pénétration française au Cayor* (Dakar, 1976), 1:378. For more on naming practices in West Africa, see Gregory Mann, "What's in an Alias? Family Names, Individual Histories, and Historical Method in the Western Sudan," *History in Africa* 29 (2000): 309–20.

49. In the histories of industrialization and capitalism in nineteenth-century Western Europe (England and France specifically) and the United States, Africa is typically relegated to the role of producers, not consumers, especially in materialist analysis. Recent studies of domesticity in Africa are bringing to light the ways in which the nineteenth century created new patterns of consumerism for continental Africans, particularly in Indian Ocean and Atlantic coastal areas. For example, Jeremy Prestholdt, *Domesticating the World: African Consumerism and the Genealogies of Globalization* (Berkeley: University of California Press, 2008), and Laura Fair, *Pastimes and Politics: Culture, Community, and Identity in Post-Abolition Zanzibar, 1890–1945* (Athens: Ohio University Press, 2001).

50. A number of works on history, sociology, culture, art history, and architectural history examine the creation of a bourgeois aesthetic in nineteenth-century France. Leora Auslander uses the terms *taste professionals* and *bourgeois style regime* to define the changing politics of French consumption of furnishings in nineteenth-century France. See Leora Auslander, *Taste and Power: Furnishing Modern France* (Berkeley: University of California Press, 1996). She defines 1830–80 as the introduction of a bourgeois style regime and 1880–1930 as the period of mature bourgeois stylistic regime.

51. For more on the relationship between republican political culture and home furnishings, see Philip Nord, *The Republican Moment: Struggles for Democracy in Nineteenth-Century France* (Cambridge: Harvard University Press, 1995), 237–44.

52. "Annual Report, Asile des Esclave Fugitifs de Saint Louis (Sénégal), 1879–1909," Bibliothèque IFAN, Dakar.

53. The portrait photographs that I consider come from the private collections of the Crespin family (courtesy Georges Crespin) and the Devès family papers, 1891–1919, 1Z11, ANS. For comparison between eighteenth-century drawings of signares and portraits of métis families of the late nineteenth century, see Xavier Ricou, *Trésors de l'iconographie du Sénégal colonial* (Paris: Riveneuve, 2007), 50–72, 127–28. For an analysis of the use of portraits among town residents, see Mark Hinchman, "African Rococo: House and Portrait in Eighteenth-Century Senegal" (PhD diss., University of Chicago, 2000).

54. Boilat, *Esquisses sénégalais*, 6–7, and Mireille Desirée, interview with author, Sor, Senegal, 16 February 2001.

55. For a discussion of the concept of sincérité with regard to the ideal comportment of men in Third Republic France, see Nord, *The Republican Moment*, 230. For comparison with men's styles among the Krio elite of Freetown, Sierra Leone, in the same period, see Leo Spitzer, *The Creoles of Sierra Leone*, 15–16, and Leo Spitzer, *Lives in Between*, 139–41.

56. Descendants of Francois "Farah" Parsine (born 16 April 1892) recall him keeping a house in Saint Louis and one in the peanut basin, where he spent a great deal of time. Marie Parsine's second son, Abdoulaye Seck Marie Parsine, became well known in Senegal as the first director of the postal service for Senegal and Mauritania (1893–1924). "François Parsine," Parish Registry of Baptisms, 11 Décembre 1897.

57. Métis women commonly contributed their jewelry for colonial exhibitions in Paris and Marseille. Marian Johnson's offers an in-depth study of the techniques and history of goldsmiths in Senegal with specific reference to métis women's collections in colonial exhibits. See Marian Johnson, "Black Gold: Goldsmiths, Jewelry, and Women in Senegal" (Ph.D. diss., Stanford University, 1980) and "Sketches of bracelet, hair ornament and necklace," 1Z11, #22, #23, #27, ANS. For a comparison with Wolof and Tukolor styles, see Marian Ashby Johnson, "Gold Jewelry of the Wolof and the Tukulor of Senegal," *African Arts* 27 (January 1994): 36–49.

58. Building regulations enforced by the administration in the 1820s also sought to make the local population conform to French customs. Many of the laws cited public health concerns like fire, flood, and disease as the main reasons for eliminating adobe and straw buildings. In 1828, there were 200 brick homes in Saint Louis. By 1838, there were approximately 320 brick homes, and most were two-story dwellings. For more on this transformation, see Sinou, *Comptoirs et villes coloniales du Sénégal,* 151–64; Bonnardel, *Saint Louis du Sénégal,* 97–98; and Boilat, *Esquisses sénégalais,* 97–98.

59. Saint Louis homes are known for the unique horseshoe double curved stairways that lead from the inner courtyard to the second-floor apartments. Floor plans show the layout of rooms on the top floor and two or three retail stores on the ground floor opening on to the street. The floor plans also show the close proximity that métis families lived to one another. The Immeuble (premises) G. Devès bordered Immeuble Descemet on the east and Immeuble Carpot on the south. See "Immeuble G. Devès à Saint Louis and Immeuble Pécarrère," 1Z11, #25, #26, ANS.

60. The first photographic studios appeared in Senegal in the 1880s. See Philippe David, "Hostalier-Noal: Un duel de photographes au Journal Officiel du Sénégal il y a cent ans," http://www.imagesetmemoires.com/doc/Articles/Hostalier_Noal_Duel_de_photographes.pdf. For a discussion of nineteenth-century African portrait photography, see Christreaud Geary, *In and Out of Focus* (National Museum of African Art, 2002), 103–18.

4. EDUCATION, ASSOCIATION, AND AN INDEPENDENT PRESS

1. Stoler forcibly makes the case for interrogating the supposed homogeneity of European communities. Scholarship on this subject over the past decade has revealed the tensions, paradoxes, and competing interests and class positions of European communities in Asia and Africa, from settlers to traders, petit colons, civil servants, and the officer corps. Ann Laura Stoler, "Rethinking Colonial Categories: European Communities and the Boundaries of Rule," in *Colonialism and Culture,* ed., Nicholas B. Dirks (Ann Arbor: University of Michigan Press, 1992), 1–27. See also Alice Conklin, "Redefining Frenchness": Citizenship, Race Regeneration, and Imperial Motherhood in France and West Africa, 1914–1940," in *Domesticating the Empire,* ed. Julia Clancy-Smith and Frances Gouda (Charlottesville: University Press of Virginia, 1998), 65–83, and Stephanie Newell, *The Forger's Tale: The Search for Odeziaku* (Athens: Ohio University Press, 2006).

2. The orphanage continued to operate discreetly through the twentieth century. "Brochure—Anne-Marie Javouhey," La Mission des Sœurs de Saint Joseph de Cluny, Saint Louis, Sénégal; and Brigaud and Vast, *Saint Louis du Sénégal,* 85–88.

3. The Falloux Law created a national standard for school curriculum and instruction. In addition to girls' schools, the law also introduced kindergartens and adult classes. Raymond Grew and Patrick J. Harrigan, *Schools, State, and Society: The Growth of Elementary Schooling in Nineteenth-Century France* (Ann Arbor: University of Michigan Press, 1991); Françoise Mayeur, *L'education des filles en France au XIXe siècle* (Paris: Hachette, 1979), 17–33; Linda Clark, *Schooling the Daughters of Marianne* (Albany: State University of New York, 1984), 5–11; and J. David Knottnerus and Frederique Van de Poel-Knottnerus, *The Social Worlds of Male and Female Children in the Nineteenth-Century French Educational System* (New York: Edwin Mellen Press, 1999), 88–91.

4. École des sœurs de St. Joseph de Cluny, Programme des études année scolaire, 1881–82, J6, #14, ANS, and École primaire de Gorée, dirige par les religieuses de St. Joseph de Cluny, Liste des élèves, 1892–93, J6, #19, ANS.

5. "École des sœurs de St. Joseph de Cluny, Programme des etudes année scolaire, 1881–82, J6, #14, ANS, and Denise Bouche, "L'enseignement dans les territoires français de l'Afrique Occidentale de 1817 à 1920," 410.

6. Boilat, *Esquisses sénégalaises*, 12–14.

7. Descemet published his work at the same time that Faidherbe published his Wolof dictionary and grammar. While Faidherbe's work was geared to soldiers and officials, Descemet's seems to have been directed toward educating *les enfants indigènes*. Descemet argued for more French schools, but maintained that children could not learn French through memorization, the method used in the schools. Louis Descemet, *Recueil d'environ 1,200 phrases françaises usuelles avec leur traduction en regard en ouolof de Saint-Louis* (Saint Louis: Imprimerie du Gouvernement, 1864), and Louis Léon Faidherbe, *Vocabulaire d'environ 1,500 mot français avec leurs correspondants en Ouolof de Saint Louis, en Pular, Toucouleur du Fouta* (Saint Louis, 1864).

8. "Allocution de Leopold Angrand," J6, #27, ANS.

9. Women constituted a large population of the town's elite. Many women were adversely affected by the economic crisis of the 1840s, as they depended on their fathers or husbands for their livelihood. The General Council commonly heard requests from widows for financial assistance. Métis women were among the first women to hold high positions in Senegal's judiciary, educational system, and medicine after independence. "Mort de Mme veuve J. B. d'Erneville," *L'Afrique Occidentale* 27 (23 July 1897), JO 7679 BN, "Decision raising salary of dames and demoiselles employed in service of posts and telegraphs," *Bulletin Administratif*, 1881.

10. Durand Valantin, son of a Marseille merchant, studied in France in the early 1820s, which aided him in his political career in Senegal in the 1830s and 1840s. Gaspard Devès studied in Bordeaux, and métis habitant Germain Crespin sent his son Jean Jacques to school in France in the 1840s. See Reyss, "Saint Louis du Sénégal," annexe 1, journal privée de Germain Crespin.

11. The School for Hostages was closed in 1871 and reopened in 1892 by Governor Henri de Lamothe under the name "School for the Sons of Chiefs and Interpreters." One of the early "hostages," Sidia Diop, born around 1850, was the son of the Brak and Linguer of Walo. A note next to his entry reads, "next in line to the throne of the Trarzas taken in Cayor and sent to Galam." See Leon-Celestin (Sidia) Diop, bap. 14 May 1864, entree 6 June 1864, Registre des élèves à l'école des frères, Sor diocese, Senegal.

12. Leland Barrows, "General Faidherbe," 472–76. For an analysis of the creation of Muslim education by French administrators in Senegal and the failure of Faidherbe's policy, see Denise Bouche, "L'école française et les musulmans au Sénégal de 1850–1920," *Revue française de l'histoire d'outre-mer*, 61, no. 223 (1974): 222–25, and Bouche, "L'enseignement," 154–56.

13. For examples of students listed as "Mahometan," see Lamine Diop, Abdoulaye Diaw, Pierre Diouf, Souleymane Diop (greffier tribunal musulman), Iba Ndiaye, Djibril Diallo, Massouba Diack (night class), Amadou Marone, and Abdoulaye Seck in "Registre des élèves a l'école des frères," Sor diocese, Senegal.

14. Early experiments with the mutual school and the college run by Boilat failed, causing officials in Paris to turn to the order. Maurice Lallemand, *Comme un long fleuve tranquille, 150 ans de présence à l'enseignement en Afrique des Frères de Ploërmel* (Paris: FF. de l'instruction chrétienne de Ploërmel, 1992), 19.

15. The law of 28 March 1882 established compulsory and free primary education for all French children and outlined a new curriculum for the schools. Religious orders continued to serve as the main providers of public education until 1905, when the government put in place secularization laws. These changes, however, followed at a slower pace in the colonies. For implementation in Senegal, see "letter from director of the school to the director of the interior," St. Louis, 21 March 1884, J6, #5, ANS.

16. The enrollment registry gives information on the students, their "affiliation," when they entered and left, and observations. Métis and grumets were enrolled by their parents and left to become civil servants or soldiers. Of the four students listed as "raised by" habitants, two left for Rio Nunez and Sierra Leone. Most métis received scholarships to attend Lycée Carcassonne or Lycée de Bordeaux. See William Blaise Dumont, Pierre André, Alfred Dodds, François Jupiter, and Edouard Bambara in "Registre des élèves de l'école primaire des Freres," Sor diocese, Senegal.

17. Three Muslims listed as "hostage" entered the school in 1844. Nafe Bakary, "Mahometan from Galam," entered in 1852 and died four years later in Alger. Mouhamed Saloum, born in Portendick, entered the school in 1856, left in 1869, and became an interpreter at the tribunal. Sidia Leon Celestin Diop, the son of the ruling family of Walo, was a hostage enrolled in the school briefly in 1864 when métis habitants François Valantin, Charles Carpot, Justin Devès, and Hyacinthe Devès also attended. In the 1870s and 1880s, the sons of Muslim traders attended the school. Abdoulaye Seck left for France in 1883, and grumet Jules Demba left for France in August 1886, possibly for higher education. "Registre des élèves de l'école primaire des Freres," Sor diocese.

18. The Falloux law introduced reforms for public secondary education. Religious orders provided most public instruction, but some state-sponsored and private secular schools also existed. Robert Gildea, "Education and the Classes Moyennes in the Nineteenth Century," in *The Making of Frenchmen: Current Directions in the History of Education in France,* ed. Donald N. Baker and Patrick J. Harrigan (Waterloo, Ontario: Historical Reflections Press, 1980), 278–80, and Grew and Harrigan, *School, State, and Society,* 191–92.

19. Boilat, *Esquisses sénégalaise,* 211.

20. Between 1853 and 1874, students Duchesne, Paul Holle, Abel Descemet, Frederic Michas, and Valantin received scholarships from the governor. *Arbre généalogique des familles Descemet-Guillabert.* On the scholarship program and early recipients, see Bouche, "L'enseignement," 260–71.

21. "Procès-verbal," General Council, ordinary session, 24 November to 6 December 1879.

22. Instruction in Latin defined secondary education in the mid-nineteenth century, since Latin served as the language of instruction in universities. Métis families pushed for teaching of Latin in primary school to prepare their children to enter lycée, where students were required to learn Latin. Robert L. G. Geiger, "Prelude to Reform: The Faculties of Letters in the 1860s," and George Weisz, "The Anatomy of University Reform, 1863–1913," both in *The Making of Frenchmen,* ed. Baker and Harrigan, 338–49, 363–81.

23. Reform of the university system began in the 1860s. The three main professional fields were law, medicine, and pharmacy. On scholarships for girls, see "Arête concerning rules for scholarship concessions from the colony for institutions in the metropole," J5, #3, ANS; "Arête #247 giving scholarships to young girls," *Bulletin Administratif du Senegal,* 1881. On the École Coloniale and its training program for colonial

administrators, see Cohen, *Rulers of Empire*, 37–44. For more on secondary education for women, see Françoise Mayeur. *L'enseignement secondaire des jeunes filles sous la troisième république* (Paris: Presse de la Fondation Nationale des Sciences Politique, 1977).

24. In 1884, the administration announced plans to develop a lycée in Saint Louis. "École Spéciale Secondaire de St. Louis: Notes générales sur les élèves sortis de l'École depuis sa fondation jusqu'au 30 Octobre 1889, J6, #11, ANS, and Bouche, "L'enseignement," 272–73.

25. Research on race in modern French history is beginning to break through the notion that race did not exist in France because of its embrace of universal and racially neutral policies. We know that people of color from Louisiana to Reunion sent their students to France for education in the nineteenth century, yet racial identity was not generally marked in school records or other bureaucratic documents. On race and French history, see Sue Peabody and Tyler Stovall, eds. *The Color of Liberty: Histories of Race in France* (Durham: Duke University Press, 2003), and Miller, *The French Atlantic Triangle*. For a treatment of the circulation of French literary and cultural ideas in the French West Indies and its impact on shaping the identity of free people of color in Louisiana, see Caryn Cossé Bell's *Revolution, Romanticism, and the Afro-Creole Protest Tradition in Louisiana, 1718–1868* (Baton Rouge: Louisiana State University Press, 1997).

26. One of the students, Ernest Piecentin, was the son of a Gorée merchant who ran a trading house. Two of the students were children of Hubler, an employee in the post and telegraph department. In addition to Carpots, Devès, and Valantins, métis students Ernest and Frederic Michas and Louis and Jean Duchesne appear in the register. Students who entered the school between 1875 and 1879 were likely chosen by the governor and his private council, whereas students listed from 1880 and 1881 likely were named by the General Council. "Registres des entrées et des sorties des élèves," 1875–81, ADG, Bordeaux.

27. Ibid.

28. "Livres d'inscription des nouveaux élèves," series T, dossier 4, ADG, Bordeaux.

29. This assertion has been proven by a number of social science studies on the making of democratic regimes in history. Jürgen Habermas is most noted for his theories on the role of associations in the development of the public sphere; see also Larry Diamond, "Persistence, Erosion, Breakdown, and Renewal," in *Democracy in Developing Countries,* ed. Diamond, Juan J. Linz, and Seymour Martin Lipset (Boulder: Lynne Rienner, 1990). Philip Nord shows that associations, especially trade unions, played a critical role in the development of democratic regimes in nineteenth-century France by challenging state power. Nord, *The Republican Moment,* 5–9.

30. I am grateful to Roger Pasquier for bringing these references to my attention in the 27 September 1887 *Bulletin Administratif,* the weekly newsletter published by the administration.

31. "Cahier de l'association des mères de familles sous le patronage de Ste. Monique 1910–1923," 312.16 Journaux des Communautés et Divers 1845–1994, Archives of the Spiritains, Chevilly La Rue, France, and "Pages d'Histoire," *Unir: L'Echo de Saint Louis* 3 (September 1967).

32. "Monsieur Le Gouverner," Saint Louis, 15 March 1887, 3G3/4, ANS.

33. For more on Freemasonry in Third Republic France, see Nord, *The Republican Moment,* 197–99.

34. "Particular rules of the lodge Union Sénégalaise" (Saint Louis, 17 and 19 October 1874; FM 2, 863 dossier 7, Bibliothèque Nationale, Paris.

35. For a history of Masonic lodges in Senegal, see Georges Odo, "Les quatre Loges de St. Louis du Senegal de 1781 a 1899" (courtesy Sylvain Sankale, in author's possession) and Odo, *La franc-maçonnerie en Afrique francophone, 1781–2000* (Paris: Editions maçonnique, 2000). For a comparison on masonry in nineteenth-century West Africa, see Augustus Casley-Hayford and Richard Rathbone, "Politics, Families, and Freemasonry in the Colonial Gold Coast," in *People and Empires in African History*, ed. J. F. Ajayi and J. D. Y. Peel (New York: Longman, 1992), 143–60.

36. "Decision authorizing the opening of a Masonic lodge in Saint Louis under the title Union Sénégalaise," Saint Louis, 30 July 1874, 3G3/4, #304, ANS, and "Union Sénégalaise request for a diploma," Saint Louis, 15 October, 1875, 153 dossier 3, BN FM, Paris.

37. Gouverneur du Sénégal, "Décision rapportant celle du 30 Juillet 1874," 30 March 1876, 3G3, #305, ANS; "Letter from P. LePennec, curé of the Parish to the Governor of Senegal," Saint Louis, 29 March 1876, Journal of Ministerial Dispatch, Reports Circulars and Letters, Sor diocese, Senegal, and "Letter from Venerable Blaixe, Saint Louis, to Grand Orient, Paris," 1876, FM 153, dossier 3, BN, Paris.

38. "Union Sen soumet un projet de création d'une école," 22 July 1882, FM 153, dossier 3 BN, Paris.

39. "Procès-verbal Séance 11 Mars 1881, Diplômes grade maitre 5 June 1882 and 29 Novembre 1882, Diplômes qualité maçon régulier au grade maitre," 8 September 1884, FM 153, dossier 3 BN, Paris.

40. This problem is certainly not unique to the métis of Senegal. The tension between democratic principles and slavery is a theme that dominated the thinking and actions of political elites in North and South America and the formation of liberal democracy in Western Europe. The publication of the decree authorizing the closing of the lodge was followed by the announcement of the liberation of slaves Boye, Diop, and Thiam declared by J. P. Floissac and confided to his wife, Catherine Pellegrin. "Arête rapportant celle du 30 Juillet 1874," *Moniteur du Sénégal*, 4 April 1876. On members of the lodge implicated in a forced labor scheme for construction of a railway in Belgian Congo, see "Affaire LaPlène, 1890–1994," K31, ANS.

41. Between 1877 and 1914, lawyers dominated the legislative assemblies of the Third Republic. Because members of the Paris Bar prided themselves on their own discipline, self-government of their professional association, and high esteem for objectivity, rationality, and independence, they considered themselves the best suited to govern newly democratic France. See Nord, *The Republican Moment*, 115–38.

42. I am grateful to Sylvain Sankale for clarifying this term as it applied to Crespin in Senegal.

43. "La nécrologie de Germain Jean Jacques Crespin," courtesy Georges Crespin, Paris.

44. For the most comprehensive work on the origins of an independent press in Senegal, see Roger Pasquier, "Les débuts de la presse au Sénégal," *Cahiers d'etudes Africaines* 7 (1962): 477–91. See also Marguerite Boulègue, "La presse au Sénégal avant 1939: Bibliographie," ANS, and Fadel Dia, *Expositions: La presse au Sénégal des Origines a L'Independence (1856–1960)*, Saint Louis: Center for Research and Documentation of Senegal (CRDS), 1978.

45. "Dépêche ministérielle, application au Sénégal du décret du 26 Février 1880 sur la presse," *Bulletin Administratif du Sénégal*.

46. I suspect that this paper may have taken its name from *Le Réveil*, a publication that appeared in Paris in 1868 after Bonaparte loosened restrictions on the press. The founder of the journal, Charles Delescluze, and a number of other journalists were charged and convicted for their criticism of the Second Empire and remained outspoken advocates for freedom of the press. See Nord, *The Republican Moment*, 130.

47. *Le Réveil du Sénégal* is listed as "incommunicable" in the collections of the Bibliothèque Nationale in Paris. I was unable to locate copies of the journal in Senegal. For information on *Le Réveil du Sénégal* I relied on the text of the 1978 exposition of the origins of the free press in Senegal organized by Fadel Dia for CRDS.

48. *Le Petit Sénégalais*, no.1–40, J.O. 5966, BN, Paris.

49. "L'Enseignement Laïque," no. 16, 18 November 1886, "Les droits civils des femmes," no. 21, 30 Décembre 1886, and "Une fête Maçonnique a la Réunion," no. 16, 18 November 1886, *Le Petit Sénégalais*.

50. "Transformation du Petit Sénégalais," no. 21, 30 December 1886, and "Avis," no. 24.

51. On this incident and events surrounding the closing of both papers, see Dia, "Expositions" and Pasquier, "Les débuts de la presse," 478–83.

52. The newspapers that appeared from the late 1890s until 1914 were *L'Union Africaine*, *Le Radical Sénégalais*, *Le Petit Sénégalais* (1908–13), and *L'Afrique Occident*.

5. FROM OUTPOST TO EMPIRE

1. Fifty-four of the eighty-six women who signed the letter belonged to métis families, and most were married or widowed. The remaining thirty-two names appear to belong to French women married to metropolitan civil servants (judiciary), colonial officers, or merchants. Jean-Bernard Jauréguiberry was the governor of Senegal from 1861 to 1863. "Monsieur le Gouverneur," Saint Louis, 15 March 1887, 3G3/4, #272, and "Monsieur Ministre de la Marine," Saint Louis, 19 March 1887, 3G3/4, #336, ANS.

2. Jürgen Habermas's definition of the public sphere as a space of critical discourse generated in a stage of capitalist development in which private individuals create a critical mass that acts as a check on state power is useful for understanding urban politics at this time in Senegal's history. Benedict Anderson's argument that print capitalism and vernacular languages played a central role in building modern democracies also applies to this case. These transformations made the emergence of civil society in the late nineteenth century distinct from earlier periods of political life in Senegal's colonial towns. Jürgen Habermas, *The Structural Transformation of the Public Sphere*, trans. Thomas Burger (Cambridge: MIT Press, 1989), and Benedict Anderson, *Imagined Communities*, rev. ed. (London: Verso, 1991).

3. Debate over the effectiveness of this term for Africa has generated scholarship on its meaning and usefulness. The idea of civil society has been described as something that is elusive, that refers to everything and nothing, and that is inherently Eurocentric; others have described it as an accurate representation of the role of nonstate actors in African states today. On the idea of civil society in Africa, see John L. and Jean Comaroff, *Civil Society*, 1–44.

4. Hegel is most often identified with the post-Renaissance concept of civil society. For Hegel, civil society was part of the spread of commodity relations that liberated the economy from the sphere of politics and replaced civil law with the force of the state. Recent scholarship considers theories of civil society advanced by Marx and Gramsci to understand the reaction to fascism and communism in eastern bloc countries as well as in emerging democracies from Turkey to Latin America and Africa. See Jean Cohen and

Andrew Arato, *Civil Society and Political Theory* (Cambridge: MIT Press, 1992), and Stepan, *Rethinking Military Politics.*

5. For political scientists' approach to the legacy of the colonial state and state-society relations in postcolonial Africa, see Bayart, *The State in Africa;* Crawford Young, *The African Colonial State in Comparative Perspective* (New Haven: Yale University Press, 1994); and Mamdani, *Citizens and Subject.*

6. Political theorists have advanced different definitions of civil society. The broadest constructions view civil society as including all nonstate activity between the government and the family, taking into account spontaneous activities like strikes or riots that influence state action. Others prefer a more narrow definition limited to actions in which members of civil society challenge the state. Bayart sees civil society as the relationship between state and society specifically when society is in confrontation with the state. See Nelson Kasfir, "The Conventional Notion of Civil Society: A Critique," in *Civil Society and Democracy in Africa: Critical Perspectives,* ed. Kasfir (London: Frank Cass, 1998), 3–8.

7. Faidherbe graduated from the École Polytechnique in 1838. He was appointed governor of Senegal at age 36. He served in Guadeloupe before arriving in Senegal, which contributed to his thoughts on abolition and his support for the French abolitionist Victor Schoelcher. After his military career, Faidherbe entered politics, seeking Senegal's legislative seat. He wrote extensively about his experiences in Senegal and the importance of French colonialism generally. See Louis Léon Faidherbe, *Le Sénégal: La France dans l'Afrique Occidentale* (Paris: L'Hachette, 1889).

8. Faidherbe's two terms as governor (1854–61 and 1863–65) of Senegal corresponded with Napoleon III's rule. Napoleon III supported French imperialism in Algeria and Asia, which influenced how Faidherbe and the military approached Islam. On Faidherbe's Islamic policy, see Harrison, *France and Islam in West Africa,* and Saint-Martin, *Le Sénégal sous le second empire.*

9. Faidherbe's friendly relationship with the Bordeaux commercial lobby is well documented. Leland Barrows and Joan Casey's study of correspondence between Faidherbe and Maurel and Prom shows that he consulted the company on almost all economic issues regarding France in Senegal. Barrows, "General Faidherbe," and Casey, "The Politics of French Imperialism," 115–18.

10. Médine is a Khassonke town located at the head of the Senegal River, near the town of Kayes in present- day western Mali. The Khassonke kingdom was founded by Pulaar speakers in the seventeenth century who migrated to the area and mixed with Malinke and Soninke peoples. France built a fort in an attempt to secure territory to build a railway from Saint Louis to Niger, part of the grand idea for a trans-Saharan railway. In 1881, France finally completed the railway line from Saint Louis to Kayes, making the town the capital of French Soudan.

11. Robinson presents the military conflict at Médine in terms of the clash of two expansionist forces—the French of Saint Louis, led by Faidherbe, and Al Hajj Umar Tal of the middle Senegal. Both were seeking to capture control over the upper Senegal. For a chronicle of Umar Tal's jihad and rivalry with the French at Saint Louis, see Robinson, *The Holy War of Umar Tal,* 204–41.

12. Diouf, *Le Kajoor au XIXe siècle,* 217–23, 227–31; Lucy Colvin, "Kajoor and Its Diplomatic Relations with Saint Louis, Senegal, 1763–1861" (PhD diss., Columbia University, 1972).

13. On wars of conquest and resistance in Sine and Saloum, see Martin Klein, *Islam and Imperialism in Senegal* (Stanford: Stanford University Press, 1968), 130–49.

14. Brière de l'Isle arrived in Senegal at age 49. He had been trained at the St. Cyr naval academy and had served in several campaigns in Asia. He had a reputation as a strong military man who could not tolerate civilian rule in the colonies. Francine Ndiaye, "La colonie du Sénégal au temps de Brière de l'Isle, 1876–1881," Bulletin de l'IFAN, série B, 30 (1968) 462–512.

15. Brière de l'Isle sent Paul Soleillet to negotiate with Amadou Sheku at Segu. Sheku was the eldest son of Umar Tal. He took over the Tokolor empire after Tal's death. By the time of his father's death, Umar Tal's movement had expanded as far east as Segu, the Bambara kingdom on the middle Niger. Kanya-Forstner, *The Conquest of the Western Sudan,* 45–50, 72–83, and 176–83.

16. In the 1820s, geographic societies promoted the first major French explorations in the interior of West and North Africa, forming the basis for colonial expansion. Interest in these societies increased tremendously in the 1870s and was accompanied by novels, magazines, and illustrations. In the late 1870s and 1880s, a colonial lobby grew among abolitionists and key members of the Paris legislature. Cohen, *French Encounter with the Africans,* 264–66, and Robert Aldrich, *Greater France: A History of French Overseas Expansion* (New York: St. Martin's Press, 1996), 97–100.

17. While Brière de l'Isle eliminated all civilian administrators, he was constantly at odds with the merchant lobby and elected officials in Saint Louis. The details of this conflict are discussed in chapter 6. Ndiaye, "La colonie du Sénégal," 462–512.

18. A royal ordinance of 7 September 1840 established this system.

19. The severity of forced labor and summary justice varied from colony to colony in French West Africa. I find that the existence of republican institutions and the systems of accommodation that developed in Senegal lessened the severity of these systems as officials in the interior had to contend with an activist judiciary and an urban community that was mindful of abuses of power in the colony. On application of forced labor and a comparison between Senegal and other colonies in French West Africa, see Babacar Fall, *Le travail forcé en Afrique-Occidentale française* (Paris: Karthala, 1993), 19–20, 47–52. For a critical examination of summary justice, see Gregory Mann, "What Was the Indigénat? The 'Empire of Law' in French West Africa," *Journal of African History* 50 (2009): 331–53.

20. The direct administration territories under the jurisdiction of the first arrondissement included Richard Toll, Dagana, Podor, Saldé, Matam, and Bakel on the Senegal. The direct administration territories of the second arrondissement included Thies, Kaolack, Foundiougne, and Fatick; Portudal, Joal, and Nianing on the Petit Côte; Sedhiou, Zuiganchor, and the island of Carabane on the Casamance River; and the Southern Rivers territories of Boké on the Rio Nunez, Boffa on the Rio Pongo, and Benty on the Mellacorie. Saliou Mbaye, *Histoire des institutions coloniales françaises en Afrique de l'Ouest, 1816–1960* (Dakar: Imprimerie Administratif, 1990), 30, and Bonnardel, *Saint Louis du Senegal,* 135–36.

21. The decree of 4 February 1879 took the administration of direct-rule areas from the governor and placed it under the General Council's authority. In 1890, the direct administration territories were modified by a governor's decree that reduced the area to the communes, their suburbs, and the land along the Dakar–Saint Louis railway corridor.

22. Guy Thilmans, *L'Hôtel du Conseil general a Saint Louis du Sénégal: Documents pour server a son histoire et sa réhabilitation* (Dakar: IFAN, 2004), 9.

23. The council also selected a delegate to the naval ministry's advisory council in Paris. Since Saint Louis served as the commercial and administrative capital of the colony, the decree excluded inhabitants of Gorée by limiting representation to residents of Saint Louis. See Johnson, *Emergence of Black Politics*, 79–80; H. O. Idowu, "Assimilation in Nineteenth-Century Senegal," *Bulletin IFAN*, série B, no. 30 (1968): 1421–25.

24. Mbaye, *Histoire des institutions coloniales française*, 139–41, 152–53, and 178–79. See also H. O. Idowu, "The Establishment of Elective Institutions in Senegal 1869–1880," *Journal of African History* 9, no. 2 (1968): 261–77.

25. At this time women did not possess the right to vote or hold office in metropolitan France. The ordinance of 21 April 1944 granted suffrage to women in France. A 1947 decree gave women the right to vote in Senegal's elections.

26. Mbaye, *Histories des institutions coloniales française*, 180–81.

27. H. O. Idowu and François Zuccarelli claim that Alfred Gasconi was the descendant of a French man from Marseille and a signare. Educated in Marseille, Gasconi participated in the Franco-Prussian War. His death certificate calls him a French man in France. Idowu, "Café au Lait," 272, and Zuccarelli, *La vie politique sénégalaise*, 54.

28. "Décret instituant un Conseil général au Sénégal et dépendances du 4 février 1879," *Moniteur du Sénégal*, 4 April 1879, 64–69.

29. Mbaye, *Histoire des institutions coloniales française*, 152–53.

30. In 1889, the councilors voted for permission to construct a building solely for the business of the assembly. In 1890, the office and private residence of the director of the interior moved to the General Council. The building was also used to host dinners for dignitaries such as Minister of Colonies Andre Lebon when he visited the capital in 1897. See "L'inauguration de l'hôtel du Conseil Générale," *Moniteur du Sénégal*, 2 February 1888, 40. On the history of the building, original architectural plans, and the project that restored the building to its original characteristics, see Guy Thilmans, *L'Hôtel du Conseil général*.

31. "Procès-verbal de la séance 24 novembre 1879 à 6 décembre 1879," 4E4, ANS.

32. "Bacre Waly Gueye (1834–1904)," courtesy Mansour Thioye, Saint Louis. Bacre Waly was the son of Saint Louis trader Bandia Waly. He developed his own business trading at the escale in Bakel and as an agent for Rabaud et cie, then established his own trade house in Podor. See the biographies of Bacre Waly Gueye and other Saint Louis traders in Fall and Sow, "Les traitants Saint-Louisiens," 187.

33. Zuccarelli, *La vie politique sénégalaise*.

34. François Manchuelle, "Le rôle des Antillais dans l'apparition du nationalisme culturel en Afrique Noire Francophone," *Cahiers d'etudes Africaines* 32, no. 3 (1992): 375–409.

35. The decree specified that these rights were to be enjoyed in the colony. This decree occurred before the administrative structure, in an attempt to unify metropolitan and colonial policy. Originaires and judicial advocates subsequently used this clause to argue that all residents of Senegal's towns were citizens rather than subjects. For the language of the decree, see its reproduction in Régine Bonnardel, *Saint Louis du Senegal: Mort ou Naissance?* 136.

36. Mbaye, *Histoire des institutions coloniales française*, 83–87; Dominique Sarr and Richard Roberts, "The Jurisdiction of Muslim Tribunals in Colonial Senegal, 1857–1932," in *Law in Colonial Africa*, ed. Kristin Mann and Richard Roberts (Portsmouth, NH: Heinemann, 1991), 132–35; and Rebecca Shereikis, "From Law to Custom: The

Shifting Legal Status of Muslim Originaires in Kayes and Médine, 1903–1913," *Journal of African History* 42 (2001): 261–83.

37. Lydon, "Les péripéties d'une institution financière"; Mbaye, *Histoire des institutions coloniales française*, 246–48.

38. The new bank was guided by the interests of metropolitan monopoly firms that operated throughout the federation and could offer credit directly to their local agents. "Situation of the Bank of Senegal," 30 April 1901, Q40, #47, ANS.

39. Members of the chamber of commerce were wholesalers (négociants), licensed traders, or agents of metropolitan firms who had lived in the colony for at least a year. This relegated membership to the French and métis until 1890, when African traders were admitted. The chamber of commerce in Saint Louis was the most important until the founding of additional institutions in Gorée and the peanut basin. In 1920, new laws removed the governor's power to determine the chamber of commerce's budget, giving it more autonomy. See Bonnardel, *Saint Louis du Sénégal: Mort ou Naissance?* 140.

40. In 1900, only 125 European merchants and company employees lived in Dakar. The highpoint of *petit blanc* settlement in Senegal occurred from 1945 to 1960, long after the decline of métis power in commune politics. For more on French settlers in twentieth-century Senegal, see O'Brien, *White Society in Black Africa,* 54–55, 66–71.

41. "Lettres et Mémoires," Fonds Chambre de Commerce de Bordeaux, Bibliothèque Municipale de Bordeaux, 1894–1900.

42. Mamadou Diouf's biography of Hamet Gora Diop (1846–1910) sheds valuable light on the little-understood strategies and capital investments of Muslim traders. Diop traded in gum, millet, and other goods. His position in Russo led him to develop ties with leading Sufi clerics. In 1882, he relocated his business to Médine and developed a network of employees who conducted trade in the upper Senegal and into areas of French expansion along the Niger. See Diouf, "Traitants ou négociants?"

43. The administration used métis habitant Raymond Martin and Muslim habitant Pedre Alassane Mbengue to mediate with the Futanke after launching expeditions of conquest. David Robinson, *Chiefs and Clerics: Abdul Bokar Kane and the History of Futa Toro, 1853–1891* (Oxford: Oxford University Press, 1975), 130, 136–37.

44. The Saint Louis traders who emerged as key players in the 1860s include Bacre Waly Gueye, Ndiaye Saar, Pedre Alassane Mbengue, Hamet Gora Diop, Abdoulaye Seck, and Abdoulaye Mar. Their children attended the brothers' school or the secular school, joined the Jeunes Sénégalais, and played key roles in the local assemblies after 1900. For more on Saint Louis traders, see Fall and Sow, "Les traitants Saint-Louisiens."

45. Seck trained as an interpreter at the School for Hostages, where he handled all correspondence, treaties, and relations with chiefs in the interior. He also maintained close connections with the Moors on the north bank of the Senegal and made the pilgrimage to Mecca. David Robinson, Interview with Swadou Seck and daughter Aby Diop, Saint Louis 29 and 30 June 1997, author present; David Robinson, *Paths of Accommodation,* 79–85, 117–39.

46. Bacre Waly Gueye's son, Lamine Gueye, founded one of Senegal's first political parties and became Senegal's representative to Paris in 1945. Abdoulaye Mar occupied key roles in the municipal assemblies and as mayor of Saint Louis. Almamy Mathieu Fall, interview with author, 27 May 2000, Saint Louis, and Andre Guillabert, interview with author, 19 February 2000.

47. Two examples of métis who pursued this path are Roger Descemet, who led the battle of Médine, and his brother Louis. Both attended St. Cyr. Louis Descemet became

secretary to General Faidherbe. Faidherbe's Senegalese son became part of the officer corps. Others served as administrators in districts of the interior in the 1860s. Georges Crespin, commandant de Boffa and Gorée, "Cercle du Rio Pongo," Poste de Boffa, #34–36, and "Affaire Valluet," 7G14, #221, #231, ANS.

48. France long relied on local inhabitants to form armies of conquest. The tirailleurs were modeled after a similar regiment of North African troops, called Spahi, which were mobilized in Algeria in the 1830s. In the 1820s, the naval ministry called for the recruitment of African soldiers in Senegal. Officials in Saint Louis turned to slaves, which presented a public relations problem for French abolition policy. Runaway slaves and individuals recruited from territories subject to wars of conquest were enlisted in the school Faidherbe founded to train African soldiers and bolster their reputation in the colony. Lieutenant Macodou M'baye from Dagana and Captain Mahmadou Racine Sy and his nephew Abdel-Kader Mademba were among the distinguished graduates of the École des Enfants de Troupe who rose to high rank in the era of conquest. Myron Echenberg, *Colonial Conscripts: The Tirailleurs Sénégalais in French West Africa, 1857–1960* (Portsmouth, NH: Heinemann, 1991), 7–24.

49. "Colonel Dodds à M. Le Gouverneur du Senegal," 17 October 1890, 3G3/4, #358, ANS, and Omar Bâ, *La pénétration française au Cayor,* vol. 1 (Dakar, 1976).

50. This includes the unique status of the originaires. Coquery-Vidrovitch, "Nationalité et citoyenneté en Afrique occidentale française."

51. Passage of the Blaise Diagne laws is commonly viewed as a deal that Diagne struck with the French in return for providing his cooperation in recruiting Africans from the protectorate to join the frontlines of the war effort. See Johnson, *Emergence of Black Politics.*

52. *Moniteur du Senegal,* 4 April 1871, #786, ANS.

6. ELECTORAL POLITICS AND THE MÉTIS (1870–90)

1. François Zucarelli contends that the first "electoral clans" appeared in the 1875 municipal council elections. It consisted of one clan led by Gaspard Devès and the other by Auguste de Bourmeister. The period from 1871 to 1882, in his view, was dominated by Bordeaux. After 1882 he divides politics into three clans: followers of merchants, followers of Alfred Gasconi, and followers of Gaspard Devès. The period from 1884 to 1902 he considers to have been dominated by the métis. François Zuccarelli, *La vie politique sénégalaise,* chaps. 3 and 4.

2. I contend that corruption was part of urban politics from Paris to Tammany Hall and not an aberration of métis domination of commune politics in Senegal before 1914. See William B. Cohen, *Urban Government and the Rise of the French City* (New York: St. Martin's Press, 1998) and James C. Scott, "Corruption, Machine Politics, and Political Change," *American Political Science Review* 63 (December 1969): 1142–50.

3. The civil act of marriage refers to Gaspard Devès as the son of Sylvie Bruno, who I believe was named Coumbel Peul Ka or Coumbel Ardo Ka. Little is known about Sylvie Bruno except that she went by that name in Saint Louis, since the union was not an official one. "Pierre Gaspard Devès and Madeleine Tamba," 9 May 1889, Commune of Saint Louis, ANS, and Madeleine Devès Senghor, interview with author, 20 March 2000, Dakar. Devès and Chaumet established an anonymous company, located on rue Ferrère in Bordeaux, called La Sénégalaise, which specialized in transportation of goods and people on the Senegal River. On the Bordeaux company, see "Annonces, Formation de

Société M.M Devès et G. Chaumet, négociants," *Moniteur du Sénégal,* 13 April 1869, "Devès et G. Chaumet, négociants-armateurs," Annuaire de la Gironde, 1888–89, ADG; "Devès, Lacoste et cie, arête autorisant l'huilerie," 5–9, series M, ADG; and "Etablissements Devès et Chaumet, Bordeaux, à Centre de Recherches et de Documentation du Sénégal, Saint Louis," 3 April 1981, courtesy Fadel Dia.

4. Guillaume Foy was one of the most successful gum merchants in the Senegal River trade. He served on the governor's private council between 1842 and 1852 and held a number of important positions in the commune during the 1830s and 1840s. His wife, Henriette, was Louis Descemet's sister. Gaspard Devès remained his daughter Elisabeth's guardian throughout her life. The details of the estate are elaborated in records of G. Devès and Company's liquidation. "Report of Liquidation of G. Devès," 21 June 1901, 1Z10, #107, ANS.

5. Sleight was elected deputy when Durand Valantin stepped down. Shortly after arriving in France, Napoleon III eliminated Senegal's representation in the National Assembly.

6. "Messieurs le président et juges composant le tribunal de commerce de Bordeaux de G. Devès," Bordeaux, 2 December 1895," 1Z9, #17, ANS; Johnson, *Emergence of Black Politics,* 50–51; Hargreaves, *Prelude to the Partition of West Africa,* 131–32; and "Le Sénégal et les guinées de Pondichéry," 1879, Bordeaux Chamber of Commerce.

7. For a full list of Devès's business investments, see the documents pertaining to his judicial liquidation (1895–1901) in 1Z9, ANS. See also "Ely Ould Mohamed El Abib to Monsieur Gaspard Devès," notarized document, Saint Louis, 2 June 1880, ANS; Thilmans, "Lat Dior: Cheikh Saad Buh et le Chemin de Fer," *Saint-Louis, Lille, Liège* 1 (December 1992): 15.

8. Madeleine Fatma Daba Daguisery, called Madeleine Tamba, was born in 1837, the daughter of Tamba Daba Daguisery and Dame Awa Souleymane N'diaye. The family lived in the fishing village of Guet-Ndar on the Atlantic coast. "Pierre Gaspard Devès and Madeleine Tamba," 9 May 1889, Civil Registry of Marriage, Commune of Saint Louis, ANS; Madeleine Devès Senghor, interview with author, 20 March 2000, Dakar, and personal correspondence, Ibrahima Diallo, Saint Louis.

9. Leopold Angrand shored up the Devès family's influence in the second arrondissement. Like Crespin, Angrand was known as a lawyer with radical political leanings. He argued on behalf of workers and peasants. Alexandre Issac was a proponent of assimilation as colonial policy and took a serious interest in Senegal during the 1880s and 1890s. Alexandre Issac, *Questions coloniales: Constitution du sénatus-consultes* (Paris: Librairie Guillaumin, 1887); Manchuelle, "Le rôle des Antillais dans l'apparition du nationalisme culturel en Afrique Noire Francophone," 390–96.

10. An 1886 report cites Louis Descemet as an agent for A. Teisseire, suggesting that he may have also served as an employee of Buhan and Teisseire. Bordeaux merchant Auguste Teisseire married Marianne d'Erneville. Raymond Martin, a French agent of the Bordeaux firms, also married a d'Erneville, suggesting that Louis Descemet had both business and familial ties to the French trade houses. Commandant, Cercle du Podor à Monsieur le Director d'Affaires Politique, 24 August 1886, 4E4, #23, ANS; Teisseire, "La famille d'Erneville"; Guillabert, "Arbre généalogique des familles Descemet-Guillabert"; Bâ, *La pénétration française du Cayor;* and Yves Pehaut, "A l'époque de la 'traite,'" 49–52.

11. Zuccarelli, *La vie politique sénégalaise,* 47–58.

12. When Sleight arrived at the Chamber of Deputies in Paris, he faced scrutiny as to his eligibility as a legislator, possibly because of his racial identity. Although little is known of

this incident, this may explain why Devès chose to advance metropolitan candidates for the legislative position. The Descemet group called a meeting of "illiterate" (African) voters to protest the candidacy of Clement de Ville Suzanne, whom they referred to as a "cousin" of G. Devès. "Declaration by E. d'Erneville, E. Sleigth, L. Descemet, L. d'Erneville, and declaration by le comité G. Devès," *Moniteur du Sénégal*, 15 March 1871, 58, and "Election results," *Moniteur du Sénégal*, 4 April 1871.

13. The 1871 petition contained 230 signatures, of which 79 were French (only 7 or 8 were recognized as French men; the others were *métis*) and the rest African. The petition rejected the idea of a quota system for "mulattos, whites, and Negroes," and instead called for universal suffrage for all three groups and defended the rights of Muslim taxpayers to participate in these institutions. Although I did not find evidence to substantiate this, Idowu claims that Muslim Saint Louis residents pushed for their inclusion in these proposals. Johnson, *Emergence of Black Politics,* 43–46; Idowu, "Assimilation in Nineteenth-Century Sénégal," 1436.

14. "Délibération séance de 2–3 Mai 1878," 4E4, #1, ANS.

15. Brière de l'Isle faced strong opposition from the merchant lobby during his time as mayor. The proposal to suppress the municipal council and subsume it under a newly constituted general council sought to pacify metropolitan businessmen, who criticized Brière de l'Isle for appointing Devès mayor. Members of the council were elected by the registered voters, but until 1880 the governor appointed the mayor. J. J. Crespin was named as Devès's deputy mayor. On Brière de l'Isle's deteriorating relationship with the Saint Louis elite, see Ndiaye, "La colonie du Sénégal," 477–79, and Zuccarelli, *La vie politique sénégalaise,* 52.

16. "Rapport au président de la République française," *Moniteur du Sénégal*, 4 April 1879.

17. Zuccarelli, *La vie politique sénégalaise,* 55.

18. Ibid., 52–69. Wolof speakers called Gasconi *borom robinets,* which meant chief of the water taps, for putting the water system in place in houses and public streets in the capital. Even though the African electorate did not hold formal political power in this period, they put pressure on elected officials to deliver practical results. Gasconi enjoyed the support of the clergy until he voted for secularism in education in the Chamber of Deputies. However, he shored up support among the merchant lobby by voting to reduce customs duties for guinées.

19. For the debate in the Bordeaux Chamber of Commerce on these import duties, see the 1879 report presented to the colonial ministry, "Le Senegal et les guinées de Pondicherry," in Fonds Chambre de Commerce de Bordeaux.

20. The Indian guinées became more valuable after 1860 as a result of the disruption of U.S. cotton production during the American Civil War. As the price of Indian cotton and textiles increased, Bordeaux merchants turned to the cheaper British textiles to supply their African market. Consequently, the 1877 decision introducing a tariff on foreign textiles had significant implications for French merchant firms who had contracts with British textile manufacturers. This example underscores the globalization of commerce in the mid- and late nineteenth century and its impact on markets of the so-called periphery.

21. "Le Sénégal et les guinées de Pondichéry," Fonds Chambre de Commerce de Bordeaux.

22. Procès-verbal Conseil General Session Ordinaire, *Moniteur du Senegal,* 24 November 1879, 55–60, and "Le Senegal et les guinées de Pondichéry," Fonds Chambre de Commerce de Bordeaux.

23. This letter was written by Brière de l'Isle ten years after his departure from Senegal and kept in the Devès family's private papers. He wrote, "Monsieur, votre père M. Gaspard Devès est le seul notable du Sénégal pour qui j'ai garde un excellent souvenir." Ministre de la Marine et des Colonies, Inspecteur Générale des Troupes d'Infanterie de Marine, General Brière de l'Isle à Monsieur le Conseilleur Générale, 18 July 1892, 1Z11, #4, ANS.

24. Mamadou Diouf, *Le Kajoor au XIXe siècle*, 217–22, 228–31, 240–53.

25. Ibid., 263–80. The construction of the railroad facilitated the introduction of monocrop agriculture in Cayor and Baol. To impose peanut cultivation for export, the merchant lobby needed the administration's assistance in suppressing resistance in Cayor and subjecting the kingdom to French authority.

26. Quoted in Guy Thilmans, "Lat Dior, Cheikh Saad Bou, et le Chemin de Fer," 15. Thilmans claims that Muslims in Saint Louis rallied around Lat Dior because of his ties to Saad Buh, a Mauritanian cleric who had a popular following among the Trarza and among Muslim interpreters and scholars in Saint Louis. Saad Buh enjoyed good relations with the administration and maintained networks with métis merchants who operated among the Trarza such as the Devès. For a biography of Saad Buh, see Robinson, *Paths of Accommodation*, 161–77.

27. The administration reported on the debts Lat Dior owed to Gaspard Devès for provisions when the damel fled from Amadu Seku's forces. In 1910, when the administration launched an attack on Justin Devès, they solicited verification of his relationships with rulers in the interior. In 1910, Mbakane Diop, a chief in Cayor under protectorate rule, reported to the colonial inspector on Gaspard Devès's influence on Cayor under Lat Dior. Réponse aux observations présentées par M. L'Inspecteur des Colonies, and handwritten note, Damel Cayor, Gestion Municipale de Justin Devès, IZ8, #26, #27, ANS.

28. Personal communications between the Devès family, officials in Saint Louis, the governor general of French West Africa, and the ministry in Paris show that this issue remained unresolved and persisted long after Gaspard Devès's death in 1901. Arguin Achat de l'Isle par Gaspard Devès Contestations de Propriété entre lui et ses héritiers et le gouvernement Français, Bordeaux 11 August 1899; Lt. Gouverneur à M. receveur de l'enregistrement des domaines, August 1903; François Devès à M. Guy, Paris, 12 September 1905; and Henri Louis Guillabert, notaire of M. Becay ould Babacar ould Zraima, 17 November 1916, 1Z5, ANS.

29. Confidentiel, Commandant cercle de Podor à Monsieur le Directeur des Affaires Politiques, Podor, 24 August 1886, 4E4, #23, ANS.

30. Note sur M. Descemet, 4E4, #7, ANS.

31. Monsieur le Gouverneur, 27 August 1886, 4E4, #21, ANS.

32. Fadel Dia, "La Presse au Sénégal des Origines a L'Independence, 1856–1960," Série Expositions Centre de Recherches et Documentation du Sénégal, Saint Louis, 1978, and personal communication; "Au Ministre M. Genouille, Gouverneur," *Le Petit Sénégalais* 16 (December 1886): 20. Mamadou Diouf gives evidence from oral tradition that confirms the Saint Louis trading community's claims about the death of Samba Laobe reported in the *Reveil du Senegal*. See Diouf, *Le Kajoor au XIXe siècle*, 278–80.

33. Brière de l'Isle held the office from June 1876 to April 1880. After that, Paris appointed three governors who served one year. Aristide Vallon served five months. Appointed on 15 April 1884, Alphone Seignac-Lesseps served as governor for two years.

34. Pasquier, "Les débuts de la presse," 481–82.

35. Pierre Gaspard Devès à Magdeleine Tamba, 9 May 1889, Commune of Saint Louis, and Devès, Jean Lazare Hyacinthe à dlle Crespin, Charlotte Louise, 22 June 1889, ANS.

36. The naval ministry appointed Aristide Vallon governor of Senegal in June 1882. He returned to France in November for health reasons. In the second round of elections, Vallon received 1,773 votes to Gasconi's 1,484 votes. Zuccarelli, *La vie politique sénégalaise,* 66.

37. For the scandal surrounding the Gasconites and Bourmeister's municipal council and the 1889 election, see ibid., 65–68.

7. URBAN POLITICS AND THE LIMITS OF REPUBLICANISM (1890–1920)

1. Georges Crespin was responding to a book by Sonolet entitled *L'Afrique occidentale française,* which criticized the existence of democratic institutions in Senegal. Sonolet traveled to French West Africa and wrote this report of his observations. He launched a virulent critique of electoral politics in Senegal and praised William Ponty's efforts to eliminate it and reorganize the colonial bureaucracy to take power out of the hands of what he called "barbarous blacks" and the "mulattos," whom he accused of monopolizing positions in the colonial bureaucracy and leading anti-French political agitation, using the slogan "Senegal for the Senegalese." "Allocution presented by M. Georges Crespin, Extraordinary Session of the General Council," Saint Louis, February 1912 (Dakar: Imprimerie Ternaux, 1913), courtesy Georges Crespin; Louis Sonolet, *L'Afrique occidentale française* (Paris: Librairie Hachette, 1912), 12–16.

2. Cohen, *French Encounter with Africans,* 263–82.

3. Think tanks of the metropolis such as the École Coloniale, the Colonial Ministry, and geographic societies played a role in defining colonial policy. Recent research shows, however, that officers in Dakar and Saint Louis had a more important role in designing and implementing policy. The continuity of governors and governor generals who served in political affairs bureaus and in military campaigns of the 1880s and 1890s confirms this. For a classic approach to association as an intellectual idea, see Raymond Betts, *Assimilation and Association in French Colonial Theory, 1890–1914* (New York: Columbia University Press, 1961). On the role of Dakar in shaping colonial policy, see Conklin, *A Mission to Civilize,* 23.

4. François Manchuelle, "Métis et colons: la famille Devès et l'émergence politique des Africains au Sénégal, 1881–1897," *Cahiers d'études africaines* 96 (1984): 477–594.

5. A fourth son, Guillaume, was also registered at the school in 1880. He pursued studies in medicine and married a woman of the French nobility. Blaise Dumont was a property owner and gum merchant. In the 1850s, he was appointed mayor of Saint Louis. Albert Laplène, a French businessman, was involved in a number of ventures, including sale of materials for the construction of the General Council building in 1888. Their union shows that for many French men who arrived in Senegal in this period, marriage into a métis family could mean marrying up in status and wealth. Mme. Laplène (born Adéle Dumont) inherited her father's property. Vente d'immeuble par les Dames Dumont à M. W. Dumont, 10 May 1881, Actes Notaires, Saint Louis, ANS; "Marie Virginie Elisabeth Devès," 1 July 1897, Parish Registry of Baptisms, Saint Louis diocese, Sor, Senegal; Thilmans, *L'Hôtel du Conseil générale,* 34–38. On the Devès family, see "Notes of Credit Given by Constance Devès," 1912, 1Z10, ANS; "Guillaume Gomis," 11 December 1890, "Justine Diop," 3 July 1900, and "Emmanuel Correa," 1905, in Parish Registry of Baptisms, Sor diocese, Senegal; Madeleine Devès Senghor, interview with author.

6. M. Louis Huchard à Mon cher F. Devès, 28 June 1916, 1Z11, #19, ANS; Ankersmit and Co. to M. François Devès Conseiller Générale, Saint Louis, Sénégal," 28 February 1919, 1Z11, #32, ANS.

7. The dispute appears to have concerned funds owed to the Crespin family for legal services provided by J. J. Crespin. The conflict had particular repercussions for Hyacinthe, who sided with his in-laws and found himself ousted from the family business for a short time. "Hérités JJ Crespin, G. Devès et Vernon, 20 June 1896 Tribunal du Première Instance Saint Louis," 1Z10, #119, ANS; "Gaspard et Justin Devès contre JJ Crespin," 1Z10, ANS, and Gaspard Devès à Justin Devès, Bordeaux, 20 September 1896, 1Z11, #12, ANS.

8. The north bank of the Senegal where the Trarza and Brakna operated remained an important network for métis habitants until the early twentieth century. Durand Valantin acted as an agent for the Devès family in Mauritania. According to an official report, the trade house called Devès Frères de Saint Louis traded with guinées to the Trarza rulers for livestock, weapons, and possibly slaves. The extent of the family's reputation was noted by the commandant, who wrote that the family was known in the region as "ahel Gaspard," the Arabic term meaning "the people of Gaspard." Territoire Civil de la Mauritanie, Saint Louis à GG AOF, Gorée, 3 April 1907, ANS GG AOF; Valantin, Durand Prosper à dlle Crespin, Rose Marie, 11 February 1888, Actes de Mariage Commune de Saint Louis, ANS; "Justin Devès and associates," 1Z11, #8, ANS; Robinson, *Paths of Accommodation*, 113–15.

9. "Gisements Aurifères du Sirimana 1907," 1Z7, #3, ANS; "Salines du Trarza, 1904–1912," 1Z6, #2–14, ANS.

10. Louis Huchard served as Justin Devès's personal lawyer and played a role in defending clients of the Devès family in the protectorate during the 1900s. Correspondance, Gestion Municipal de Justin Devès, 1Z8, #40–42, ANS. On Hyachinthe Devès's reputation in the General Council, see Idowu, "Café au Lait," 281.

11. Galandou Diouf was born in Saint Louis to a Muslim family. He attended Catholic school and became a clerk for the administration before leaving to become a trader in Nianing. It appears that Justin Devès mentored Diouf in politics. In 1909, Diouf became the first originaire elected to the General Council since Bacre Waly Gueye and the first originaire representing Rufisque. In a letter to the editor of the newspaper *Le Petit Sénégalais*, Diouf accused Devès of supporting Mody Mbaye and others over him in the 1913 General Council elections. Devès sued Diouf for libel. "Galandou Diouf, Conseiller General du Sénégal à Nianing à Monsieur le Directeur du Petit Sénégalais, Dakar," *Le Petit Sénégalais*, 16 December 1912; "Note sur l'affaire Post de Ngalandou Diouf," and "Cour d'Assises du J. Devès et Galandou Diouf," Gestion Municipale Justin Devès, 1Z8, #39, #53, ANS.

12. "Charles Carpot entrée Octobre 1862," and "François Carpot, entrée Novembre 1868," *Registre de l'école primaire des Frères Ploërmel* and *Registre Lycée Michel Montaigne*, séries T, dossier 4, ADG. A fourth brother, Ernest, is also listed on the register.

13. Theodore Carpot married Georginie Pecarrère, who came from an eighteenth-century métis family with links to Gorée. François Carpot married Marguerite Teisseire of the Bordeaux merchant house. "Carpot, Jean Marius Theodore à dlle Pecarrère, Marie-Louise Adèle Georginia," 5 March 1887, Acte de Mariage Commune de Saint Louis, ANS.

14. When François Carpot was elected Senegal's representative in Paris, Governor Roume raised concern over his support of African interests and questioned his loyalty to the administration. See Johnson, *Emergence of Black Politics*, 110–11.

15. These practices were not specific to the colonies alone. Until 1882, mayors were appointed by the prefect in the municipalities of metropolitan France. The prefect could also dissolve the municipal council, and he controlled voter registration. As a result, conflicts commonly arose between appointed mayors and elected municipal councils from the opposition party. Cohen, *Urban Government*, 21–41.

16. In 1887, the colonial ministry created an office of the inspection des colonies when it was still housed under the ministry of commerce and the naval ministry. The role of the inspector became more effective after 1894 when Paris created an independent ministry of colonies. The inspector could examine any civil or military office and was responsible only to the official ordering the mission. With the creation of the Government General, a permanent inspector was assigned to Dakar. The presence of the inspector not only caused problems for the assemblymen but also could be a point of contention within the administration. Chaudié required the inspector to sit in the General Council session, causing a conflict with the director of the interior, who traditionally represented the administration in the assembly. "Podor affaire de meurtre administrateur Jeandet," 13G, #135, ANS; Mbaye, *Histoire des institutions coloniales française*, 15–20.

17. The Conseil d'Etat served as the central administrative court in Paris. The court routinely heard complaints of voter fraud and corruption by prefects in municipal elections of late nineteenth-century France. Citizens in the colonies had the same right to redress as candidates for public office in the metropolis. Cohen, *Urban Government*, 39.

18. Searing offers a useful treatment of conquest and the policy of disannexation as it impacted the Wolof kingdoms in "Accommodation and Resistance," 56–75.

19. The account of the Jeandet affair is contained in a report called "Affaire de Podor Meutre de l'amiral Jeandet, 1890–1892," 13G, #135, ANS. The dossier contains a report of the event in its immediate aftermath as well as documents pertaining to the court cases brought against French officials on behalf of the widow of Lam Toro Sidikh. For historians' interpretation of the event, see Manchuelle, "Métis et colons," 485–92, and Robinson, *Paths of Accommodation*, 65–66.

20. Descemet had commercial interests in Fouta, and Sidikh was a client of Descemet. Podor served as the main base of operations for Bacre Waly Gueye. The Devès family also operated out of Podor. The administration supported Descemet's clients over Devès's when appointing chiefs in the period of conquest. Gaining support among deposed Futanke chiefs may have motivated Gaspard Devès to get involved in the conflict. "Traduction de Hamet Fal lettre de la part de Louis Descemet à Lam Toro Sidick," Podor, 13 February 1884, 4E4, #8, ANS; David Robinson, *Chiefs and Clerics*.

21. Alexandre Issac was a member of the human rights group *Ligue des Droits de l'Homme*. Admiral Vallon was the Devès candidate who was elected to the Chamber of Deputies in 1889, effectively giving the Devès family allies in both houses of the national legislature.

22. Manchuelle argues that the Antillian justices posed a particular threat to the governor and director of political affairs because they tended to be more liberal and concerned with humanitarian issues like forced labor and summary justice. De Lamothe's account of the judiciary in his private papers confirms this. "De Lamothe to undersecretary of state, Saint Louis, 6 February 1891," Papiers Henri de Lamothe, 4 PA/1, 112, CAOM.

23. In a letter to the undersecretary of state regarding "certain personalities" that instigated the Podor affair, de Lamothe gives a detailed assessment of Devès and Crespin

and their influence in the colony. He accuses them of giving "bad advice" to the African population and maintains that Crespin was "sous la dépendance de la maison Devès." See à M. Sous-secrétaire d'Etat, 16 January 1891, 4PA/2 d.4 50, CAOM.

24. H. de Lamothe à Monsieur le Ministre des Colonies, 25 September 1896, 4PA/2 d.4 8, CAOM.

25. Manchuelle provides evidence to show that Couchard, de Lamothe, and the French merchant firms joined together to defeat the Devès group in this election. De Lamothe's report stated that the African electorate in Saint Louis was angered over the outcome of the election. Although little is known of this protest, Zuccarelli found that African women in Saint Louis protested the results by marching in the streets. See à Monsieur le Sous-secrétaire d'Etat, 7 April 1891, 4PA/5, CAOM, and à M. Chef de Cabinet du Sous-secrétaire d'Etat, Saint Louis, 24 Décembre 1892, 4PA/2 d.4, 7, CAOM. Also Zuccarelli, *La vie politique Sénégalaise,* 68, and Manchuelle, "Métis et colons," 493–94.

26. De Lamothe opened the School for the Sons of Chiefs and Interpreters shortly after announcing the new budget for the protectorate. On the arête establishing the budget for the protectorate, see Mbaye, *Histoires des institutions coloniales française,* 154.

27. Although the councilors could not reverse the governor's decision, they responded by adopting two resolutions protesting the policy of disannexation started by Clément-Thomas and continued by de Lamothe. De Lamothe's decree separated the interior posts and towns of the Southern Rivers region (later French Guinea) and the French Soudan from direct administration of the second arrondissement. "H. de Lamothe a M. le Ministre des Colonies, Mesnil-sur-Oge, 23 Septembre 1896," 4PA/2 d.4, 8 CAOM.

28. Sénateur A. Issac à Gaspard Devès, Saint Louis, 19 August 1894, 1Z11, #15, ANS. On the investigation into Justin Devès's involvement in the Belgian Congo emigration scheme, see Rapport Affaire Laplène, Dakar, 4 March 1894, K31, #47, ANS, and Telegram Dakar, 24 February 1894, K31, #77, ANS.

29. Charles Molinet was appointed by Brière de l'Isle to replace Gaspard Devès as mayor of Saint Louis in 1880. A native of Gorée, Molinet married a member of the Guillabert family and had strong ties to Descemet's group. He worked as treasurer of the bank from 1872 to 1884 before he was appointed director in 1885.

30. Commissaire colonial Pinder à M. Ministre des Colonies, Saint Louis, 30 November 1895, Q40, #6, ANS.

31. Molinet was offered a position in the department of colonial treasuries or financial services in Paris. Ministre des colonies to GG AOF, Paris, 2 June 1899, Q40, #38, ANS.

32. Banque du Sénégal Situation des débiteurs, 31 Décembre 1896, Q40, #31, ANS.

33. The Devès group backed Crespin in the first round but not in the second when Gasconi pulled out and it became apparent that Crespin could not win. Couchard had the support of the French merchants, the administration, and the Church. Zuccarelli, *La vie politique sénégalaise,* 69–71.

34. Crespin died on 3 January 1895. "Obit Jean Jacques Crespin" (courtesy Georges Crespin, in author's possession).

35. The two independent journals that appeared in this period were *L'Union Africaine* and *L'Afrique Occidentale. L'Union Africaine* started its run in 1895. It contained less editorial information and focused on reports of the commercial activities of French firms and the state of the economy in Senegal. It was called "an organ of commercial interests of the French colonies on the West Coast of Africa." *L'Union Africaine* J.O. 6936, BN.

36. "Le Syndicat des Arachides: Illégalité? Immoralité?" and "Informations Couchard," *L'Afrique Occidentale* 1 (14 July 1896), JO 7679, BN; L. Houchard, "Le Conseil General," *L'Afrique Occidentale* 14 (15 February 1897), all in JO 7679, BN. They specifically complained that the protectorate system allowed colonial officials to ignore abuses by appointed African rulers against the peasant population.

37. *L'Afrique Occidentale* 1 (14 July 1896), JO 7679, BN.

38. "Préjugé," *L'Afrique Occidentale* 8 (31 October 1896), JO 7679, BN.

39. Lebon made a tour of the French administrative towns along the Dakar–Saint Louis railway corridor. The visit involved the organization of delegations of the tirailleurs then called Spahi, students of the School of the Sons of Chiefs, and elected officials who greeted the minister according to the customs reserved for a visit of a high official of the Republic. The phrase reportedly chanted by the demonstrators translates as "In the water with the Whites! Down with the French! We are the masters! Senegal is ours!" On Lebon's 1897 tour, see Voyage de Mr. Lebon, Ministre des Colonies au Sénégal, 10D6.9, ANS. For an account of the demonstration, see "Senegal," *Le Temps* (Paris), 28 November 1897.

40. Ibid. The account of the event says the mob attacked Bacre Waly Gueye's home, destroying windows and doors. Durand Valantin, pictured in figure 13, was identified in the report as one of the two people arrested for starting the incident.

41. Malik Sy campaigned on Carpot's behalf in the communes. Christian Valantin, interview with author, Dakar, 16 May 2000. For an overview of François Carpot's 1898 and 1902 campaigns, see Zuccarelli, *La vie politique sénégalaise,* 80–85, and Johnson, *Emergence of Black Politics,* 110–11.

42. O'Brien, *White Society in Black Africa,* 54.

43. Secularization had already begun before Roume announced the policy in French West Africa. In the 1880s, the administration created a secular lycée in Saint Louis for originaires. These education reforms prohibited government subsidies for higher education in France. The Brothers of Ploërmel left the colony, but the Sisters of Saint Joseph de Cluny remained and continued to operate private schools for girls in Senegal. On Roume's secularization policy, see Conklin, *A Mission to Civilize,* 40–51.

44. In 1902, French West Africa consisted of Senegal, French Guinea, French Soudan, and Ivory Coast. In 1904, Dahomey was included in the federation. Mauritania and Niger were designated military territories, but in 1904 France designated southwest Mauritania as civil territory and located its administration in Ndar Toute, the coastal village adjacent to the island of Saint Louis. The Adrar remained military territory. The finance commission of the General Council debated the proposal for the 1900 financial law, which had implications for Senegal's customs revenue, and it eventually supported the budget law implemented by Roume. *Session Ordinaire de 1900, Conseil General Sénégal et Dépendances* (Saint Louis: imprimerie du Gouvernement), and Mbaye, *Histoire des institutions coloniales française,* 154.

45. Guy mentions that French representatives from Dakar and Rufisque complained about Carpot's election having "ruinous consequences" for their region and even resigned from the General Council in protest of the last election, which gave the métis a majority in the assembly. Guy came to Senegal from the ministry of colonies in Paris, unlike others with a history of military service during wars of conquest, which meant that he was more in touch with the bureaucratic priorities of Paris and less concerned about satisfying the interests of the Saint Louis community. See Lieutenant Governor of Senegal to the Governor General of French West Africa, 18 April 1903, 4E6, #4, ANS.

46. The governor proposed creating an assembly that would be a compromise between the departmental assemblies in metropolitan France, the Colonial Council of Indochina, and the financial delegations of Algeria. In the proposal, control of the budget rested with the Conseil Supérieur of the government and the minister of colonies. Governor General of French West Africa to the Minister of Colonies, 4E6, #2, ANS.

47. By the 1900s, a number of African commune residents worked as traders, clerks, or elementary school teachers in the administrative and commercial districts of the interior. In practice, this group was afforded the same privileges as French citizens. They were not subject to the indigénat, they could seek the protection of French courts, and they maintained local voting rights. In the 1900s, the protectorate administration purposefully denied commune residents their ability to exercise these rights in districts and towns of the interior.

48. GG AOF à M. le Ministre des Colonies, Dakar, projet de création d'un Conseil Colonial, 1903–1907, 4E6, #2, ANS; "Mon Cher Amiral," Saint Louis, 7 Décembre 1892, and "Envoi d'un projet de décret réglementant les conditions de l'électorat au Sénégal," Saint Louis, 7 April 1891, 4PA, CAOM.

49. Président du Conseil Générale Th. Carpot à Président Conseils Généraux, Saint Louis, 21 November 1904, 4E6, #10, ANS.

50. Lt. Gouverneur à M. Gouverneur Générale AOF, Saint Louis, 21 November 1904, 4E6, #27, ANS.

51. Télégramme Lt. Gouverneur à Gouverneur Générale AOF, Saint Louis, 30 November 1904, 4E6, #48, ANS.

52. The Devès family seems to have always been under surveillance. Scrutiny of their affairs tended to increase at specific times, a situation that was still evident in 1907. Territoire Civil de la Mauritanie à Gouverneur General AOF, Saint Louis, 3 April 1907, GG AOF ANS and 13G66 Actions des maures sur le Senegal, 1908–11, ANS (notes courtesy David Robinson).

53. Lt. Gouverneur Sénégal à Gouverneur Générale AOF, Saint Louis, 28 May 1905 4E6, #68, ANS.

54. Hyacinthe Devès mentioned Guillaume, evoking the name of the German emperor, Wilhelm I, who reigned during the Franco-Prussian War when France lost many casualties in their defeat in battle. *Colonie du Sénégal Conseil General, Session Ordinaire de Mai 1905* (Saint Louis: Imprimerie du Gouvernement).

55. The meeting was held in the building of "citizen Hamet Gueye." "Ordre du Jour, les membres du Bureau Justin Devès, Pierre Chimère, Jaques Blondin," Saint Louis, 29 July 1906, 4E6, #86, ANS.

56. This letter was an effort to counter the efforts of H. Devès and J. Devès to mobilize support against the administration. Lt. Gouverneur du Sénégal à M. Gouverneur General de l'A.O.F, Saint Louis, 15 August 1906, 4E6, #109, ANS.

57. Johnson found that the Saint Louis youth founded the Aurora to discuss intellectual issues, perform plays, and hold sporting events. They formed a musical group called La Lyre de Saint Louis, admired Booker T. Washington, and read about blacks participating in local politics in Guadeloupe, Martinique, and French Guiana. Other humanistic groups like the brass band La Faidherbe appeared in Saint Louis between 1900 and 1910. Johnson, *Emergence of Black Politics*, 149–53, and "Page d'Histoire, La Faidherbe," *UNIR: Echo de Saint Louis.*

58. Louis Huchard served as Mbaye's lawyer in his disputes with the administration. Huchard (perhaps aided by the Devès family's connection to Alexandre Issac)

persuaded the Ligue de Droits de l'Homme to investigate the situation and put pressure on the administration to recognize Mbaye's rights. On the administration's concerns that Mbaye was radicalizing people in Baol, the case brought against him, and the Ligue's involvement, see Johnson, *Emergence of Black Politics*, 133–38, and Manchuelle, "Le rôle des Antillais dans l'apparition du nationalisme," 395–96.

59. The decision by the judiciary was part of the court's effort to deny black commune residents the right to vote. Zuccarelli, *La vie politique sénégalaise*, 89–90.

60. Lt. Gouverneur à Gouverneur General AOF, Saint Louis, 16 April 1910, 1Z8, #4, ANS.

61. Lt. Gouverneur à Justin Devès, Saint Louis, 30 May 1910, and Justin Devès, maire, à Lt. Gouverneur, Saint Louis, 2 June 1910, 1Z8, #9, #10, ANS.

62. This report launched a number of accusations against Devès. French, métis, and Africans in the Saint Louis community were known to have clients among chiefs of the interior with whom they exchanged favors. Justin Devès's actions may have been part of the established relationship of clientage. His actions helped to demonstrate to chiefs the importance of the political institutions in the communes to affairs in the protectorate. "Report by M. Fouque, Inspector of Colonies," 13 June 1910, 1Z8, #23, ANS, and "Telegram, Governor to Administrators," 1Z8, #25, ANS.

63. Télégramme Lt. Gouverneur Sénégal à Gouverneur General AOF, Saint Louis, 13 July 1910, and télégramme, July 15 1910, 1Z8, #30, #31, ANS.

64. Searing, "Accommodation and Resistance," 324–43; Johnson, *Emergence of Black Politics*, 133–38, 144–49.

65. Blaise Diagne was born in Gorée in 1872. His mother came from Lebou and Afro-Portuguese origins. His father was Serer from Joal. Adolphe Crespin brought Diagne into his Saint Louis household, sponsored his education in the Brothers of Ploërmel's school and the secular lycée in Saint Louis, and then followed the young Diagne's career as a customs officer in various regions of the French Empire. "Oncle Adolphe," private correspondence, Diagne to Charlotte Devès, Paris, 11 March 1933 (courtesy Georges Crespin, Paris). For a biography of Diagne, see Johnson, *Emergence of Black Politics*, 154–59, and Amady Aly Dieng, *Blaise Diagne: Député noir de l'Afrique* (Paris: Editions Chaka, 1990).

66. Zuccarelli, *La vie politique sénégalaise*, 110–11.

67. The Diagne laws were the culmination of a masterful political negotiation in which Diagne took advantage of Paris lawmakers' desire to mobilize West African soldiers for service on the front lines in World War I. Johnson, *Emergence of Black Politics*, 154–59.

68. Martial Merlin began his career in Senegal as political affairs director under Henri de Lamothe. From 15 December 1907 to 9 March 1908, Merlin served as acting governor general. He became governor general of French West Africa on 16 September 1919 and remained in office until March 1923. One of his first acts was to request the closing of the General Council. Closing the assembly accomplished one final act of the consolidation of political power and the reorganization of the colonial bureaucracy. It did away with an institution seen as meddlesome and a thorn in the side of French officials in Dakar and Saint Louis since the 1890s. Gouverner Générale de l'Afrique occidentale française à Monsieur Ministre des Colonies, 4E6, #2, ANS.

69. *Règlement Intérieur du Conseil Colonial* (Saint Louis: Imprimerie du Gouvernement, 1930), chaps. 1 and 2; Ruth Morgenthau, *Political Parties in French-Speaking West Africa* (Oxford: Clarendon Press, 1964), 127.

70. H. J. Ankersmit, a business partner in the guinée trade in Antwerp, informed François Devès that he was sending a contribution of 1,000 francs toward a reception honoring the Senegalese soldiers who participated in the war. Ankersmit and Co. à M. François Devès, Conseiller Générale, Saint Louis, 28 February 1919, 1Z11, #32, ANS.

71. Télégramme L. Guillabert, président General Council, à Monsieur le Gouverner Générale, Dakar, Saint Louis, 12 March 1920, 4E14, #79, ANS.

72. Blaise Diagne, Députe du Sénégal, à Louis Guillabert, Président du Conseil Colonial du Sénégal, 29 September 1916, 1Z129, #1, ANS.

73. Discours prononce par M. H. L. Guillabert, Président du Conseil Colonial du Sénégal, à M. Albert Sarraut, Ministre des Colonies, 11 October 1921, 1Z129, #2, ANS.

CONCLUSION

1. "Extrait de la délibération du conseil municipal," 26 August 1916, 1Z11, #9, ANS.

2. While historians have examined the history of Brazilians returning to Benin and Nigeria and the history of Americo-Liberians, relatively little attention has been paid to the migration and settlement of individuals from the French Caribbean to Senegal, and yet there is evidence of Antillean migration in the late eighteenth and early nineteenth centuries, and Antilleans played roles in Senegal's judiciary and military force in the nineteenth and early twentieth centuries. Future research on French Caribbean contributions to Senegal's history may yield important insights. On the distinct form of cosmopolitanism that emerged in Senegal's Atlantic towns and for a theoretical approach to cultural mixing in Africa's colonial cities, see Mamadou Diouf, "The French Colonial Policy of Assimilation and the Civility of the Originaires of the Four Communes (Senegal): A Nineteenth-Century Globalization Project," *Development and Change* 29, no. 4 (1998): 671–96, and Catherine Coquery-Vidrovitch, "La ville colonial 'lieu de colonisation' et métissage culturel," *Afrique contemporaine* 4 (1993): 11–22.

3. Stoler, *Race and the Education of Desire.*

4. One important example of this is Mbodj, "The Abolition of Slavery in Senegal, 1820–1890."

5. A labor historian, David Roediger describes the privileges conferred to white workers in the antebellum South who he argues received a cultural bonus from a belief in the inherent racial superiority of whites over nonwhites, even though they did not benefit from any economic advantage. I am not suggesting that working-class racism operated in the same way in Senegal as in the United States. However, the notion of a psychological wage offers analytical insight about how the métis in Senegal benefited from the privilege of cultural proximity to whiteness in a way that African town residents of Africans in the countryside could not. David R. Roediger, *The Wages of Whiteness: Race and the Making of the American Working Class* (New York: Verso, 1991).

6. Marks, *The Ambiguities of Dependence in South Africa.*

7. Vergès, *Monsters and Revolutionaries.*

BIBLIOGRAPHY

ARCHIVAL SOURCES

Senegal National Archives (ANS)

Series E, Electoral
4E4 Conseil Général du Sénégal, 1878–94

Séries G, Politique et Administration Générale
3G2, 3G3 Institutions Municipales
7G Guinée
7G3 Rivières du Sud, 1882–89
13G, Affaire de Podor Meurtre de l'amiral Jeandet, 1890–92.

Series J, Enseignement
J5 Enseignement Laïque, 1876–95
J6 Ecoles secondaires de Saint Louis, Ecoles primaires de Saint Louis, Gorée, Dakar, et
    Rufisque

Séries K, Travail et main d'œuvre
K31 Emigration d'ouvriers indigènes pour la construction du chemin de fer du Congo-
    Belge, 1890–1894

Series Q, Affaires Economiques
Q27 Chambre de Commerce de Saint Louis
Q40 Banque du Sénégal, 1895–1901

Series Z, Archives privées
1Z1-1Z3 d'Erneville Papers
1Z5–1Z18 Devès Papers
1Z129 Documents André Guillabert
2Z Annales Religieuses

Actes Notaires
1Z107 Gorée, 1880
Saint Louis, 1881

Etat Civil, Commune de Saint Louis
8 M/52 Actes de Naissances, 1861–63
Actes de Mariage, 1887–90

Archives Départementale de la Gironde (Bordeaux) (ADG)

Séries T, Registres des entrées et des sorties des élèves
Dossier 4 (1875–77)
Dossier 5 (1875–81)

14 J, Fonds Clamageran et Delile-Jay

Séries M, Sante Publique

Fonds Chambre de Commerce de Bordeaux (Bibliothèque Municipale de Bordeaux)

Extraits des Procès-verbaux Lettres et Mémoires, 1894–1900
Procès-verbaux, Séance, "Guinées des Pondichéry," 1871
Bulletin de Chambre de Commerce de Bordeaux, 1878–83, 1892, 1900

Centre d'archives d'outre Mer, Aix-en-Provence (CAOM)

Archives privées
4 PA 1, papiers d'Henri de Lamothe

Bibliothèque Nationale, Paris (BN)

Le Petit Sénégalais. J.O. 5966.
L'Afrique Occidentale. J.O. 7679.
L'Union Africaine. J.O. 6936.
Le Temps, 28 November 1897.

Catholic Church, Saint Louis Diocese, Sor, Senegal

Registry of Students of the Primary School of the Ploërmel Brothers in Saint Louis, 1843–1892
    Dépêches Ministérielle, Rapports, Circulaires, Lettres Officielles, Août 1852–Novembre 1910
    Registre Paroissial des baptêmes et Ondoiements, 1854–63, 1891–1908
    Unir: L'Echo de Saint Louis, n.s., nos. 3–142, 3 September 1967–June 1995

Bibliothèque, IFAN, Dakar

Asile des Esclaves Fugitifs de Saint Louis (Sénégal) 1879–1909.
L'Eurafricain: Bulletin d'Information et de liaison de l'union des Eurafricains de l'A.O.F. et du Togo, no. 7 (Dakar)

Bibliothèque, CRNS, Saint Louis

"Etablissements Maurel et Prom à M. Directeur du Centre de Recherches et de Documentation du Sénégal," Bordeaux, 10 Mars 1981. Courtesy Fadel Dia.
"Etablissements Devès et Chaumet, Bordeaux à Centre de Recherches et de Documentation du Sénégal, Saint Louis," 3 Avril 1981. Courtesy Fadel Dia.

OFFICIAL PUBLICATIONS

Moniteur du Sénégal et Dépendances
Journal Officiel du Sénégal et Dépendances
Bulletin Administratif du Sénégal et Dépendances

GENEALOGIES

Crespin, Georges. "Liste de descendance de Benjamin Crespin." Courtesy Georges Crespin, in author's possession.

Guillabert, Guillaume. "Arbre généalogique des familles Descemet-Guillabert." Courtesy Andre Guillabert, in author's possession.

Ricou, Xavier. "Sénégalmétis." http://senegalmetis.com/Senegalmetis/Accueil.html.

Teisseire, Yves. "La famille d'Erneville."

INTERVIEWS

Interviews in Senegal and Paris by Hilary Jones

Bonet, Georgette. With Louis Camara. Sor, 1 and 17 December 2000 and 4 and 10 January 2001.

Brigaud, Ferdinand. Saint Louis, 4 December 2000.

Crespin, Georges. Paris, 8 June 2001.

Fall, Almamy Mathieu. Saint Louis, 27 May 2000.

Désiré, Mireille. Sor, 16 February 2001.

Guillabert, Andre. Saint Louis, 19 February 2000.

Sankale, Sylvain. With David Robinson. Dakar, 3 July 1997.

Senghor, Madeleine Devès. Dakar, 18 March 2000 and 30 March 2001.

Valantin, Christian. Dakar, 16 May 2000.

Watara, Paul. Saint Louis, 2 December 2000.

Interviews in Senegal by David Robinson

Diange, Mame Latir. With Aboubakar Diop. Saint Louis, 11 April 1985.

Dieye, Demba Matalibé. Sor, 12 June 1985.

Diop, El Hadj Amadou. Saint Louis, 11 June 1985.

Swadou Seck and her daughter, Aby Diop. Saint Louis, 29 and 30 June 1997.

Primary Sources in French and English

Adanson, Michel. *Voyage au Sénégal: Relation abrégée d'un Voyage fait en ce pays, pendant les années 1749, 50, 51, 52, 53*. Edited by Denis Reynaud and Jean Schmidt. Publications de l'Université de Saint-Etienne, 1996.

Boilat, Abbé David. *Esquisses sénégalaises*. Paris: P. Bertrand, 1853; reprint, with introduction by Abdoulaye Bara Diop. Paris : Karthala, c1984.

Bruë, André. *Au long des Côtes Occidentales d'Afrique 1697. Histoire Générale des Voyages ou Nouvelle Collection de Toutes les Relations de Voyages par mer et par terre qui ont été publiées jusqu'à présent dans les différentes langues de toutes les nations connue*. Edited by Antoine François Prévost. Holland: Pierre de Hondt, 1747.

Carrère, Frédéric, and Paul Holle. *De la Sénégambie française*. Paris: Librairie de Firmin Didot Frères, 1855.

D'Anfreville de la Salle, Docteur. *Notre Vieux Sénégal: Son histoire, son état actuel ce qu'il peut devenir*. Paris: Librairie Maritime Coloniale, 1909.

Descemet, Louis. *Recueil d'environ 1,200 phrases françaises usuelles avec leur traduction en regard en ouolof de Saint-Louis*. Saint Louis: Imprimerie du Gouvernement, 1864.

Durand, Jean Baptiste Léonard. *A Voyage to Senegal*. London: Richard Phillips, 1806.

Faidherbe, Louis Léon. *Le Sénégal: La France dans l'Afrique Occidentale*. Paris: l'Hachette, 1889.

———. *Vocabulaire d'environ 1,500 mot français avec leurs correspondants en Ouolof de Saint Louis, en Pular, Toucouleur du Fouta, en Soninké, Sarakhollé de Bakel*. Saint Louis, 1864.

Golbéry, Silvester Meinrad Xavier. *Travels in Africa*. Translated by W. Mudford. 2nd ed. London, 1808.

Hargreaves, John, ed. *France and West Africa: An Anthology of Historical Documents*. London: Macmillan, 1969.

Hulstaert, G. "Le Problème des Mulâtres." *Africa* 15, no. 3 (1945): 129–44

———. "Le Problème des Mulâtres (suite)." *Africa* 16, no. 1 (1946): 39–44.

Issac, Alexandre. *Questions coloniales: Constitution des sénatus-consultes*. Paris : Librairie Guillaumin, 1887.

Labarthe, Pierre. *Voyage au Sénégal pendant les années 1784–1785*. Paris, 1802.

Lamiral, M. *L'Afrique et le peuple Afriquain considères sous tous leurs rapports avec notre Commerce et nos Colonies*. Paris: Chez Dessenne, Libraire au Palais Royale et Chez les Marchands de Nouveautés, 1789.

Lindsay, Reverend John. *A Voyage to the Coast of Africa in 1758*. London, 1867.

Loti, Pierre. *Le roman d'un spahi*. Paris, 1873.

Mandelou, Tita. *Signare Anna*. Dakar: NEAS, 1991.

Mollien, Gaspard Theodore. *Travels in Africa to the Sources of the Senegal and Gambia in 1818*. London, 1820.

Raffenel, Anne. *Nouveau Voyage dans le Pays des Nègres suivi d'études sur la colonie du Sénégal*. Paris: Imprimerie de Napoléon Chaix, 1856.

———. *Voyage dans l'Afrique occidentale française*. Paris, 1846.

Richards, Robert Samuel, trans. *Code Napoléon: Being the French Civil Code*. London: Wildy and Sons, 1851.

Sadji, Abdoulaye. *Nini: Mulâtresse du Sénégal*. Paris: Présence Africaine, 1988.

Sonolet, Louis. *L'Afrique occidentale française*. Paris: Hachette, 1912.

Villeneuve, Geoffroy. *L'Afrique ou histoire, mœurs et coutumes des Africaines*. Paris, 1814.

UNPUBLISHED THESES

Barrows, Leland. "General Faidherbe, the Maurel and Prom Company, and French Expansion in Sénégal." PhD diss., UCLA, 1974.

Bouche, Denise. "L'enseignement dans les territoires français de l'Afrique occidentale de 1817 à 1920: Mission civilisatrice où formation d'une élite?" PhD diss., Université de Paris I, 1974.

Casey, Joan Droege. "The Politics of French Imperialism in the Early Third Republic: The Case of Bordeaux." PhD diss., University of Missouri, Columbia, 1973.

Colvin, Lucy. "Kajor and Its Diplomatic Relations with Saint Louis, Sénégal, 1763–1861." PhD diss., Columbia University, 1972.

Hinchman, Mark. "African Rococo: House and Portrait in Eighteenth-Century Sénégal." PhD diss., University of Chicago, 2000.

Johnson, Marian. "Black Gold: Goldsmiths, Jewelry, and Women in Senegal." PhD diss., Stanford University, 1980.

Marcson, Michael David. "European-African Interaction in the Pre-Colonial Period: Saint Louis, Sénégal, 1758–1854." PhD diss., Princeton University, 1976.

Mouser, Bruce L. "History of Trade and Politics in the Guinea Rivers, 1790–1865." PhD diss., Indiana University, 1971.

Pasquier, Roger. "Le Sénégal au milieu du XIXe siècle: la crise économique et sociale." Thèse de doctorat d'état, Paris IV, 1987.

Pehaut, Yves. "Les oléagineux dans les pays d'Afrique Occidentale associes au marché commun." Thèse de doctorat, Université de Bordeaux III, 1973.

Ray, Carina. "Policing Sexual Boundaries: The Politics of Race in Colonial Ghana." PhD diss., Cornell University, 2007.

Reyss, Natalie. "Saint Louis du Sénégal a l'époque précoloniale: l'émergence d'une société métisse originale, 1658–1854." Thèse de 3eme cycle, Université Paris I, 1983.

Sackur, Amanda. "The Development of Creole Society and Culture in Saint Louis and Gorée, 1719–1817." PhD diss., University of London, 1999.

Sankale, Sylvain. "A la mode du pays . . . chroniques Saint Louisiennes d'Antoine François Feuiltaine, Saint Louis du Sénégal, 1788–1835." Thèse de doctorat, l'Université de Montpellier II, 1998.

Searing, James. "Accommodation and Resistance: Chiefs, Muslim Leaders, and Politicians in Colonial Senegal, 1890–1934." PhD diss., Princeton University, 1985.

SECONDARY WORKS

Aïdara, Abdoul Hadir. *Saint Louis du Sénégal: d'hier à aujourd'hui.* Brinon-sur-Sauldre, France: Editions Grandvaux, 2004.

Ajayi, Jacob. *Christian Missions in Nigeria, 1841–1891: The Making of a New Elite.* London: Longman, 1965.

Aldrich, Robert. *Greater France: A History of French Overseas Expansion.* New York: St. Martin's Press, 1996.

Amin, Samir. "La politique coloniale française à l'égard de la bourgeoisie commerçante Sénégalaises, 1820–1960." In *The Development of Indigenous Trade and Markets in West Africa,* ed. Claude Meillassoux, 361–76. Oxford: Oxford University Press, 1971.

Amselle, Jean-Loup. *Mestizo Logics: Anthropology of Identity in Africa and Elsewhere.* Translated by Claudia Royal. Stanford: Stanford University Press, 1990, 1998.

Anderson, Benedict. *Imagined Communities.* Rev. ed. London: Verso, 1991.

Auslander, Leora. *Taste and Power: Furnishing Modern France.* Berkeley: University of California Press, 1996.

Austen, Ralph. *African Economic History: Internal Developments and External Dependency.* Portsmouth: Heinemann, 1987.

Aw, Mansour. "Saint Louis, chef-lieu de la Concession du Sénégal et sa place dans la traite négriere aux XVIIᵉ et XVIIIᵉ siècles." In *Saint Louis et l'esclavage,* ed. Djibril Samb, 85–94. Dakar: IFAN, 2000.

Bâ, Omar. *La pénétration française au Cayor.* Vol. 1. Dakar, 1976.

Barber, Karen, ed. *Africa's Hidden Histories: Everyday Literacy and the Making of the Self.* Bloomington: Indiana University Press, 2006.

Barrera, Giulia. "Patrilinearity, Race, and Identity: The Upbringing of Italo-Eritreans during Italian Colonialism." *Quaderni Storici* 37, no. 1 (April 2002): 21-53.

Barry, Boubacar. *Le royaume du Waalo: Le Sénégal avant la conquête.* Paris: Karthala, 1972.

———. *Senegambia and the Atlantic Slave Trade.* Translated by Ayi Kwei Armah. Cambridge: Cambridge University Press, 1998.

Barry, Boubacar, and Leonhard Harding, eds. *Commerce et commerçants en Afrique de l'Ouest: Le Sénégal.* Paris: Harmattan, 1992.

Bathily, Abdoulaye. Portes de l'or: le royaume de Galam, Sénégal de l'ère musulmane au temps de négriers, VIIe au XVIIᵉ siècle. Paris : L'Harmattan, 1989.

Bayart, Jean Francois. *The State in Africa: The Politics of the Belly.* Translated by Mary Harper. New York: Longman, 1993.

Becker, Charles, Saliou Mbaye, and Ibrahima Thioub, eds. *AOF: Réalités et héritages: Sociétés ouest africaines et ordre coloniale, 1894–1960.* 2 vols. Dakar: Direction des Archives du Sénégal, 1997.

Becker, C., V. Martin, J. Schmitz, and M. Chastanet. *Les premiers recensements au Sénégal et l'évolution démographique.* Dakar: ORSTOM, 1983.

Bell, Caryn Cossé. *Revolution, Romanticism, and the Afro-Creole Protest Tradition in Louisiana, 1718–1868.* Baton Rouge: Louisiana State University Press, 1997.

Benoist, Joseph-Roger de. *Histoire de l'église catholique au Sénégal.* Paris: Karthala, 2008.

Berlin, Ira. "From Creole to African: Atlantic Creoles and the Origins of African American Society in Mainland North America." *William and Mary Quarterly* 53 (April 1996): 251–88.

Berman, Bruce, and John M. Lonsdale. *Unhappy Valley: Conflict in Kenya and Africa.* Athens: Ohio University Press, 1992.

Betts, Raymond F. *Assimilation and Association in French Colonial Theory, 1890–1914.* New York: Columbia University Press, 1961.

Bhabha, Homi K. *The Location of Culture.* London: Routledge, 1994.

Biondi, Jean Pierre. *Saint Louis du Sénégal: mémoires d'un métissage.* Paris: Edition Denoël, 1987.

Bonnardel, Régine. *Saint Louis du Sénégal: Mort ou Naissance?* Paris: Harmattan, 1992.

Bouche, Denise. "L'école française et les musulmans au Sénégal de 1850 à 1920." *Revue française de l'histoire d'outre-mer* 61, no. 223 (1974): 222–25.

Boulègue, Jean. *Les Luso-Africains de Sénégambie XVI–XIXe siècle.* Senegal: Université de Dakar, 1972.

Bouquillon, Yvon, and Robert Cornevin. *David Boilat: Le Précurseur.* Dakar: Les Nouvelles Editions Africaines, 1981.

Bourdieu, Pierre. *Outline of a Theory of Practice.* Translated by Richard Nice. Cambridge: Cambridge University Press, 1977; reprint, 1995.

———. *The State Nobility: Elite Schools and the Field of Power.* Translated by Lauretta C. Clough. Stanford: Stanford University Press, 1989.

Bouteiller, Paul A. *Le Chevalier de Boufflers et le Sénégal de son temps, 1785–1788.* Paris : Editions Lettres du Monde, 1995.

Brigaud, Felix, and Père Jean Vast. *Saint Louis du Sénégal: ville aux mille visages.* Dakar: Editions Clairafrique, 1987.

Brooks, George E. *EurAfricans in Western Africa.* Athens: Ohio University Press, 2003.

———. "Peanuts and Colonialism: Consequences of the Commercialization of Peanuts in West Africa, 1830–1870." *Journal of African History* 16, no. 1 (1975): 29–54.

———. "*Signares* of Saint Louis and Gorée: Women Entrepreneurs in Eighteenth-Century Sénégal." In *Women in Africa,* ed. Nancy Hafkin and Edna G. Bay, 19–44. Stanford: Stanford University Press, 1976.

Camara, Camille. *Saint Louis du Senegal.* Dakar: IFAN, 1968.

Casely-Hayford, Augustus, and Richard Rathbone. "Politics, Families, and Freemasonry in the Colonial Gold Coast." In *People and Empires in African History,* ed. J. F Ajayi and J. D. Y. Peel. New York: Longman, 1992.

Clancy-Smith, Julia, and Frances Gouda, eds. *Domesticating the Empire: Race, Gender, and Family Life in French and Dutch Colonialism.* Charlottesville: University Press of Virginia, 1998.

Clark, Linda L. *Schooling the Daughters of Marianne*. Albany: State University of New York, 1984.

Cohen, Abner. *Custom and Politics in Urban Africa: A Study of Hausa Migrants in Yoruba Towns*. Berkeley: University of California Press, 1969.

Cohen, Jean, and Andrew Arato. *Civil Society and Political Theory*. Cambridge: MIT Press, 1992.

Cohen, William B. *The French Encounter with Africans*. Bloomington: Indiana University Press, 1980.

———. *Rulers of Empire: The French Colonial Service in Africa*. Stanford: Stanford University Press, 1971.

———. *Urban Government and the Rise of the French City*. New York: St. Martin's Press, 1998.

Comaroff, Jean, and John Comaroff, eds. *Civil Society and the Political Imagination in Africa*. Chicago: University of Chicago Press, 1999.

———. *Of Revelation and Revolution*. Vol. 1, *Christianity, Colonialism, and Consciousness in South Africa*. Chicago: University of Chicago Press, 1991.

———. *Of Revelation and Revolution*. Vol. 2, *The Dialectics of Modernity on a South African Frontier*. Chicago: University of Chicago Press, 1997.

Conklin, Alice. *A Mission to Civilize: The Republican Idea of Empire in France and West Africa, 1895–1930*. Stanford: Stanford University Press, 1997.

———. "Redefining 'Frenchness': Citizenship, Race Regeneration, and Imperial Motherhood in France and West Africa, 1914–40." In *Domesticating the Empire: Race, Gender, and Family Life in French and Dutch Colonialism*, ed. Julia Clancy-Smith and Frances Gouda, 65–83. Charlottesville: University Press of Virginia, 1998.

Cooper, Barbara. *Marriage in Maradi: Gender and Culture in a Hausa Society in Niger, 1900–1989*. Portsmouth, NH: Heinemann, 1997.

Cooper, Frederick. "Between Metropole and Colony: Rethinking a Research Agenda." In *Tensions of Empire: Colonial Cultures in a Bourgeois World*, ed. Frederick Cooper and Ann Laura Stoler, 1–56. Berkeley: University of California Press, 1997.

———. *Colonialism in Question: Theory, Knowledge, History*. Berkeley: University of California Press, 2005.

Coquery-Vidrovitch, Catherine. "La ville coloniale 'lieu de colonisation' et métissage culturel." *Afrique Contemporaine* 4 (1993): 11–22.

———. "Nationalité et citoyenneté en Afrique occidentale français: originaires et citoyens dans le Sénégal colonial." *Journal of African History* 42, no. 2 (2001): 285–305.

Crowder, Michael. *Senegal: A Study in French Assimilation Policy*. London: Methuen, 1967.

Curtin, Philip D. *Cross Cultural Trade in World History*. Cambridge: Cambridge University Press, 1984.

———. *Economic Change in Precolonial Africa: Senegambia in the Era of the Slave Trade*. Madison: University of Wisconsin Press, 1975.

David, Philippe. "Hostalier-Noal: Un duel de photographes au Journal Officiel du Senegal il y a cent ans." http://www.imagesetmemoires.com/doc/Articles/Hostalier_Noal_Duel_de_photographes.pdf.

Davis, Natalie Zemon. *Society and Culture in Early Modern France*. Stanford: Stanford University Press, 1975.

Delacourt, Jean. *Histoire Religieuse du Sénégal*. Dakar: Editions Clairafrique, 1976.

Deschamps, Hubert. *Le Senegal et la Gambie*. Paris: Presses Universitaires, 1968.

Dia, Fadel. *Expositions: La presse au Sénégal des Origines à l'Independence (1856–1960).* Saint Louis: Center for Research and Documentation of Senegal, 1978.

Diamond, Larry. "Persistence, Erosion, Breakdown, and Renewal." In *Democracy in Developing Countries: Comparing Experiences with Democracy,* ed. Larry Diamond, Juan J. Linz, and Seymour Martin Lipset. Boulder, CO: Lynne Rienner, 1990.

Dieng, Amady Aly. *Blaise Diagne, député noir de l'Afrique.* Paris: Editions Chaka, 1990.

Dike, K. O. *Trade and Politics in the Niger Delta, 1830–1885.* Oxford: Oxford University Press, 1956.

Diop, Abdoulaye Bara. *La famille Wolof.* Paris: Karthala, 1985.

———. *La société Wolof.* Paris: Karthala, 1981.

Diouf, Mamadou. "Assimilation coloniale et identitaires religieuses de la civilité des originaires des Quatre Communes (Sénégal)." *Canadian Journal of African Studies* 34, no. 2 (2000): 565–87.

———. "The French Colonial Policy of Assimilation and the Civility of the Originaires of the Four Communes (Senegal): A Nineteenth-Century Globalization Project." *Development and Change* 29, no. 4 (1998): 671–96.

———. *Le Kajoor au XIXe siècle: Pouvoir ceddo et conquête coloniale.* Paris: Karthala, 1990.

———. "Traitants ou négociants? Les commerçants Saint Louisiens (2ᵉ moitié du XIXe–début XXe): Hamet Gora Diop (1846–1910), étude de cas." In *Commerce et commerçants en Afrique de l'Ouest: Le Sénégal,* ed. Boubacar Barry and Leonhard Harding, 107–53. Paris: Harmattan, 1992.

Dirks, Nicholas B, ed. *Colonialism and Culture.* Ann Arbor: University of Michigan Press, 1992.

Dominguez, Virginia R. *White by Definition: Social Classification in Creole Louisiana.* New Brunswick, NJ: Rutgers University Press, 1986.

Dubois, Laurent. *A Colony of Citizens: Revolution and Slave Emancipation in the French Caribbean, 1787–1804.* Chapel Hill: University of North Carolina Press, Omohundro Institute, 2004.

Echenberg, Myron. *Colonial Conscripts: The Tirailleurs Sénégalais in French West Africa, 1857–1960.* Portsmouth, NH: Heinemann, 1991.

Fair, Laura. *Pastimes and Politics: Culture, Community, and Identity in Post-Abolition Zanzibar, 1890–1945.* Athens: Ohio University Press, 2001.

Fall, Babacar. *Le travail forcé en Afrique-Occidentale française.* Paris: Karthala, 1993.

Fall, Babacar, and Abdoul Sow. "Les traitants Saint-Louisiens dans les villes escales du Sénégal, 1850–1930." In *Commerce et commerçants en Afrique de l'Ouest: Le Sénégal,* ed. Boubacar Barry and Leonhard Harding, 155–86. Paris: Harmattan, 1992.

Fields, Barbara J. "Ideology and Race in American History." In *Region, Race, and Reconstruction: Essays in Honor of C. Vann Woodward,* ed. J. Morgan Kousser and James M. McPherson, 143–77. New York: Oxford University Press, 1982.

Fuchs, Rachel. "Seduction, Paternity, and the Law in Fin de Siècle France." *Journal of Modern History* 72, no. 4 (2000): 944–89.

Gann, L. H., and Peter Dunigan. *Colonialism in Africa, 1870–1900.* London: Cambridge University Press, 1969.

Gaspar, David Barry, and David Patrick Geggus, eds. *A Turbulent Time: The French Revolution and the Greater Caribbean.* Bloomington: Indiana University Press, 1997.

Geary, Christreaud. *In and Out of Focus.* National Museum of African Art, 2002,

Geiger, Robert L. G. "Prelude to Reform: The Faculties of Letters in the 1860s." In *The Making of Frenchmen: Current Directions in the History of Education in France,* ed. Donald N. Baker and Patrick J. Harrigan, Waterloo, Ontario: Historical Reflections Press, 1980.

Gildea, Robert. "Education and the Classes Moyennes in the Nineteenth Century." In *The Making of Frenchmen,* ed. Donald N. Baker and Patrick J. Harrigan. Waterloo, Ontario: Historical Reflections Press, 1980.

Glassman, Jonathon. *War of Words, War of Stones: Racial Thought and Violence in Colonial Zanzibar.* Bloomington: Indiana University Press, 2011.

Gocking, Roger. *Facing Two Ways: Ghana's Coastal Communities under Colonial Rule.* Lanham, MD: University Press of America, 1999.

Grew, Raymond, and Patrick J. Harrigan. *School, State, and Society: The Growth of Elementary Schooling in Nineteenth-Century France.* Ann Arbor: University of Michigan Press, 1991.

Guillard, Pierre. "Cheri Peyrissac." *UNIR: Echo de Saint Louis* 140 (December 1994): 7–11.

Guyer, Jane I., and Samuel M. Eno Belinga. "Wealth in People as Wealth in Knowledge: Accumulation and Composition in Equatorial Africa. *Journal of African History* 36 (1995): 91–120.

Habermas, Jürgen. *The Structural Transformation of the Public Sphere.* Translated by Thomas Burger. Cambridge: MIT Press, 1989.

Hargreaves, John. "Assimilation in Eighteenth-Century Sénégal." *Journal of African History* 6, no. 2 (1965): 177–84.

———. *Prelude to the Partition of West Africa.* London: Macmillan, 1963.

Harrell-Bond, Barbara E., Allen M. Howard, and David E. Skinner. *Community Leadership and the Transformation of Freetown.* The Hague: Mouton, 1978.

Harrison, Chris. *France and Islam in West Africa, 1860–1960.* Cambridge: Cambridge University Press, 1988.

Hinchman, Mark. "House and Household on Gorée, Senegal, 1758–1837." *Journal of the Society of Architectural Historians* 65 (June 2006): 164–87.

———. "The Travelling Portrait: Women and Representation in Eighteenth-Century Senegal." In *Interpreting Colonialism,* ed. Byron R. Wells and Philip Stewart, 33–66. Oxford: Voltaire Foundation, 2004.

Hopkins, Anthony G. *An Economic History of West Africa.* New York: Columbia University Press, 1973.

Hunt, Lynn. *The Family Romance of the French Revolution.* Berkeley: University of California Press, 1992.

Idowu, H. O. "Assimilation in Nineteenth-Century Sénégal." *Bulletin de l'IFAN,* série B, no. 30 (1968): 1421–47.

———."Café au Lait: Sénégal's Mulatto Community in the Nineteenth Century." *Journal of the Historical Society of Nigeria* 6 (December 1972): 271–88.

———. "The Establishment of Elective Institutions in Sénégal, 1869–1880. *Journal of African History* 9, no. 2 (1968): 261–77.

Jean-Baptiste, Rachel. "Miss Eurafrica: Men, Women's Sexuality, and Métis Identity in Late Colonial French West Africa, 1945–1960. *Journal of the History of Sexuality* 20, no. 3 (2011): 568–93.

Johnson, G. Wesley. *The Emergence of Black Politics in Senegal: The Struggle for Power in the Four Communes.* Stanford: Hoover Institution, 1971.

————. "Introduction: Reciprocal Influences between French and Africans in the Age of Imperialism." In *Double Impact: France and Africa in the Age of Imperialism,* ed. G. Wesley Johnson. Westport, CT: Greenwood Press, 1985.

————. "The Senegalese Urban Elite, 1900–1945." In *Africa and the West: Intellectual Responses to European Culture,* ed. Philip D. Curtin. Madison: University of Wisconsin Press, 1972.

Johnson, Marian Ashby. "Gold Jewelry of the Wolof and the Tukulor of Senegal." *African Arts* 27, no. 1 (January 1994): 36–49, 94–95.

Jones, D. H. "The Catholic Mission and Some Aspects of Assimilation in Senegal, 1817–1852." *Journal of African History* 21 (1980): 323–40.

Kandé, Sylvie, ed. *Discours sur le métissage: identités métisses en quête d'Ariel.* Paris : L'Harmattan, 1999.

Kanya-Forstner, A. S. *The Conquest of the Western Sudan.* London: Cambridge University Press, 1969.

Kasfir, Nelson, ed. *Civil Society and Democracy in Africa.* London: Frank Cass, 1998.

Klein, Martin A. *Islam and Imperialism in Sénégal: Sine-Saloum, 1847–1914.* Stanford: Stanford University Press, 1968.

————. "Servitude among the Wolof and Serrer of Senegambia." In *Slavery in Africa,* ed. Suzanne Miers and Igor Kopytoff. Madison: University of Wisconsin Press, 1977.

————. *Slavery and Colonial Rule in French West Africa.* Cambridge: Cambridge University Press, 1998.

————, ed. *Breaking the Chains: Slavery, Bondage, and Emancipation in Modern Africa and Asia.* Madison: University of Wisconsin Press, 1993.

Knottnerus, J. David, and Frederique Van de Poel-Knottnerus. *The Social Worlds of Male and Female Children in the Nineteenth-Century French Educational System.* New York: Edwin Mellen Press, 1999.

Lacroix, Jean Bernard. *Les français au Sénégal au temps de la compagnie des Indes.* Vincennes: Service Historique de la Marine. 1986.

Lallemand, Maurice. *Comme un long fleuve tranquille, 150 ans de présence à l'enseignement en Afrique des Frères de Ploërmel.* Paris: FF. De l'instruction chrétienne de Ploërmel, 1992.

Landers, Jane G. *Atlantic Creoles in the Age of Revolutions.* Cambridge: Harvard University Press, 2010.

Law, Robin. *Ouidah: A Social History of a West African Slaving Port, 1727–1892.* Athens: Ohio University Press, 2004.

Lawrence, Benjamin N., Emily Lynn Osborn, and Richard L. Roberts, eds. *Intermediaries, Interpreters, and Clerks: African Employees in the Making of Colonial Africa.* Madison: University of Wisconsin Press, 2006.

Lecuir-Nemo, Genevieve. *Anne-Marie Javouhey: Fondatrice de la congrégation des sœurs de Saint Joseph de Cluny, 1779–1851.* Paris: Karthala, 2001.

Lee, Christopher Joon-Hai. "The 'Native' Undefined: Colonial Categories, Anglo African Status, and the Politics of Kinship in British Central Africa, 1929–38." *Journal of African History* 46, no. 3 (2005): 455–78.

Lionnet, Françoise. *Autobiographical Voices: Race, Gender, and Self-Portraiture.* Ithaca: Cornell University Press, 1999.

Loum, Daouda. "Métis et métissages: L'Eclairage littéraire en miroir." *French Colonial History* 9 (2008) : 79–102.

Lovejoy, Paul. "The Impact of the Atlantic Slave Trade on Africa: A Review of the Literature." *Journal of African History* 30, no. 3 (1989): 365–94.

Ly, Abdoulaye. *La compagnie du Sénégal.* Dakar: Présence Africaine, 1958.

Lydon, Ghislaine. "Les péripéties d'une institution financière: La Banque du Sénégal,
1844–1901." In *AOF: réalités et heritages,* edited by Charles Becker, Saliou Mbaye, and
Ibrahima Thioub. Dakar: Direction Archives du Sénégal, 1997.

———. *On Trans-Saharan Trails: Islamic Law, Trade Networks, and Cross-Cultural Exchange in Nineteenth-Century Western Africa.* Cambridge: Cambridge University Press,
2009.

Lynn, Martin. "Technology, Trade, and a 'Race of Native Capitalists': The Krio Diaspora of
West Africa and the Steamship, 1852–95." *Journal of African History* 33 (1992): 421–40.

Mamdani, Mahmood. *Citizen and Subject: Contemporary Africa and the Legacy of Late
Colonialism.* Princeton: Princeton University Press, 1996.

Manchuelle, François. "Métis et colons: la famille Devès et l'émergence politique des Africains au Sénégal, 1881–1897." *Cahiers d'études africaines* 24, no. 96 (1984): 477–504.

———. "Le rôle des Antillais dans l'apparition du nationalisme culturel en Afrique
Noire Francophone." *Cahiers d'etudes Africaines* 32, no. 127 (1992): 375–409.

———. *Willing Migrants: Soninke Labor Diasporas, 1848–1960.* Athens: Ohio University
Press, 1997.

Mann, Gregory. "What Was the Indigénat? The 'Empire of Law' in French West Africa."
Journal of African History 50 (2009): 331–53.

———. "What's in an Alias? Family Names, Individual Histories, and Historical Method
in the Western Sudan." *History in Africa* 29 (2000): 309–20.

Mann, Kristin. *Marrying Well: Marriage, Status, and Social Change among the Educated
Elite in Colonial Lagos.* Cambridge: Cambridge University Press, 1985.

———. *Slavery and the Birth of an African City: Lagos, 1760–1900.* Bloomington: Indiana
University Press, 2007.

Mann, Kristin, and Richard Roberts, eds. *Law in Colonial Africa.* Portsmouth: Heinemann, 1991.

Marfaing, Laurence. *L'évolution du commerce au Sénégal, 1820–1930.* Paris: Harmattan, 1991.

Mark, Peter. "The Evolution of 'Portuguese' Identity: Luso-Africans on the Upper
Guinea Coast from the Sixteenth to the Early Nineteenth Century." *Journal of African
History* 40 (1999): 173–91.

———. *"Portuguese" Style and Luso-African Identity: Precolonial Senegambia, Sixteenth–
Nineteenth Centuries.* Bloomington: Indiana University Press, 2002.

Marks, Shula. *The Ambiguities of Dependence in South Africa: Class, Nationalism, and the
State in Twentieth-Century Natal.* Baltimore: Johns Hopkins University Press, 1986.

Marseille, Jacques. *Empire colonial et capitalisme français: Histoire d'un divorce.* Paris:
Albin Michel, 1984.

Mayeur, Françoise. *L'éducation des filles en France au XIXe siècle.* Paris: Hachette, 1979.

———. *L'enseignement secondaire des jeunes filles sous la troisième république.* Paris:
Presses de la Fondation Nationale des Sciences Politiques, 1977.

Mbaye, Saliou. *Histoire des institutions coloniales française en Afrique de l'Ouest, 1816–1960.*
Dakar: Imprimerie Administratif, 1990.

———. "L'esclavage domestique à Saint Louis à travers les archives notariés, 1817–1848."
In *Saint Louis et l'esclavage,* ed. Djibril Samb, 139–58. Dakar: IFAN, 2000.

Mbodji, Mohamed. "The Abolition of Slavery in Sénégal, 1820–1890." In *Breaking the Chains: Slavery, Bondage, and Emancipation in Modern Africa and Asia,* ed. Martin A. Klein, 197–215. Madison: University of Wisconsin Press, 1993.

———. "D'une frontière à l'autre où l'histoire de la marginalisation des commerçants sénégambiens sur la longue durée: la Gambie de 1816 à 1979." *In Commerce et commerçants en Afrique de l'Ouest: Le Sénégal,* ed. Boubacar Barry and Leonhard Harding, 191–241. Paris: Harmattan, 1992.

McClintock, Anne. *Imperial Leather: Race, Gender, and Sexuality in the Colonial Contest.* New York: Routledge, 1995.

McLaughlin, Fiona. "On the Origins of Urban Wolof: Evidence from Louis Descemet's 1864 Phrase Book." *Language in Society* 37, no. 5 (2008): 713–35.

Miers, Suzanne, and Igor Kopytoff, eds. Introduction to *Slavery in Africa.* Madison: University of Wisconsin Press, 1977.

Miller, Christopher L. *The French Atlantic Triangle: Literature and Culture of the Slave Trade.* Durham, NC: Duke University Press, 2008.

Mintz, Sidney, and Richard Price. *The Birth of African American Culture.* Boston: Beacon Press, 1976.

Moitt, Bernard. "Slavery, Flight, and Redemption in Senegal, 1819–1905." *Slavery and Abolition* 14, no. 2 (1993): 70–86.

Morgenthau, Ruth Schachter. *Political Parties in French-Speaking West Africa.* Oxford: Clarendon Press, 1964.

Ndiaye, Francine. "La colonie du Sénégal au temps de Brière de l'Isle, 1876–1881." *Bulletin de l'IFAN,* série B, no. 30 (1968): 463–512.

Newell, Stephanie. *The Forger's Tale: The Search for Odeziaku.* Athens: Ohio University Press, 2006.

Nord, Philip. *The Republican Moment: Struggles for Democracy in Nineteenth-Century France.* Cambridge: Harvard University Press, 1995.

O'Brien, Donal B. Cruise, Momar Coumba Diop, and Mamadou Diouf. *La construction de l'état au Sénégal.* Paris: Karthala, 2002.

O'Brien, Rita Cruise. *White Society in Black Africa: The French of Senegal.* Evanston, IL: Northwestern University Press, 1972.

Odo, Georges. *La franc-maçonnerie en Afrique francophone, 1781–2000.* Paris: Editions maçonnique, 2000.

———. "Les quatre loges de St. Louis du Sénégal de 1781–1899" (courtesy Sylvain Sankale, in author's possession).

Pasquier, Roger. "Les débuts de la presse au Sénégal." *Cahiers d'etudes Africaines* 7 (1962): 477–90.

———. "Les traitants des comptoirs du Sénégal au milieu du XIXe siècle." In *Actes du Colloque Entreprises et Entrepreneurs en Afrique,* ed. Catherine Coquery-Vidrovitch, 141–63. Paris: Harmattan, 1983.

Peabody, Sue, and Tyler Stovall, eds. *The Color of Liberty: Histories of Race in France.* Durham: Duke University Press, 2003.

Pedersen, Jean Elisabeth. "'Special Customs': Paternity Suits and Citizenship in France and the Colonies, 1870–1912." In *Domesticating the Empire,* ed. Julia Clancy-Smith and Frances Gouda, 43–65. Charlottesville: University Press of Virginia, 1998.

Pehaut, Yves. "A l'époque de la 'traite' de l'arachide: les 'bordelais' au Sénégal." *Revue historique de Bordeaux et du Département de la Gironde* 30 (1883–84): 48–69.

Phillips, Roderick. *Putting Asunder: A History of Divorce in Western Society.* Cambridge: Cambridge University Press, 1988.

Prestholdt, Jeremy. *Domesticating the World: African Consumerism and the Genealogies of Globalization.* Berkeley: University of California Press, 2008.

Ricou, Xavier. *Trésors de l'iconographie du Sénégal colonial.* Paris: Riveneuve, 2007.

Roberts, Richard. "History and Memory: The Power of Statist Narratives." *International Journal of African Historical Studies* 33, no. 3 (2000): 513–22.

Robinson, David. *Chiefs and Clerics: Abdul Bokar Kane and the History of Futa Toro, 1853–1891.* Oxford: Oxford University Press, 1975.

———. "France as a Muslim Power in West Africa." *Africa Today* 46, no. 3 (1999): 105–27.

———. *The Holy War of Umar Tal: The Western Sudan in the Mid-Nineteenth Century.* New York: Oxford University Press, 1985.

———. *Paths of Accommodation: Muslim Societies and French Colonial Authorities in Sénégal and Mauritania, 1880–1920.* Athens: Ohio University Press, 2000.

Robinson, David, and Jean Louis Triaud, eds. *Le Temps des marabouts: Itinéraires et stratégies islamique en Afrique occidentale français, v. 1880–1960.* Paris: Karthala, 1997.

Robinson, Ronald. "Non-European Foundations of European Imperialism: Sketch for a Theory of Collaboration." In *Studies in the Theory of Imperialism,* ed. Roger Owen and Bob Sutcliffe. London: Longman, 1972.

Roediger, David R. *The Wages of Whiteness: Race and the Making of the American Working Class.* New York: Verso, 1991.

Saada, Emanuelle. *Les enfants de la colonie: Les métis de l'Empire français entre sujétion et citoyenneté.* Paris: Editions La Découverte, 2007.

Saint-Martin, Ives-Jean. *Le Sénégal sous le second empire: naissance d'un empire colonial, 1850–1871.* Paris: Karthala, 1989.

Samb, Djibril, ed. *Saint Louis et l'esclavage.* Dakar: IFAN, 2000.

Sarr, Dominique, and Richard Roberts. "The Jurisdiction of Muslim Tribunals in Colonial Sénégal, 1857–1932." In *Law in Colonial Africa,* ed. Kristin Mann and Richard Roberts. Portsmouth, NH: Heinemann, 1991.

Scott, James C. "Corruption, Machine Politics, and Political Change." *American Political Science Review* 63 (December 1969): 1142–58.

Searing, James. *West African Slavery and Atlantic Commerce: The Senegal River Valley, 1700–1860.* Cambridge: Cambridge University Press, 1993.

Shereikis, Rebecca. "From Law to Custom: The Shifting Legal Status of Muslim Originaires in Kayes and Médine, 1903–1913." *Journal of African History* 42 (2000): 261–83.

Siga, Fatou Niang. *Reflets de modes et traditions Saint-Louisiennes.* Dakar: Khoudia, 1990.

Sinou, Alain. *Comptoirs et villes coloniales du Sénégal.* Paris: Karthala, 1993.

Sparks, Randy. *The Two Princes of Calabar: An Eighteenth-Century Atlantic Odyssey.* Cambridge: Harvard University Press, 2004.

Spitzer, Leo. *The Creoles of Sierra Leone: Responses to Colonialism, 1870–1945.* Madison: University of Wisconsin Press, 1974.

———. *Lives in Between: The Experience of Marginality in a Century of Emancipation.* New York: Hill and Wang, 1999.

Stepan, Alfred. *Rethinking Military Politics: Brazil and the Southern Cone.* Princeton: Princeton University Press, 1988.

Stoler, Ann Laura. *Carnal Knowledge and Imperial Power: Race and the Intimate in Colonial Rule.* Berkeley: University of California Press, 2002.

———. "Making Empire Respectable: The Politics of Race and Sexual Morality in Twenti-eth-Century Colonial Cultures." *American Ethnologist* 16 (November 1989): 634–60.

———. *Race and the Education of Desire.* Durham, NC: Duke University Press, 1995.

———. "Rethinking Colonial Categories: European Communities and the Boundaries of Rule." In *Colonialism and Culture,* ed. Nicholas B. Dirks, 319–52. Ann Arbor: University of Michigan Press, 1992.

Suret-Canale, Jean. *French Colonialism in Tropical Africa, 1900–1945.* Translated by Till Gottheiner. New York: Pica Press, 1971.

Swigart, Leigh. "Cultural Creolisation and Language Use in Post-Colonial Africa: The Case of Sénégal." *Africa* 64 (1994): 175–89.

Tamari, Tal. "The Development of Caste Systems in West Africa." *Journal of African History* 32 (1991): 221–50.

Thilmans, Guy. *L'Hôtel du Conseil général à Saint Louis du Sénégal: Documents pour servir à son histoire et sa réhabilitation.* Dakar: IFAN, 2004.

———. "Lat Dior, Cheikh Saad Bou, et le Chemin de Fer." *Saint Louis, Lille, Liège* 1 (December 1992): 3–41.

Thioub, Ibrahima. "Juvenile Marginality and Incarceration during the Colonial Period: The First Penitentiary Schools in Senegal, 1888–1927." In *A History of Prison and Confinement in Africa,* ed. Florence Bernault and Janet L. Roitman. Portsmouth, NH: Heinemann, 2003.

Trouillot, Michel-Rolf. *Silencing the Past: Power and the Production of History.* Boston: Beacon Press, 1995.

Vansina, Jan. *Oral Tradition as History.* Madison: University of Wisconsin Press, 1985.

Vergès, Françoise. *Monsters and Revolutionaries: Colonial Family Romance and Métissage.* Durham: Duke University Press, 1999.

Villalon, Leonardo. *Islamic Society and State Power in Sénégal: Disciples and Citizens in Fatick.* Cambridge: Cambridge University Press, 1995.

Webb, James L. A., Jr. *Desert Frontier: Ecological and Economic Change along the Western Sahel, 1600–1850.* Madison: University of Wisconsin Press, 1994.

Weisz, George. "The Anatomy of University Reform, 1863–1914." In *The Making of Frenchmen,* ed. Donald N. Baker and Patrick J. Harrigan. Waterloo, Ontario: Historical Reflections Press, 1980.

White, Luise, Stephan F. Miescher, and David William Cohen, eds. *African Words, African Voices: Critical Practices in Oral History.* Bloomington: Indiana University Press, 2001.

White, Owen. *Children of the French Empire: Miscegenation and Colonial Society in French West Africa, 1895–1960.* Oxford: Oxford University Press, 1999.

Wilder, Gary. *The French Imperial Nation-State: Negritude and Colonial Humanism between the Two World Wars.* Chicago: University of Chicago Press, 2005.

Young, Crawford. *The African Colonial State in Comparative Perspective.* New Haven: Yale University Press, 1994.

Young, Robert J. C. *Colonial Desire: Hybridity in Theory, Culture, and Race.* London: Routledge, 1995.

Zuccarelli, François. *La vie politique sénégalaise: 1798–1940.* Paris: CHEAM, 1987.

———. Le régime des engagés à temps au Sénégal (1817–1848). *Cahiers d'Etudes Africaines* 2, no. 7 (1962): 420–61.

INDEX

Page numbers for illustrations are in *italic.*

HILARY JONES is Assistant Professor of West African and African diaspora history at the University of Maryland, College Park. Her research examines political and cultural history, nineteenth-century Senegal, colonialism, and the Atlantic world. She is currently working on a project that investigates the role of women in the development of modern Senegalese nationalism. She has taught at the University of Notre Dame and Macalester College and received generous support for her scholarship from the Erskine Peters fellowship in Africana studies from Notre Dame, the Dubois-Mandela-Rodney postdoctoral fellowship from the Center for African and African American Studies at the University of Michigan, and a Graduate Research Board award from the University of Maryland, College Park.

Printed and bound by CPI Group (UK) Ltd, Croydon, CR0 4YY

13/04/2025